Prairie Mosaic

Prairie Mosaic
An Ethnic Atlas of Rural North Dakota

William C. Sherman

Introduction to Second Edition by Thomas D. Isern

NDSU NORTH DAKOTA STATE
UNIVERSITY PRESS

Sherman, William C.
        Prairie mosaic: an ethnic atlas of rural North Dakota /
William C. Sherman. —Fargo, N.D.: North Dakota Institute
for Regional Studies, 1983.

        Includes index.
        1. Ethnology — North Dakota. 2. Ethnology —
North Dakota — Maps. 3. North Dakota — Emigration and
Immigration — Maps. 5. North Dakota — History. 6. North
Dakota— Population, Rural. I. Title.

F 645.A1 S52   978.4   UND

Library of Congress Catalog Card Number: 82-61305
ISBN (First Edition): 0-911042-27-X
ISBN (Second Edition): 978-0-911042-88-7

Cover photograph and insert photographs provided by Father William C. Sherman Photograph
Collection (110) © 2017, Germans from Russia Heritage Collection.

Cover and interior design for *Prairie Mosaic: An Ethnic Atlas of Rural North Dakota*
Second Edition are by Amanda Booher.

PRINTED IN THE UNITED STATES OF AMERICA

The publication of *Prairie Mosaic: An Ethnic Atlas of Rural North Dakota*, Second Edition, is a
collaborative effort of NDSU Press and Germans from Russia Heritage Collection.

 NDSU Press
North Dakota State University
Dept. 2360, P.O. Box 6050
Fargo, ND 58108-6050
(701) 231-8338
www.ndsu.edu/ahss/ndirs

 GERMANS FROM RUSSIA
GRHC
HERITAGE COLLECTION

Germans from Russia Heritage Collection
North Dakota State University Libraries
Dept. 2080, P.O. Box 6050
Fargo, ND 58108-6050
(701) 231-6596
www.ndsu.edu/grhc

DEDICATED TO:
The first edition of *Prairie Mosaic* is
dedicated to Seth Russell and Carle C.
Zimmerman—friends, teachers, and guides
on the Great Plains "frontier."

The second edition is dedicated especially to
John Guerrero, who helped for many years
to put the whole thing together.

Table of Contents

Acknowledgment

The many bits and pieces of information that combined to make the maps and commentary included in this atlas were collected through the labors of at least a hundred students at North Dakota State University. To each, I owe a debt of gratitude. The several hundred residents in various communities throughout the state who furnished local information are also gratefully remembered. A special thanks is due to Mary Anne Kinane, whose artistic talents brought forth the maps contained in this volume.

The discussion of methodology is taken from the author's article, "Problems and Possibilities in North Dakota Ethnic Settlement Analysis," published in Volume 28 of *Association of North Dakota Geographers Bulletin*. A large part of the southwestern state commentary was published in *North Dakota History*, Volume 46, Number 1, under the title, "Ethnic Distribution in Western North Dakota." To Dr. Kang-tsung Chang, editor of *North Dakota History*, I give my thanks for permission to use the published materials.

The preparation of this book was done with the assistance of Dr. Lillie Francis, Department of English, University of North Dakota, and Dr. Thomas Howard, Department of History, University North Dakota. They read the manuscript and made many helpful suggestions. To them I give special thanks. Dr. Archer Jones, Dean of Humanities and Social Sciences at North Dakota State University, has been a constant source of encouragement over the years. I appreciate, too, the help of both Dr. Michael Lyons and Dr. Larry Peterson, of the Department of History, North Dakota State University.

I'm indebted to Mark Strand and especially to Gerald Richardson of the Communications Office at North Dakota State University. I'm grateful to John Guerrero for his considerable archival assistance. Finally, I wish to say thanks to four people who typed the various revisions: Elaine Lee, Lori Beckstead, Pat Lanes, and Ethel Mohn. Their patience and diligence proved to be exceptional. Daniel Rylance, Colleen Oihus, and Audrey Kazmierczak of the Special Collections Department of Chester Fritz Library at the University of North Dakota were of great help in the gathering of reference materials. The same is true of John Bye at the Institute of Regional Studies at North Dakota State University.

In particular, I express my gratitude to Kathy Foss-Bakkum who designed the entire volume and assisted at every stage of the final publication process.

William C. Sherman
1983

Introduction to the Second Edition By Thomas D. Isern

In 1983 the Institute for Regional Studies, a little-known academic publisher headquartered at North Dakota State University, issued the title, *Prairie Mosaic: An Ethnic Atlas of Rural North Dakota*, by the little-known prairie scholar, William C. Sherman. Distribution was limited. Editorial files have not survived, and so it is unknown what evaluations and expectations prevailed at time of publication. Promotion was rudimentary at best. The work was simply released to make its mark, or not.

Evident at the time was the dedication of the scholar behind the book, Father Bill Sherman, and the enormous amount of work that must have gone into completion of the meticulous local compilations and cartographic depictions of ethnic immigrant settlements on the northern plains, as well as the author's affectionate familiarity with the landscape and its people. Evident in hindsight, however, is how Sherman's study took its place—a prominent and leading place—in the belated development of ethnic studies on the plains, becoming a touchstone for a rising generation of scholars uncovering the region's immigrant past. The writing of *Prairie Mosaic*, by Father Bill and his associates, and its publication by the Institute for Regional Studies, constituted a contribution to ethnic studies on the Great Plains that was remarkable in its own right and significant in advancement of the field. Thus it is a fine thing that North Dakota State University Press, the lineal descendant of the Institute for Regional Studies and its publishing arm today, has restored Fr. Bill's landmark work to print with this second edition.

With the exception of American Indians—an exception best left for anthropologists and native historians to argue—the history of the Great Plains is all immigrant history. Discounting popular beliefs as to early Norse penetration of the middle of North America, immigrant arrival on the plains dates from the sixteenth century. The processional arrival of European agents of conquest and capitalism was prologue to a mass migration of European, Latin American, Native American, Asian, and African peoples whose motivations were both diasporic and aspirational—or, to put them in terms generated by the work of E. G. Ravenstein in the 1880s and still deployed by sociologists in the generation of Fr. Bill, combined both push factors and pull factors.[1]

This immigrant occupation of the Great Plains was modest until the late nineteenth century, and it colored only corners of the greater region—Hispanics colonizing its southwest, for instance, dispossessed eastern Indians its southeast, and Métis its northeast. The stimulation of a mass migration to the plains originated during the American Civil War, when a nation-building Republican administration provided both subsidies for railroads, which would provide transportation for immigrants and infrastructure for their settlements, and homesteads for farmers, who would come from across the United States and from across oceans. The great majority of the immigrants to the plains conformed to the rude classifications of "new immigrants" and "old immigrants" popularized by sociologists of the early twentieth century. The old immigrants, they said, arrived during the late nineteenth century from northern and western Europe, their numbers peaking during the 1880s. The new immigrants arrived during the early years of the twentieth century from southern and eastern Europe. These generalizations about immigrant origins can be taken as sound, without accepting the nativist prejudices of the writers who generated them.[2]

Consider more specifically the northern plains state, North Dakota (until 1889, the northern half of Dakota Territory): during the late nineteenth century, North Dakota, like most states of the Great Plains, partook heavily of the old immigration from northern and western Europe. This influx included, among other nationalities, Norwegians, Swedes, Danes, Dutch, Finns, Germans, Austrians, English, Scots, and Irish, along with that large and anomalous group, the Germans from Russia (ethnic Germans immigrating from czarist Russia). In the last years of the nineteenth century and the early years of the twentieth, North Dakota also received many of the so-called new immigrants—Poles, Ukrainians, and Russian Jews, for instance. Nebraska's ethnic historian, Frederick C. Luebke, writes, "In the latter part of the nineteenth century the United States was the beneficiary of the largest mass movement of peoples in the history of the world."[3] Luebke later observes as to percentage of population that was immigrant or of foreign parentage in 1900, "in north Dakota the proportion reached 78 percent, the highest figure registered for any state in the union."[4] Thus, as Fr. Bill says in his introduction, "That national origins should be of special significance in North Dakota is not surprising"—but there remained terrific complications to sort out and complexities to delineate, which became the task of his book.[5]

When Fr. Bill initiated his ethnic studies of the northern plains in the 1960s, the scholarship on the history of ethnic immigrants on the Great Plains was thin. The foundational work of regional history, Walter Prescott Webb's *The Great Plains*, 1931, famously focused on the physical environment in the formation of regional culture and ignored the influence of immigrant ethnicity.[6] North Dakota's scholarly priest, however, labored contemporary with scholars of immigration on the southern and central plains who gathered considerable acclaim for their contributions—such as the historian, Luebke, of the University of Nebraska, and the geographer, Terry G. Jordan, of the University of North Texas (later University of Texas). Indeed, in his landmark

1 D. B. Grigg, "E. G. Ravenstein and the 'Laws of Migration,'" *Journal of Historical Geography* 3 (January 1977): 41–54.

2 See, for instance, Julius Weinberg, "A. A. Ross: The Progressive as Nativist," *Wisconsin Magazine of History* 50 (Spring 1967): 242–53.

3 Frederick C. Luebke, *Immigrants and Politics: The Germans of Nebraska, 1880–1900* (Lincoln: University of Nebraska Press, 1969), vii.

4 Frederick C. Luebke, "Ethnic Group Settlement on the Great Plains," *Western Historical Quarterly* 8 (October 1977): 406.

5 William C. Sherman, *Prairie Mosaic: An Ethnic Atlas of Rural North Dakota* (Fargo: North Dakota Institute for Regional Studies, 1983), 7.

6 Walter Prescott Webb, *The Great Plains* (Boston: Ginn and Co., 1931).`

1966 book, *German Seed on Texas Soil*, Jordan invokes the term, "mosaic," in framing his study: his work on German immigrants, says Jordan, "seeks to discover on the basis of their experience whether rural Texas became a mosaic bearing the marks of the various ethnic groups which inhabited it, or whether the agricultural individuality of the immigrants was erased through the process of assimilation."[7] Both Jordan and Luebke, who published his book on Germans and politics in Nebraska in 1969, argue for acknowledging the complexity of ethnic assimilation, acculturation, and persistence, and for the need to examine processes at the grass roots, using local sources. Both authors, too, consider ethnic persistence a neglected factor in regional history. "In his heart," writes Luebke, "the acculturating immigrant often remained a German, an Italian, or a Swede."[8] A few years later Luebke would publish, in the *Western Historical Quarterly*, the single most influential article on Great Plains ethnicity. In "Ethnic Group Settlement on the Great Plains" he declaims, "The importance of foreign-born immigrants and their children for the settlement of the Great Plains has been largely overlooked by historians of the frontier and of the trans-Mississippi West."[9]

It is a commonplace among prairie academics to acknowledge an earlier awareness among Canadian scholars of the importance of regional ethnicity, and it is true that bi-culturalism, followed by multi-culturalism, was an article of faith among them. A retrospective examination of the literature nevertheless reveals that Canadian knowledge of prairie ethnicity was not much better than American. The Canadian scholars, at least to the time of publication of Gerald Friesen's *The Canadian Prairies* in 1984, too often concerned themselves with ethnicity as an issue and failed to focus on immigrants as a subject.[10]

The point of examining the state of the scholarship on immigrants and ethnicity in the late twentieth century is to establish that when Fr. Bill pitched into the subject, he was doing pioneering work. He came to such work via an interesting path. William C. Sherman was born in 1927 in Detroit, Michigan, of somewhat mixed parentage: his father, William Alfred Sherman,

the son of a steam engineer and himself an engineering graduate of Montana State College, had no particular religion, while Bill's mother, Ellen, was a fervent Roman Catholic. She also was a strong-willed, vigorous woman. "My mother was Irish Catholic. That's why I'm Catholic," says Fr. Bill.[11] William A. Sherman came home from Marine Corps service in the Great War with a slight disability and went to college using veteran's benefits. After that he worked for the Indian Service. His postings took him first to Chemawa Indian School, Salem, Oregon, and then to Cherokee Indian School, in North Carolina, in which two places young Bill got his early schooling. With the outbreak of the Second World War, William A. entered the army, while young Bill went with his mother to stay with relatives in Richland County, North Dakota. Somehow, then, he received an appointment to the United States Naval Academy, but being color blind, flunked the physical. Enlisting in the army, Bill served in the Philippines and with occupation forces in Japan.[12]

On a troop transport en route stateside from Japan, Bill learned about the GI Bill. The result was his enrollment at St. John's University, Collegeville, Minnesota, where he earned his baccalaureate and continued on for his divinity degree. "Here were all these darned priests around the place," muses Fr. Bill. "I began to think, geez, maybe I should become a priest. I didn't want to, because once you become a priest, you have to say goodbye to all the girls. But after eight years they made a priest out of me."[13]

Ordained and assigned to St. Mary's Cathedral of Fargo in 1955, Fr. Bill next shifted to Grand Forks, where he was encouraged by the bishop to get a master's in rural sociology at the University of North Dakota while also teaching religion and staffing UND's Newman Center. His thesis for the Master of Arts, completed August 1965, was "Assimilation in a North Dakota German-Russian Community." The study area was a group of German-Russian settlements centered in Pierce County and stretching, Fr. Bill explains, "from Karlsruhe on the west to Esmond on the east, from Harvey northward to Rugby."[14] He positions his work as part of the movement among sociologists

7 Terry G. Jordan, *German Seed on Texas Soil: Immigrant Farmers in Nineteenth-Century Texas* (Austin: University of Texas Press, 1966), 3.

8 Luebke, *Immigrants and Politics*, 34.

9 Luebke, "Ethnic Group Settlement on the Great Plains," 405.

10 Gerald Friesen, *The Canadian Prairies: A History* (Toronto: University of Toronto Press, 1984), devotes a chapter to "Immigrant Communities." Another handy index to late twentieth-century knowledge of ethnicity on the Canadian Prairies is R. Douglas Francis and Howard Palmer, eds., *The Prairie West: Historical Readings* Edmonton: Pica Pica Press, 1985). Friesen, in his contribution to this anthology, notes the increasing tendency to dwell upon "the reaction of Canadian society to the presence of the newcomers" (14–15).

11 Personal interview with Father William C. Sherman, Grand Forks, North Dakota, 19 May 2016.

12 Ibid. Other sources used for biographical statements here and in succeeding paragraphs include Byron L. Dorgan, "Father Bill Sherman," *capitolwords*, http://capitolwords.org/date/2003/06/18/S8123_father-william-sherman/; "Honorary Doctor of Leadership, Reverend William C. Sherman," documents from University of Mary Commencement, 3 May 2003, http://library.ndsu.edu/grhc/outreach/friends/sherman2.html; Catherine Jelsing, "Father William Sherman Continues to Research in His Beloved North Dakota," reproduced with permission from the Spring 2006 newsletter of the College of Arts, Humanities, and Social Sciences, North Dakota State University, by the Germans from Russia Heritage Collection, http://library.ndsu.edu/grhc/outreach/friends/sherman5.html/; nomination for honorary doctorate, North Dakota State University, 1990, Administrative Files, Department of Sociology-Anthropology, North Dakota State University (thanks to Kate Ulmer for assistance locating pertinent files in the department); and the "Biographical Sketch" appended as page 160 of Fr. Bill's master's thesis, cited in footnote 14.

13 Sherman interview, 19 May 2016.

from "Anglo-conformity" and "melting pot" ideas about immigration toward viewing immigrant assimilation "as a very complex thing."[15]

A key reason for focusing on the Germans from Russia was that Fr. Bill had become acquainted with, sometimes exasperated by, and eventually fond of the Germans from Russia, many of them railroad workers, who constituted about half the parish at St. Michael's Church of Grand Forks. Then, too, he found that his faculty mentors knew little or nothing about German-Russian culture, making it an attractive subject. In the course of his study of German-Russian country folk he became fascinated with their ways—their festive wedding ceremonies, their use of *Mischtholz* (dried manure) for home heating, and countless other homely customs. His findings were that while German-Russians readily adapted to the economic conditions of North Dakota, they were "most resistant to change in the things they had fought in Russia to avoid: inter-marriage, loss of family solidarity, loss of religion, and for a generation or two, their own particular brand of German culture."[16]

Father Bill left Grand Forks for parishes in Verona and Enderlin, where he greatly enjoyed the hunting and fishing. Although loath to leave such recreational pursuits behind, he was reassigned to Fargo, there to direct the Newman Center and teach sociology at NDSU. He continued teaching for NDSU, commuting every week, after being posted in the late 1970s to St. Michael's of Grand Forks, where he would serve twenty-six years. It was during a span of eight years in the late 1960s and early 1970s, while resident in Fargo, that he produced his path-breaking study, *Prairie Mosaic*.

The ethnic atlas was the product of an energetic, persistent mentor rallying the research efforts of a corps of student researchers. Father Bill was largely unaware of other work on Great Plains ethnicity being done by historians and social scientists at the time. His model, in fact, was a 1962 work by J. Neale Carmen, *Foreign-Language Units of Kansas*. Carmen was a linguist, and his somewhat eccentric work charted the rise and persistence of what he called "for-lings"—foreign-linguistic areas—in the Sunflower State. Most important was his method: Carmen established his database from detailed plat maps showing land ownership, and then he meticulously investigated the ethnicity of the landowners, which he proceeded to map with high specificity.[17]

Father Bill, therefore, got hold of a copy of a big, green, soft-cover plat book published in Grand Forks in 1967, entitled simply *North Dakota Farmers Directory*.[18] Its series of county-level maps depicted land ownership as of 1965. Alongside each county map appeared a "County Farmers Directory." It was Fr. Bill's ambitious intent to trace every landowner, establish ethnicity, and gather other pertinent local details of settlement and persistence. This is where the students gave service. Students in all of Fr. Bill's classes—sociology of religion, rural sociology, introductory sociology—contributed. They took over a room of the Newman Center as research headquarters. "We had big charts on the wall, had a dot for every household, had a number on there—N for Norwegian, SW for Swede, and so on," Fr. Bill recounts. "Then we drew circles around it, and then we could say, here's where the Bohemians are, and so on."[19]

A key contributor to the research effort was a Marine Corps veteran named John "DJ" Guerrero. Early in the development of *Prairie Mosaic*, Guerrero, who was taking classes at NDSU, happened into the Newman Center and was drawn into conversation with Fr. Bill about the project. Because of his military training, Guerrero had a good understanding of maps—an essential and timely contribution to the research work, as Fr. Bill, not being a farm boy, had a shaky understanding of section-range-township. Guerrero was drawn deep into the research project—and remained a research collaborator with Fr. Bill until his death in 2016. He recalled how at one point the chart on the wall was a 10x20-foot map of North Dakota crammed with data. This was the one that was cut into regional sections as the basis for the maps in the book.[20]

It was an advantage that NDSU was a land-grant university, with students from all over the state. Student directories in those days listed home addresses, and so selected students from different parts of the state were cold-called into the Newman Center to give information about the ethnic identities of people in the database. Father Bill also gave students from his classes names of landholders and sent them out to investigate, starting at the courthouses, often seeking out county commissioners for narrative data, and in particular making contact with undertakers—because, as Fr. Bill says, "they knew everybody; they buried them all."

Father Bill spent endless days in the field with students. In addition to working with the landowner data, they also pursued another line of work—documenting traditional ethnic housing. Father Bill would perch students as scouts on the running boards of his car cruising the section roads, their job being to

14   William C. Sherman, "Assimilation in a North Dakota German-Russian Community," MA thesis, University of North Dakota, copy in Germans from Russia Heritage Collection, Main Library, North Dakota State University, p. 11.

15   Ibid., 4.

16   Ibid., 145–46.

17   J. Neale Carmen, *Foreign-Language Units of Kansas: 1. Historical Atlas and Statistics* (Lawrence: University of Kansas Press, 1962).

18   *North Dakota Farmers Directory* (Grand Forks: Tel-E-Key Co., 1967). The book is rare today; thanks to Greg Gilstrap for assistance locating the copy in the Fargo Public Library.

19   Sherman interview, 19 May 2016.

20   Telephone interview with John Guerrero, 4 July 2016. Guerrero has been a respected spokesperson for veterans and participant in community affairs. For a brief sketch, see—"The Long War," *Prairie Sun Rising*, 2 June 2008, http://prairiesunrising.blogspot.com/2008/06/long-war.html.

sing out if they spotted an interesting vernacular building, particularly one built of earth. These buildings were photographed and documented—establishing the invaluable collection of photographs, now housed in the Germans from Russia Heritage Collection, from which a gallery for this new edition of *Prairie Mosaic* was drawn.[21]

The database of landowner ethnicity populated the chart-maps on the wall of the Newman Center.[22] Contemplating them, and drawing upon narrative material gathered from the field as well as from local histories, Fr. Bill composed the narratives accompanying the regional maps. In order to make the maps publication-ready, he contracted with a student at Moorhead State University, an art major named Mary Anne Kinane, who hand-drafted the maps.[23] All this material he then brought to the Institute for Regional Studies for publication. Its director, Dean Archer Jones, was much impressed with the work and shepherded it through to print. There was no launch, no particular recognition associated with release of the book in 1983.

Reviewers, however, took notice.[24] Without doubt the most notable review was that of the distinguished geographer, John C. Hudson, in *Minnesota History*. *Prairie Mosaic*, he adjudged, "is surely the most detailed set of ethnic maps ever produced for a large area within the United States," maps that "show the ethnic background of virtually every square mile of North Dakota in 1965." Hudson admired the sheer determination involved in compiling this "gem of scholarship" with no grant funding and lauded Fr. Bill's "skill, patience, and hard work." This, Hudson intimated, was work that scholars could rely on—results confirmed in specific and on the ground, not just sampled and modeled. Other reviewers in substantial journals—the *Great Plains Quarterly*, the *Journal of Geography*, *The Professional Geographer*, and the *Journal of Historical Geography*—praised the work along similar lines. Frederick Luebke, in *North Dakota History*, was duly impressed. "It is especially appropriate that this fine book should have been produced in North Dakota," he noted, "the state that, at the turn of the century, had the highest proportion of foreign-born inhabitants in the Union."

The regard of scholars was high, but what did this mean to North Dakota? Warren A. Henke, of Bismarck Junior College, hailed *Prairie Mosaic* as "the first major scholarly contribution to ethnic studies in North Dakota, and with this work," Henke allowed, "another North Dakota is coming into view." "Another North Dakota" was a phrase by which Henke intimated that the citizens of the state, absorbing themselves in Fr. Bill's maps and narratives, came to realize how distinctive their ethnic mosaic really was, and how durable—extending right into the present. Newspaper reviewers said as much, poring over the specifics and examining their own localities. There was a down side to this regional particularism. Whereas most scholars appreciated the contribution made by the book, a few, either by specific statement or by subtle rhetoric, indicated that its value was limited in that it was just about—North Dakota.

Reappraisal of *Prairie Mosaic* a generation hence confirms the positive judgements given at the time of original issue and justifies publication of a new edition today. Father Bill would agree that a fundamental value of the book is regional. It documents and defines the identity of North Dakota as the most ethnic of all Great Plains States, not only at time of settlement but also by persistence on the land. As Fr. Bill frequently says, it's not just the story of who settled here; it's the story of who stayed. The work situates North Dakotans as individuals and as communities, and it situates North Dakota in an American landscape of diversity.

Beyond considerations of regional identity, *Prairie Mosaic* stands as a monument of scholarship built with sweat equity. What possessed Fr. Bill to carry through with this daunting work? Determining an answer to that question is complicated by his self-effacing attitude. Finding the answer requires reflections on conversations, considerations of circumstances, and some triangulation. Here, then, is a reasonable conclusion.

Bill Sherman, much to his mother's satisfaction, is a priest, a pastor by profession and by inclination. It is evident from the way he speaks of his parishes that he loves the people in them. He is that shepherd of John 10:3 who "calleth his own sheep by name, and leadeth them out." Father Bill was driven to investigate every single landowner in North Dakota because he considered every one of them a member of his flock. Whereas the welter of names might have been a burden to a clinical social scientist, to him those names were to be honored, to be held almost holy—to be noted and mapped for posterity.

Pressed repeatedly to assess his own work, even at risk of deadly sin, Fr. Bill finally blurts out in exasperation—"You're damn right I'm proud of it!"

* * *

The author of the introduction to the second edition of Prairie Mosaic, *Thomas D. Isern, is Professor of History and University Distinguished Professor, North Dakota State University. Dr. Isern acknowledges research assistance by Amanda B. Biles in preparation of the introduction.*

* * *

21 Sherman interview, 19 May 2016; Guerrero interview, 4 July 2016; Father William C. Sherman Photograph Collection, Germans from Russia Heritage Collection, Main Library, North Dakota State University.

22 The original charts, which Fr. Bill took to his house at conclusion of the *Prairie Mosaic* project, unfortunately were destroyed by the Red River Flood of 1997.

23 Ms. Kinane still practices as a landscape and architectural artist. See *Mary Anne Kinane Art*, http://www.makinaneart.com/.

24 Fortunately, a substantial collection of reviews of *Prairie Mosaic* are retained in the offices of Fr. Bill's home department at NDSU. Copies now have been placed in the files of NDSU Press. All references to reviews here are to these files.

The scholarly contributions of Father Bill Sherman to ethnic studies on the northern plains did not cease with publication of *Prairie Mosaic*. It is but an early peak in a long line of meticulously researched, path-breaking studies. Most notable in the line is *Plains Folk: North Dakota's Ethnic History*, for which Bill was lead editor and first author. That work was published by the Institute for Regional Studies in 1986. Those wishing to explore the further contributions of Fr. Bill Sherman, and to be enlightened as to the rich ethnic diversity of North Dakota, may consult the selected bibliography (chronological listing) below.

Sherman, William C. "Assimilation in a North Dakota German-Russian Community." MA thesis, University of North Dakota, 1965.

Sherman, William C. *Prairie Mosaic: An Ethnic Atlas of Rural North Dakota*. Fargo: North Dakota Institute for Regional Studies, 1983.

Sherman, William C., and Playford V. Thorson, eds. *Plains Folk: North Dakota's Ethnic History*. Fargo: North Dakota Institute for Regional Studies, 1986.

Lamb, Jerome D., William C. Sherman, and Jerry Ruff. *Scattered Steeples: The Fargo Diocese, A Written Celebration of Its Centennial*. Fargo: Burch, Londergan and Lynch, 1988.

Newgard, Thomas P., and William C. Sherman. *African-Americans in North Dakota: Sources and Assessments*. Bismarck: University of Mary Press, 1994.

Sherman, William C., Paul L. Whitney, and John Guerrero. *Prairie Peddlers: The Syrian-Lebanese in North Dakota*. Bismarck: University of Mary Press, 2002.

State of North Dakota
Atlas Sectional Divisions

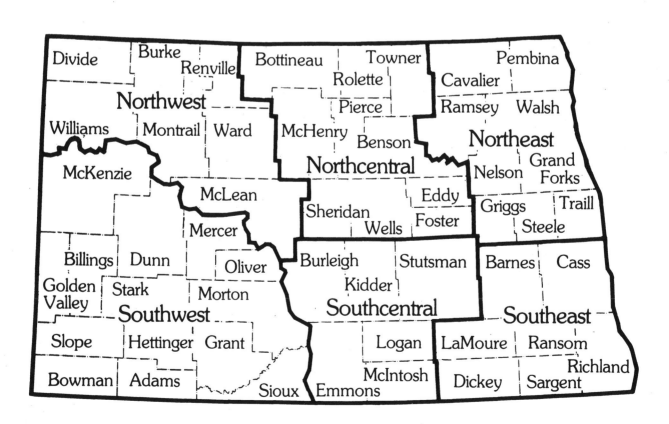

Introduction

This small volume intends to do three things. First, it provides a comprehensive list of the surprisingly large number of ethnic groups who came to early North Dakota; second, it gives the location of the many groups which remained in 1965, and finally, it presents something of both the times of settlement and the various social institutions around which the national communities were known to have rallied. Some additional information as to the settlement patterns in the earliest days and the present size and situation of the groups is also given.

In the United States, studies of national origins using a multiplicity of approaches are frequent these days. Their abundance would seem to indicate that the subject is one which involves more than just a matter of "roots" or nostalgia. There is evidence, too, that — particularly in North Dakota — the ethnic dimension still influences, in small and perhaps large ways, the personal lives of many contemporary residents. One might point to the experience of newcomers in the state. (The author was himself once in this category.) Outsiders receive a surprise when local residents seek to know not only such usual information as one's name and home address, but also one's "nationality." This is, indeed, a unique question. In much of the United States such knowledge is of little consequence, but for the North Dakotan, it can be of great significance. Nationality gives the questioner a dependable clue to such things as the person's place of origin, his religion, his occupation, and the size of his family. In fact, for more experienced observers, the ethnic answer provides a ready index to the subject's level of education, his job preference and even his hobbies, his circle of friends, his attitude toward work, and — surprisingly — such trivia as his food, alcohol, and musical tastes.

The question of national origins has for some time aroused the interest of America's professional scholars — not just historians, but those in the other social sciences as well. Some have suggested that it is a variable of significance in matters of mental health, educational performances, social mobility, religious and political behavior, certain types of deviancy, and a host of other social phenomena.

That national origins should be of special significance in North Dakota is not surprising, however, for the state is relatively young. Homesteading in many counties continued until the first World War. Furthermore, the cultural integrity of many groups, thanks to the mere fact of the geographic isolation, could and did remain undisturbed for several generations. In fact, until the 1950's, the mud of spring and snow of winter minimized outside travel except for the most venturesome. Indeed, "Little Norways," "Little Germanys," "Polands," and "Bohemias" flourished throughout the state until recent times. The maps included in this volume indicate that, even today, perhaps sixty percent of North Dakota's rural residents live on farmsteads where almost all of their immediate neighbors are of the same ethnic background.

In spite of the local interest in ethnicity, whether on a professional or personal level, very little has been written on the subject. Indeed, no one knows for sure how many kinds of people are actually in North Dakota; no list and

certainly no analysis has ever been published. Even the precise location of the major groups is a matter of conjecture. Sadly, it must be said that we know much more about the soil, crop, weed, and water conditions of any particular Dakota township than we know of the national character of the people who reside there.

Recent United States census reports provide information about the income, age, occupation, and level of education of various categories of citizens; but the portrayal of ethnic background is inadequately treated. The only helpful items are the questions which seek responses from those who are either foreign-born or of foreign-born parentage. Race, mother tongue, and Hispanic origins have been treated; but the background of the preponderantly white North Dakota population, now in the third and fourth generations, is overlooked.*

This atlas is not a land-ownership study. It records the national backgrounds of rural residents — the people who live on the land, but not necessarily those who own it. The ethnic makeup of the residents probably does, in most cases, coincide with that of the owners. The Pierce County study and the 1914 Norwegian study, found in the latter part of this volume, seem to indicate such a correlation.

This atlas is essentially a series of six basic double-paged maps. Each map should be able to stand by itself, for the available information was compressed into each regional section. In this the author must apologize to his geographer friends, for a standard rule of cartographic design has been violated: too much has been poured onto one page. As a partial excuse, the author appeals to the matter of economy in publication.

The volume's initial pages contain a state-wide map detailing the six sectional divisions. Also, since township names are often used to describe locations, maps containing North Dakota township names and designations are reprinted from the 1960 United States Census, North Dakota volume.

A commentary accompanies each sectional map for two reasons. One involves the fact that no comprehensive record exists of the many national groups who took up land and eventually left the state. These settlement clusters made up part of the dramatic North Dakota frontier. Their existence is today unheralded; sometimes not a single descendant of the original families remains. These groups have been included at least as a matter of historical record, and because there are those who believe that an analysis of the "departees" — their unwillingness and inability to persist — coupled with a corresponding study of the surviving prairie peoples may tell us something about the state and ultimately about what some have called the "North Dakota personality."

A second reason for the commentary is to give some sense of time to the process of settlement and to point out institutional focal points that may have been vital to early ethnic life. Time of arrival was often of fundamental importance to the groups' subsequent performance for

*The 1980 United States Census has introduced an "ancestry question." This new approach seems to have great potential. As the data become available and the information is analyzed, rural ethnic studies will benefit greatly. Township totals and multiple ancestry categories will be particularly helpful.

local prestige, opportunity and self-esteem were at stake. Institutional life was both a vehicle and a measure of group integrity.

Unfortunately, the commentary is the most tentative portion of the atlas. Dates and names have been gathered from hundreds of local sources, but often memories are vague and records conflict. The times were kaleidoscopic in nature, for in every settlement year a constant stream of wagons was moving out, criss-crossing and leaping ahead from rail and river dispersal points. In this commentary the author feels the general picture is, in the main, accurate; but future studies will undoubtedly correct specific factual errors.

The nomenclature presents problems. A place of origin may change its label as empires or nation-states adjust their boundaries. Name variation enables one North Dakota group to be classified as Ukrainian (emphasizing the parent culture), Galician (emphasizing the home territory), Austrian (emphasizing the political jurisdiction at the time of emigration), or Russian (the homeland's present national setting). Where possible, the atlas uses the term which the group appropriated to itself, the one they themselves considered most fitting. In several instances a less frequent but more descriptive label is used, one which distinguishes more clearly the differences between groups: Anglo-American vs. Anglo-Ontarian; Pennsylvanian Mennonite vs. German-Russian Mennonite.

Those Germans who came to America from Eastern European countries such as Russia and Austria-Hungary are described, for simplicity's sake, by using an adjective or a hyphen: Bohemian Germans, German-Russians. Characterizing the Germans who emigrated directly to the United States is also difficult. Should they be called "Imperial Germans," "Stock Germans," or "Off-the-Boat-Germans"? This volume will use the term *Reichsdeutsch*. In each case, apologies are offered to those who are offended.

As can be seen in the section on methodology, the maps are based on an analysis of all North Dakota's rural households in the year 1965. The ethnic origin of each family was ascertained, for the most part, through a local interview process. The resulting 46,486 family units have been totaled and categorized in several ways, and the data should be of help to those researchers whose needs demand quantification. Accordingly, two tables are printed in the latter part of the volume. The first is a slightly simplified portrayal of the distribution of the rural households of the thirteen largest national groups according to counties (almost ninety-five percent of the population in question). The second is a county-by-county breakdown of over fifty major and minor groups found in the study. The totals listed in the two tables portray, without doubt, the ethnic origins of that portion of North Dakota's population listed in the census category of rural-farm. The significance of the data can be even broader, however, for the proportions may possibly be valid for that larger group of citizens classed as rural-nonfarm, namely open country non-farmers and residents of towns with fewer than 2,500 inhabitants.

State and local leaders regularly act on the assumption that the social makeup of towns and villages reflects the composition of the countryside. The author agrees with this position. In fact, after a somewhat informal analysis of a dozen small cities, he would go even further and say that in towns of 3,000 or under (Air Bases, construction centers, and bedroom suburbs excepted) the ethnic makeup coincides almost exactly with the proportions of national groups found within their rural trade areas. Through the decades, a stream of young people and retired elders left the farm and gravitated to the familiar central city. Eventually the complexion of the town resembled that of the countryside. An exception to the rule is the relatively few "outsiders" who came and went as educators, clergy, and medical people, or as specialists in trade and business fields.

If the above assumption is valid, there is good reason to believe that the numerical proportions of the state's ethnic groups recorded in this atlas represent not just rural households but also those of the smaller towns. The 1960 United States census found that the North Dakota population was forty-four percent urban, twenty-five percent rural-farm, and thirty-one percent rural-nonfarm. The ethnic proportions found in this atlas could possibly represent over fifty percent of the state's population. Further, it may be suggested that the larger cities — even Bismarck, Minot, Dickinson, and Jamestown — draw most of their populations from the Dakota hinterlands, so the proportions can have an even wider significance. But such assumptions await further analysis.

The concluding pages contain several indexes, one listing the names and former locations of groups who are no longer present in the state, another indicating the geographic locations of major and minor existing groups, and finally a general index.

Those who are interested in the exact population totals represented in the various rural settlements found in the maps will be disappointed. The listing of such information would require a volume of tables. The author will gladly supply the specific data to those who request it. For those who seek only approximations, a population density table has been included.

What emerges from this study of North Dakota's ethnic groups is a virtual mosaic of ethnic settlement areas. Contrary to those who would see the state as a melting pot, it was in 1965, and probably is today, a series of large and small enclaves made up of people from similar national backgrounds. Whether these separate units still retain elements of their "old country" ways of life is a matter of conjecture. If territorial integrity contributes to the persistence of culture, some distinctive qualities should still remain.

Method

Since this volume is primarily concerned with national groups and their precise locations, a discussion of the problems involved in such analysis, and of possible solutions, is in order. The dearth of information on the subject should indicate that the matter does present difficulties. This chapter concludes with a discussion of the procedures used in developing the maps contained in this atlas.

Long-term residents of North Dakota are very much aware of the presence of various nationality groups about them, and with a moment's thought they can recite their locations. Western Dakota people will say that Bohemians are at New Hradec, Hungarians are at Lefor, Ukrainians at Belfield. Eastern residents will say Norwegians live at Mayville, French are at Oakwood, Polish are at Geneseo. So it is around the state, but the exact location of the various groups is another matter. Are they north of town? Mixed with others? In the adjoining township? Here, even the local residents begin to hedge and qualify their remarks.

Those who want precise knowledge for professional purposes — such as a social scientist with a special research project, or a student with a personal or historical curiosity — will find that a variety of approaches can be and have been used. They will also find that the results are often less than satisfying. In the following pages, various procedures for determining the location of rural ethnic groups are discussed at some length.

CENSUS REPORTS

Most researchers will initially turn to the Federal decennial census for ethnic distribution data. Some will find in the various reports the information they need, especially if general impressions are sought and large categories are satisfactory. Many will find that the census records are of mixed value. Even in urban areas a set of difficulties can arise: problems of definition, third and fourth generation responses, mixed parentage, sporadic approaches to key questions, and methods of interviewing. The unique treatment given to selected places — standard metropolitan statistical areas and regions with racial minority difficulties — helps resolve some of the problems. Unfortunately, a rural state like North Dakota has received little of this kind of special analysis.

When census data are used for sparsely settled rural areas, be they on the Great Plains or elsewhere, additional problems become apparent. Census materials do not present ethnic data in units small enough to do justice to the diversity of the population. One county may have four or five solid concentrations of differing ethnic groups, but census reports lump them together in a seemingly mixed situation.

A close look at North Dakota will indicate a complexity that is beyond the scope of any census analysis. There were (and are), for instance, at least twelve different kinds of German-speaking settlers, all with sizable settlement areas. Among the German-Russians in different parts of the state, one finds Black Sea Germans, Volhynian Germans, and Dobrudja Germans. German-Hungarians are at Fingal (Burgenland) and Lefor

(Banat). *Reichsdeutsch* settlements exist in a dozen areas. Mennonite Germans of two or three different European backgrounds are found near Langdon and Harvey. Mennonites of Pennsylvanian origin are in Pierce County. Marienburg Germans are present in Stutsman County. Bohemian Germans (Sudetenland) settled in Alice and Jessie, while Austrian Germans (Galicia) came to an area south of Langdon. Each of these groups had its own dialect, folk customs, and religious preferences. Some left the German states more than a century before they came to the United States. The assumption that the behavior of these different groups in America would be identical could lead to serious error in any ethnic investigation.

Similar variations can be found among other groups. Two radically different types of Ukrainians are in the state: Belfield and Wilton people stand in stark contrast with those of Kief and Grassy Butte. Similarly, large groups of Bohemians came from the Crimean Peninsula of South Russia (New Hradec), but several other settlements of Bohemians came directly from Bohemia (Pisek, Lankin, and Lidgerwood).

Those who use census data concerning "country of birth" face a recurring difficulty, the shifting of national boundaries. This can be a particularly acute problem in North Dakota, for a great portion of the central and western Dakota immigrants came from eastern Europe, which has seen considerable change in political boundaries in the past century. Census materials from 1910 and 1920 show Austria as the birthplace of several thousand residents of counties west of the Missouri. The author, in studying the 8,000 rural households of that region in 1965, found not even a dozen true Austrians in that area. Ukrainians, Rumanians, Bohemians, and others of the Hapsburg Empire were listed indiscriminately as Austrians. Walsh County in 1910 had 838 Austrian foreign-born residents. In 1965, few, if any, ethnic Austrians were present; Bohemians had been classified as Austrians.

The Germans from Russia are of particular interest, for they represent the second largest national group in the state. These Dakota residents, who came with the last waves of immigrants, were popularly labeled as "German" during two wars against Germany and were classed as "Russian" during the anti-Bolshevik hysteria of the 1920's and the anti-Communist period of the 1950's. They have had a particularly difficult time. Canadian sources clearly show (and North Dakota data seem to agree) that Red Scares and anti-German wars led many German-Russians to become "Russian-born" in 1920 and 1940, and "German-born" in 1930 and 1950. A large portion of the Protestant Germans came from Bessarabia, which gave them the opportunity, if need be, to declare themselves "Rumanian" in the various decennial census surveys. In the 1930 census, 2,518 North Dakota residents listed Rumania as their place of birth. At the same time, only 110 indicated Rumanian as their "mother tongue." Bessarabia, of course, was part of Rumania from the close of World War I until the Russian occupation during the second World War.

Sociologists have long observed that United States residents of southern and eastern European backgrounds rank lower on status scales than those of more northern and western European origins. In North Dakota, Ukrainians became Galicians or Austrians, Bohemians became Austrians, German-Russians became Rumanians or Germans, German-Hungarians from the Banat became Germans.

OTHER APPROACHES

Clearly, in many research projects, census information must be supplemented by data from other sources if any serious degree of accuracy is sought. Scholars, through the years, have turned to a number of outside sources to solve the problem. The procedures have varied according to the scale and focus of the particular study. Several approaches, which are of special value to the understanding of rural midwestern national groups, are discussed in the following pages.

Railroads

J. Neale Carmen's *Foreign-Language Units of Kansas, Vol. 1, Historical Atlas and Statistics* (Lawrence: University of Kansas Press) is a remarkable work. Though published in 1962, it still remains the best detailed description of the various nationalities present in a Great Plains state and can serve as a model in certain aspects of ethnic study. Carmen uses such census materials as place of birth, foreign stock, and mother tongue; but he supplements his study with a number of additional key sources. His delineation of the railroad lines which affected the dispersal of particular national groups may have some application in North Dakota. For example, the Germans from Russia, though a rural people, occasionally settled in urban centers and did so as railroad workers. Literally hundreds of families came to dwell in the "railroad part of town" in such cities as Devils Lake, Mandan, Dickinson, and Grand Forks. A railroad analysis would be helpful here. Even more, the movement of rural immigrant groups to particular parts of various states was affected by the intensity of railroad advertisement in foreign countries. The Chicago, Milwaukee and St. Paul Railroad, which passed the northern tier of South Dakota counties, was without question the favorite artery of German-Russian immigration. From its railheads in South Dakota, these people journeyed by wagon to settlements as far away as Saskatchewan. Eureka, the end of the line for several years, became the hub of the German-Russian dispersals; indeed, the so-called "German-Russian Triangle" of North Dakota finds Eureka at its central point. Germans fanned out into every neighboring county to a distance of a hundred miles on every side. A second important example is the very heavy Norwegian concentration in the north central and northwestern counties of the state. Aggressive advertisement by Great Northern Railway agents in Norway and in the Norwegian settlements of Minnesota and Wisconsin must have had a strong influence on this homestead pattern.

Ethnic Organizations

Church and synod records provide a list of the locations of early day ethnic-centered parishes and congregations. In this matter, synodal divisions usually represented nationality preference.

Thirty Augustana Lutheran churches spread through central and eastern North Dakota in 1955; this portrays, to a great extent, the dispersal of Swedish settlers throughout the state. Danes and Icelanders also had their synods. Hundreds of Norwegian Lutheran churches dotted the North Dakota countryside; the Norske Synod, Hauge's Synod, the Free Church, and others. Many reflected cultural and regional differences in Norway. The German Missouri Synod church dispersal indicates some of the *Reichsdeutsch* patterns. Evangelical United Brethren, Wisconsin Synod, and others clarify the German picture even more completely. In the Catholic tradition, Bohemian, Polish, and German national parishes can be identified. Early Methodist, Presbyterian, Episcopalian, and Congregational churches indicate the presence of either Anglo-American or Anglo-Ontarian farmers and townsmen.

The presence of national lodges — Sons of Norway, German *Vereinen*, and Bohemian ZCBJ *(Západni Česka Bratrská Jednota)* groups — are additional clues to the distribution of national groups. German-Russian Protestant settlements are even more helpful in that their rural churches tended to be named after the home colonies in the Ukraine. As can be seen in the commentary sections of this volume, the chronicle of early national churches and lodges can be most helpful in determining both the presence and the time of arrival of many North Dakota groups.

Place Names

The use of place names as an index of the location of ethnic groups has been suggested by many. Karl Raitz gives helpful suggestions in his article, "Ethnic Settlement and Topographic Maps," published in *The Journal of Geography* (November 1973). Unfortunately, such a procedure is of limited value in North Dakota. Though some thirty percent of the population of the state is of Norwegian background, few town names reflect such origins. A similar proportion of the state's population is German, yet no more than two dozen town names indicate their presence. Rather, what is clearly evident is the resounding number of towns with British or Anglo-American names. As is well known, the railroads played a decisive role in the naming of newly-established railway sidings; and the influential personnel in railroad companies were not immigrants, but tended to be of British background.

On the assumption that North Dakota townships might have been named by local immigrant and settler groups, 1,000 townships were analyzed by the author and his students; the results were disappointing. Indeed, several Viking, Skandia, and Arnegaard names were found, but they were surprisingly few. Although Russland, Berlin, Strasburg, and other German names were present in greater numbers, they were comparatively rare; conclusive patterns were difficult to establish. What became apparent was that the Anglo-American influence had been the strongest. Names such as Enterprise, Liberty, and Independence still sing the praises of the American way of life. Hamilton, Grant, Webster, and Monroe proclaim American heroes. Indian names are in abundance as are Western-type phrases such as Wagon Box and Flat Butte; but literally hundreds of townships are named McKinnon, Scotia, Sinclair, West Ontario, Avon, Albion, and the like. Generally, there was only slight evidence of the often numerically overwhelming presence of the immigrants from Europe. Township names may alert one to possible ethnic concentration, but operationally, they are of a minimum value.

Following the same line of analysis, the nicknames of local public school athletic teams were investigated since at least here, the local residents might have had a say in the matter. But it seems that a motif of competition and not heritage prevailed. Birds and beasts were in abundance: such names as "Hawks," "Eagles," "Wolves," and "Coyotes." "Vikings" and "Dutchmen" were rare. Surprisingly, occupational names appeared: "Miners" was the name for the teams in four coal mining areas; "Holsteins," "Brickmakers," and "Packers" dramatized their respective town's major industry; "Cowboys," "Ranchers," and "Roughriders" occurred in the west. ("Farmers" was never used.) Towns with residents of Indian background were the only ones which conformed to our hypothesis; invariably, "Braves," "Warriors," "Chieftains," and "Sioux" were present.*

County Land Atlases

The analysis of various county plat maps is certainly a most valuable aid in the determination of settlement patterns, making it possible to detail ethnic land holdings to within a quarter of a mile. Carmen seems to have used them extensively in Kansas. This method can also be used readily in North Dakota, for county atlases are published at regular intervals by several commercial firms. The names of owners are indicated down to the last forty-acre plots. This kind of settlement description involves a great amount of work; but, with care and diligence, a precise map of ethnic landholdings can be obtained. Indeed, Alfred Gabrielson, whose remarkable 1914 Norwegian land ownership map of North Dakota is discussed elsewhere in this volume, must have depended to a great extent on such land ownership atlases. His treatment of the entire state, indicating tracts of even eighty acres, shows how fruitful the method can be.

Several problems are evident in this approach. Ownership of the land does not necessarily mean residence, at least in the present day. Quite obviously, "Bank of North Dakota" or "Northwest Improvement Co." does not represent the resident or even the farm laborer who may live on the site. Secondly, whether working with county atlases or any other list of names, an attempt to determine national background solely by the apparent ethnic "sound" of the family name can lead to serious mistakes. Thus, in North Dakota, the name Miller is at times English, Norwegian, Polish, Swiss, German, and Swedish. Johnson can be English, Norwegian, Icelandic, Swedish, or Danish. Gregor and Gilbert can be German, Norwegian, or Old American. Alfred Gabrielson, to his great credit, resolved the difficulty by journeying personally to every North Dakota county and interviewing local residents.

Nevertheless, the "sound of the name" method has great value. Carmen uses it in much of his research, but he reinforces his "educated guess" with the following supports: (1) the character of the neighborhood (for instance, Johnson in a Swedish colony would most likely be a Swede); (2) possible state census information indicating the national background of earlier individuals with the name in question; (3) local documents, such as church records and tombstones in ethnic-centered congregations; and (4) local informants who recall the origins of the family in question.

In terms of North Dakota, one might add that local documents now include some remarkably extensive county and town histories, many of which were published during the Bicentennial year. These histories usually consist of a series of personal accounts by family members as to their origins, arrival, and subsequent activities. For example, Williams County, North Dakota, which had a population of 19,301 in 1970, published a county history containing over 2,300 pages.

Each of the above approaches to the problem of ethnic identification has some merit; each also has its limitations. Some combination of approaches and certain refinements can certainly increase their effectiveness, but difficulties still remain.

---

*In a half-serious endeavor, one of the author's students has begun an investigation of the relative consumption of certain key ethnic foods. A major wholesale grocery firm covers all of North Dakota and does its entire commerce through the use of a computer. By seeking the proportionate consumption of distinctive foods such as poppyseed (Bohemian), Halva (German-Russian), and Lutefisk (Norwegian), the investigator hopes to describe the dispersal of various national groups throughout the area.

Formation of This Atlas

The maps printed in this volume represent the ethnic characteristics of North Dakota's rural population in 1965. As mentioned before, this may or may not coincide with land ownership patterns. Aggregate personal data from published sources such as census reports being limited, a more direct and more reliable (and ultimately more laborious) method was devised for this project. Such things as land ownership information, settlement distribution mechanisms, census reports, and church records provided clues in the initial stages and assisted in verification of results; but for the most part, little additional aid was derived from these sources. The author's method and its rationale will now be described.

As a starting point, it should be pointed out that ethnicity necessarily involves a matter of perception; the individual sees himself, or is seen by others, as a special kind of person. Definitions of ethnicity may include such elements as a common language, culture, and history; but essential to it all is the matter of identification. Either the person identifies himself with that particular segment of the population, or is so identified by others. Where possible, then, it would seem that the most satisfactory approach would be to go directly to an individual (or at least to his neighbors) and seek an answer to a question which in some way says, "What is your nationality?" The first response to this question should indicate the group to which the subject is most directly related. The person's own perception of the situation thus becomes the ultimate criterion of classification. This, of course, introduces the issue of interviewing and survey techniques such as adequate phraseology and avoidance of bias, which must be given proper attention. Such an approach — self-enumeration — is often included in sociological questionnaires when information concerning ethnicity is sought, and ultimately it underlies the United States census survey which asks the individual to indicate "place of birth," "race," and "mother tongue." In North Dakota, and perhaps in much of the Great Plains, this direct approach would appear to be a valuable one. As has previously been observed, newcomers perceive, with some surprise, the special fascination North Dakota residents have for nationality backgrounds.

That national origin should have a comparatively great and long-lived significance is understandable for a number of reasons. Firstly, the ancestors of most Dakota residents arrived in America in relatively recent times; the communities themselves are young — some towns still await the celebrations of their seventy-fifth jubilees. It is, therefore, possible in many places to interview people who recall the early feverish scramble for land and the building of the new towns. Secondly, most population centers on the northern plains were widely dispersed and isolated by physical space, poor roads, and difficult winters. Ethnic groups, if they so wished, could keep contact with the outside world to a minimum. Taking advantage of their isolation, many settlements did, in fact, display a very long-lived national character. Thirdly, the personal dimension of life is strong in a rural culture. Memories are long; kinships and friendships are enduring, and traditions die slowly. Finally, a number of the national groups which settled in North Dakota had previously experienced the difficulties of living as minority groups. This is especially true of those from eastern Europe: Germans from the Ukraine, Bohemians from the Crimea, Germans from the Hapsburg Empire, and Ukrainians from Russia. Minority defense postures were already developed, and separate village life in America was not a novel experience. In-group consciousness, therefore, could remain at a high level.

Since memories tend to be long and settlement history rather short in much of the Great Plains, it is possible to ascertain the national backgrounds of residents in most areas either by a personal approach or by using knowledgeable informants. One can successfully ask a local resident either his own nationality or that of many of his neighbors. Accordingly, it would seem that the best way to develop an ethnic map of a given area would be to ask every single resident his national background, record the location of his residence, and plot the data on maps. In most cases, however, this person-to-person approach involves a great amount of interviewing and, thus, a large expenditure of time and money.

The maps in this volume were developed by using the above procedure, but in a simplified fashion. The author made extensive use of local informants. The procedure follows this line of approach. A master list of the names and locations of residents in the area under study was obtained. Informants were then asked to supply data concerning the national origins of various individuals. The resulting mass of information (verified where necessary by local documentation) was then plotted on large-scale maps. Happily, the basic ethnic settlement areas emerged. The solid concentrations were evident; the boundaries could be accurately determined; and, even more, the components of ethnically mixed areas could be calculated with precision (e.g., fifty percent Norwegian, twenty-five percent Swede, and twenty-five percent German).

The master list of names upon which this study was based was obtained from a commercial firm which specialized in North Dakota atlases (North Dakota Farmers Directory, Grand Forks: Tel-e-Key Co., 1967). This publication contains all of the rural property owners within the state, some 48,000 households (rural farm and open countryside and non-farm residents).* The publishing firm periodically obtains lists of rural taxpayers from county treasurers and publishes large-sized state maps and directories. The Tel-e-Key list, which included range, township and section, has proved to be a comprehensive one; the names of several hundred individuals known to be in rural North Dakota were checked against it, and the results were satisfactory. The use of county tax records

---

*Most owners were male (ninety-five percent). In age they probably resembled the state-wide average for farm operators which was approximately fifty years in 1969.

As to the extent of ethnically mixed marriages, only an approximation can be made. Mixed marriages should have been at a minimum in areas in which one national group extended into many contiguous townships. They should, correspondingly, have been more frequent in mixed areas. Taking into consideration the fact that the male farm owners had probably married in the 1930's (before good roads and modern mobility) and recognizing the varying degrees of ethnic cohesion, the author estimates that Germans in solidly ethnic regions embracing five or more townships had about a five percent mixed-marriage ratio. Norwegians in similar situations may have had a proportion as high as twenty percent. These marriages, however, were often unions of Norwegians and other Scandinavians.

was especially appropriate, since highly mobile farmworker families, most of whom were not "long time" residents, were absent. The only deficiency was the general lack of names of Indian farmers and ranchers who resided on tribal land. Indians on trust land do not pay county taxes. (Much of the land on reservations is, of course, farmed by whites; and their names were included in this analysis.) Reservation land in question constituted all of Sioux County and about one-sixth of Dunn, McLean, and Benson counties. The white populations of these areas are listed on the maps in a less definite fashion: "scattered Germans," "scattered Norwegians."

The study date chosen was the Tel-e-Key list of 1965 (though published in 1967). An earlier or a later date could have been selected; but it was felt that 1965 data would still reflect some second-generation ownership in the later settlement areas, and third-generation ownership in the earlier settlement areas. The date tends to avoid the major upheavals in land ownership which have ensued in the past decade as a result of large farm machinery and highly capitalized agriculture. The date is, thus, a compromise between the concerns of the historian and those of the modern-day social researcher.

In every part of North Dakota it was relatively easy to find residents who knew almost every family who lived, or had lived, within a ten-mile radius of their homes. Informants whose occupations required a knowledge of many individuals were, of course, particularly valuable: these included local funeral directors, county extension agents, and people such as sheriffs, county commissioners, and auditors — all of whom were involved in local politics. Retirement homes had many alert old-timers whose memories extended back two or three generations.

The delineation of various subdivisions within a national group was done with a degree of precision by using this local interview method. As mentioned above, North Dakota has at least a dozen different kinds of Germans. Bohemian-Germans and Hungarian-Germans are not the same as German-Russians. Sometimes their non-German neighbors call them simply "Bohemians," "Hungarians," and "Russians"; such terms often have a derogatory content, but they do, at least, indicate that variations among the German sub-groups are evident and significant, even to the general public. Census reports and most public records fail to register these inter-group distinctions, but local informants are much aware of the differences.

The method described above was helpful in solving the knotty problem of how to ascertain the national origins of third-, fourth-, and even fifth-generation Americans. The United States census question about mother tongue is an approach to the matter but its effectiveness is limited; generally, the third and subsequent generations are described as having "native parentage." The above procedure was more precise, for it made possible the eliciting of national backgrounds as long as they were perceived to be meaningful to individuals or to the community.

Ethnicity is usually a family affair. Even in ethnically mixed marriages there is a tendency to identify with the more pervasive of the inherited cultures. Local residents are usually attuned to the national allegiance prevailing in a given household. Thus, it is not too far out of line to depend on their assessment in the determination of the status of such mixed families. With this in mind, the ethnic orientation of this special kind of household was determined and recorded in the map preparation.

Verification of the map data was done in several ways. Existing published sources were used, along with the various federal and state population and census studies. Several small-scale historical land ownership surveys were brought into comparative analysis: the Pembina County Icelandic community, the Hill Township Danes of Cass County, the Pierce County German-Russians, and especially the Alfred Gabrielson 1914 Norwegian land ownership map which is portrayed in the final pages of this volume.

Finally, as each sectional map was completed, it was sent to scholars and well-versed individuals in the relevant area for their assessments. Some thirty persons reviewed the material.

County or small area portions of the maps were published locally in conjunction with newspaper articles concerning historical or civic celebrations and promotions, and comments were invited. Three minor changes which were suggested have been incorporated into the final draft.*

In summary, the approach here described was used in the preparation of the atlas maps. Regional conditions made it an effective and relatively simple tool. It bypassed problems involved in census materials; it is based on self-identity, and it thus eliminated difficulties arising in the consideration of third- and fourth-generation matters. It allowed for the study of mixed regions and showed quite conclusively the areas of solid one-nationality concentrations.

---

*The shaded portions on the various maps represent areas in which at least ninety-five percent of the residents are of the indicated ethnic group (unless otherwise noted).

The "mixed" areas indicate regions in which the ethnic composition of the groups is too diverse to describe in meaningful proportions, e.g., ten households of six or seven different backgrounds. In general, the national groups in the mixed areas are made up of the predominant groups in the surrounding townships. If a decidedly different group is in the area, some note is made to that effect.

Southwestern North Dakota

Ethnic Population Distribution
Southwest Section of North Dakota

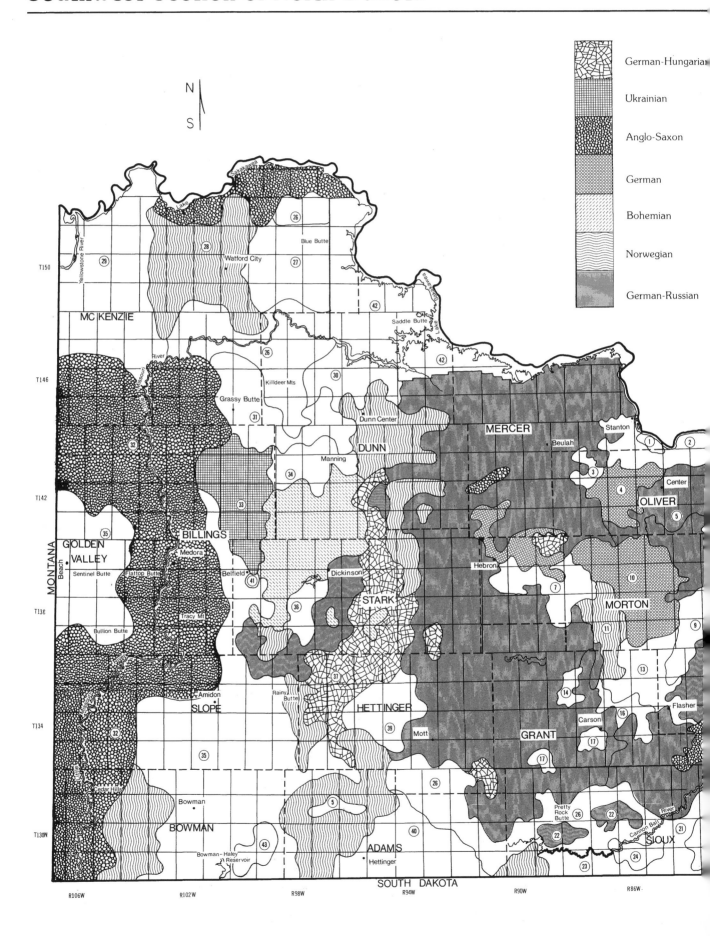

1   Anglo-American and Swedish
2   Anglo-American 25%: Norwegian 25%: German-Russian:
        Swedish: German
3   Norwegian: German-Russian: German
4   German 90%: German-Russian 10%
5   German-Russian 70%: Anglo-American 15%:
        German 15%: Norwegian
6   Anglo-American 80%: Norwegian 20%
7   German-Russian: Bohemian: German: Anglo-American
8   Bohemian 80%: German-Russian 20%
9   Norwegian 50%: Anglo-American 25%: Bohemian:
        German-Russian
10 German 90%: German-Russian 10%: Anglo-American
11 Norwegian 80%: German 20%
12 Anglo-American and Bohemian
13 German-Russian 50%: Anglo-American 25%: Bohemian:
        German: Norwegian
14 German-Russian 50%: Anglo-American and Others 50%
15 Anglo-American: German-Hungarian: German-Russian
16 Anglo-American 50%: Norwegian 45%: Others
17 Mixed
18 Anglo-American 80%: Norwegian and Irish 20%
19 Scattered German-Russian
20 Scattered Anglo-American: German: German-Russian
21 Scattered Anglo-American: Norwegian
22 German-Russian: and Others
23 Scattered Anglo-American: German-Russian: and Others
24 Scattered German Russian
25 Norwegian and Others
26 Norwegian 50%: Anglo-American 50%
27 Anglo-American 65%: Norwegian 35%
28 Norwegian 80%: Mixed 20%
29 Norwegian 40%: Anglo-American 40%: German:
        Bohemian 20%
30 Anglo-American 50%: German-Russian 50%
31 Russian 50%: Mixed: German, Norwegian, Anglo-American 50%
32 Anglo-American With a Few Irish and Others
33 Ukrainian With a Few Others
34 German-Russian 50%: Bohemian 50%
35 Anglo-American 35%: Norwegian 35%: German,
        German-Russian and Others 30%
36 German-Russian 35%: German-Hungarian 35%: Bohemian 30%
37 German-Hungarian With a Few German-Russian
38 Scattered German-Russians
39 German-Russian: Norwegian: Anglo-American:
        Bohemian: German-Hungarian: Others
40 Norwegian 35%: Anglo-American 35%: German-Russian 30%
41 French
42 Indian
43 Bohemian 35%: Polish 35%: Others 30%

Shaded Areas
Are At Least
Ninety-Five
Percent Of The
Same National
Group Unless
Otherwise Indicated

Rural Residents As Of 1965

William C. Sherman   NDSU   Fargo, ND

Township Names and Descriptions
Southwest Section of North Dakota

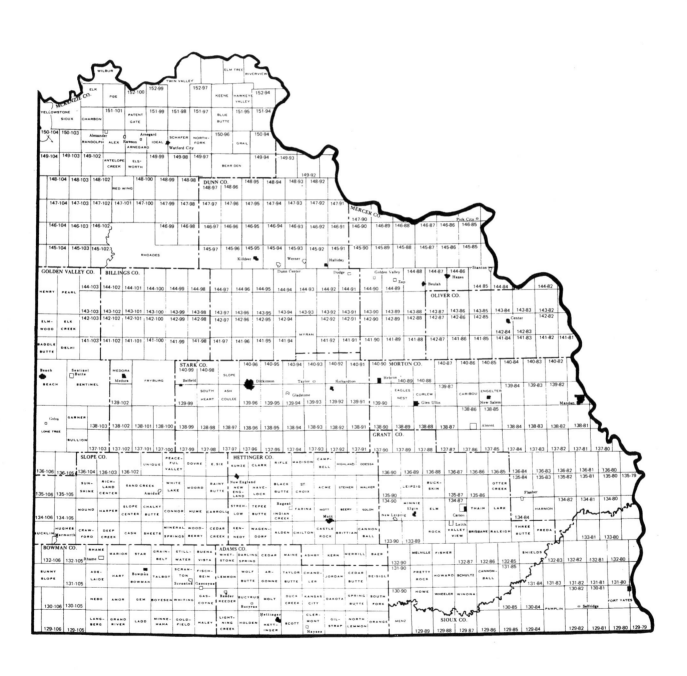

Commentary

ANGLO-AMERICAN

The term Anglo-American is used here to describe residents whose forebears, however remotely, are from the British Isles, such as English, Scots, and Welsh. Included also are occasional Irish and some few individuals whose ancestors were third and fourth generation German or French: in other words, people of Old American stock.

Without a doubt, these are the pioneer people. Their forefathers were the "Yankees" who almost invariably became the merchants and professionals of the newly founded towns and villages. On one occasion, south of Dickinson, they established their own complete town in a colonizing venture, naming it, appropriately, "Mayflower" and later "New England."

Many of the earliest homesteaders were also of this Old American background. They dotted the southwestern counties in a random fashion, generally without the need of colony-type clusters, for they were very much at home in this country; they were the "true Americans." Today, few descendants of these original Yankee farmers and village folk remain, for they moved out of the region rather rapidly. They left an occasional frame "opera house" and Congregational church, and more frequently a rambling turreted two- or three-story house. Some went into the large towns of the state, where their knowledge of American ways enabled them to prosper.

One type of Anglo-American pioneer came and did stay, however; that was the rancher of the "cowboy" tradition. These people first entered the area from Montana and South Dakota, being part of the western cattle culture which had its roots in Texas and the Southwest.

Many came with the trail herds that moved up the eastern slopes of the Rockies and often were the "hired men" of the large bonanza cattle ranches. There is one report of a small ranch in Bowman County in 1878. Some early arrivals came with the army, and some were in the region when the railroad arrived. By 1881, or shortly thereafter, names such as the Eaton Brothers, Teddy Roosevelt, the Reynolds Brothers, and William Gibbs showed up in the territory.

Today, their descendants are found wherever there is rough country: in the Badlands, along the creeks and rivers — the Little Missouri, the Knife, the Heart, the Cannonball — and in the breaks of the Missouri itself. They preceded the great movement of "dirt-farmer" immigrants by at least ten years and have a distinctly different set of traditions. Cherishing their independence, they have until recently held themselves aloof; yet, they still provide a great deal of the local color in the region. In fact, many of their cattlemen ways such as rodeos and Western wear have been adopted by the other national groups and provide an interesting "cowboy" flavor to the whole region.

The subsequent homesteading immigrants were much aware of the existence of these ranch-type Anglo-Americans. The Mercer County German-Russians called them the "Knife River Irish." They formed a distinctly different and consciously superior class during the early decades of settlement. Today, there are often Norwegian and, occasionally, German-Russian ranchers mixed among them, though they still predominate in the heart of the Badlands.

BLACKS

A township south of Alexander (T 149-R 102) had a group of Black homesteaders who came during that region's settlement era (1909-1915). At least ten individuals or families were present at one time or another. Little information is available; but within a decade, it seems, they dispersed to other areas, many going to North Dakota towns or cities.

BOHEMIANS FROM THE CRIMEA

New Hradec in southeastern Dunn County is the center of a large Bohemian community which stretches almost twenty miles to the southwest of that village and includes the South Heart area. It extends fifteen miles west, twelve miles north, and six miles east. The New Hradec settlement (Novy Hradec on early maps) was founded in 1887 by Bohemians from Czechohrad and several other villages in the northern part of the Crimea. Like their German-Russian neighbors, they had been invited to settle in the newly acquired Russian territories; after living there for part of the nineteenth century, they left to find "land and freedom" in Dakota Territory. Like some of their German neighbors, the first Czech settlers came to their homestead lands by way of Yankton, Menno and Bowdle (South Dakota). They are Catholic, and many still speak their native language. Compared to nearby Germans, their stay in the Crimea was relatively brief, a matter of one generation; the "Russian" elements of their culture, though present, are less distinctive. Perhaps this is why they were never called "Bohemian-Russians."

In New Hradec, the parish of SS. Peter and Paul was organized in 1898. A frame church was built (1898), and within a decade a parish house and a hall were erected. In 1917, a large new brick church and a grade school were built; the school was enlarged in 1948, and Czech-speaking nuns taught there until the 1960's. The school was, without doubt, a significant force in maintaining the cultural integrity of the entire Bohemian community; in 1942, records show that 143 pupils were enrolled, of which ninety-two were boarding students.

BOHEMIANS

A Bohemian settlement existed, and survives in a diminished form today, in an area which begins several miles south of Mandan and extends about ten miles to the southwest. At least until recently, this group maintained a strong cohesiveness and had, as its focal point, a Bohemian Lodge officially called *Západni Česka Bratrská Jednota* (ZCBJ), which was organized in 1904. This lodge, like its counterparts elsewhere in the state, tended to be anti-clerical and was a social, political, and even religious center. It has its own cemetery and social hall. These people were, thus, unique among the various West River groups in that the role of the church was minimal.

Another small cluster of Bohemians is found south of Scranton and Gascoyne in Bowman County. This group, mixed with Polish farmers, is probably the remnant of workers who first came as employees in the local mines.

ESTONIANS FROM THE CRIMEA

Tucked between the Norwegian settlement of Daglum and the German-Russian community of Schefield was a number of Estonian farmers (initially several dozen) who came from six colonies in Russia's Crimean Peninsula. The group homesteaded primarily in the western portion of Township 137, Range 97 — an area about two miles wide and three miles long. Like their North Dakota neighbors, the Germans and Bohemians, the Estonians had previously answered the call of the Russian government and had taken up free land in south Russia; but their stay in Russia was short, only one or two generations. A Lutheran pastor of Estonian background would come from Saskatchewan for short periods of time to baptize and instruct the original families. Almost all the settlers had moved elsewhere by World War I; today only several families remain.

FINNS

A Finnish colony developed south of New Leipzig during settlement times. These homesteaders, who occupied much of Delabarre Township, came particularly from Finnish communities in Minnesota. Most, if not all, left the New Leipzig area by the end of the thirties. They are still remembered by area residents for their saunas.

FRENCH

A small pocket of French families live on either side of Highway 85 immediately south of Belfield. They are said to have come originally in 1905 from the Wild Rice community south of Fargo. In 1912, thirty-five families were present; with others, they built the Gaylord Church some fourteen miles south of Belfield. Hard times, especially in the 1930's, caused most to leave. An occasional French family with anglicized spelling of the name is also found in the Badlands area; they are descendants of very early settlers who arrived during the original "cowboy-cattle" period.

GERMANS (Reichsdeutsch)

Though not one of the major groups in southwestern North Dakota, three distinct types of unhyphenated Germans came to the region: (1) Many were second-, third-, and even fourth-generation Germans who arrived with the "Old American" settlers. Among these, some were farmers and some engaged in ranching. Often little remained of their original German heritage; only the name betrayed their origins. Several dozen of these families remain. (2) Many Germans came as single families or small groups in a random fashion directly from the ports of immigration or from German areas of Minnesota and other eastern states. In the 1880's, they came along the railroad to Richardton and Beach. In the later settlement times, the early twentieth century decades, they came to all the mixed nationality areas. Today, they are intermingled either with Germans from eastern Europe or with Anglo-Americans. (3) Thanks to the efforts of Northern Pacific Railroad agents and various church officials, large groups of Germans came to western Dakota in an organized and systematic manner;

these remain in a relatively undispersed pattern even to the present day.

New Salem in Morton County was founded by German settlers from Illinois and Wisconsin. The date can be determined with precision, for on April 3, 1883, an initial trainload of farmers and craftsmen came to the railroad siding under the auspices of a German Evangelical Church colonization *Verein*. This region today includes the area from Blue Grass to New Salem and Judson and extends almost to Sweetbriar. In 1885 another *Evangelischer Kolonizations Verein* set up a second colony of newly arrived Germans at the railway siding which they named "Hebron." The colony expanded, but eventually other national groups moved in; today the townships to the south of Hebron are of mixed background. A concentrated German area still exists to the north.

Throughout the area's towns and countryside, small *Evangelische Kirchen* appeared. Hazen and Hebron, both in the cities and their rural neighborhoods, had Evangelical United Brethren churches. The Missouri Synod, too, was active. In Hannover, St. Peter's Church was organized at a very early date, 1889. These first settlers came from the Hannover district of Germany by way of Illinois. Churches of the same synod were eventually founded throughout the Knife River territory. Among others there were the Wittenberg and Mannhaven churches north of Hazen, the Trinity Church at Kronthal, and churches at Beulah, Zap, and Golden Valley. The last four institutions served Germans and Germans from Russia. St. Paul's Church at Halliday was another German religious center.

A separate and distinct Catholic German settlement is located near Glen Ullin and has rural Haymarsh with St. Clemens Church as its focal point. The original settlers came from Ohio in 1884 under the impetus of an energetic, letter-writing Catholic layman. An additional group of Germans, now with mixed religious backgrounds, may be found occupying part or all of several townships extending north and south of Hannover in Oliver County.

On the west side of the Badlands, in present Golden Valley County, homesteading brought another collective settlement venture to the region. The German Catholic Golden Valley Land Company encouraged many Germans from Minnesota, especially Stearns County, to take up land. This movement, starting in 1902, brought a number of second-generation German Catholic families to the southern part of the county. As a result, Catholic parishes arose in Sentinel Butte (1905), in Beach (1906), Alpha (1912), Burkey (1912), and Golva (1921). German-speaking priests from Assumption Abbey at Richardton often served these communities. Many German families remain in this area.

HUNGARIAN-GERMANS

Germans of many backgrounds came to western Dakota in pioneer days. Sometime in the middle or late 1880's a number of German homesteaders from Hungary came to the land near Gladstone in Stark County. This early contingent was followed by larger groups in the early 1890's, and the settlement expanded through Hirschville (St. Phillip's Church) and ten miles to the north. From Gladstone, the German-Hungarians homesteaded in a belt that extended south to Lefor (St. Elizabeth Church and school, 1897), eastward to St. Stephen's Church, and at least fifteen miles southwest to the vicinity of New England. This is the largest concentration of German-Hungarians in the state. The descendants of a group with a similar background who arrived in the early 1890's still live about ten miles north of Glen Ullin, while others are found southeast of Mott.

The Hungarian-Germans are, in fact, German people who came from the Banat region of what used to be the Austro-Hungarian Empire. After this territory was taken from the Turks by the Hapsburgs, Maria Theresa invited German settlers into the rich lands along the tributaries of the Danube. They and their descendants remained in that region for many generations; some live there even today. Banat is now a part of Rumania and Yugoslavia. The Gladstone families (frequently from the Temesvar section of Banat) came to North Dakota in much the same fashion as the German-Russians and other immigrants from eastern Europe. They wanted free land and, therefore, responded to the advertisements of American railroad and land companies. For the most part, they are Catholic and have a dialect that differs from the other local German people. Though initially intermarriage with German-Russian Catholics was infrequent, it became a common thing after the first generation. Many, if not most, studies combine Hungarian-Germans with German-Russians; but such a designation is inaccurate. Their origins, dialect, and traditions are quite different, since their home colonies in eastern Europe were 500 miles from the Ukraine.

Most of North Dakota's Hungarian-Germans are found west of the Missouri, although another rather large group of Austro-Hungarian (Burgenland) settlers were present at the founding of Fingal and still make up much of the population of that Barnes County town. In the west Missouri region, St. Anthony in Morton County received a group of Burgenland Germans in 1887. The Hungarian villages of Illmuetz, Halbdorf and Apetten are frequently named as their European points of origin. Only a few families of that group remain, and they are mixed with Germans from Russia. Some of the same people, however, settled and are still present in the Huff and Fort Rice communities. The Banat and Burgenland home districts are separated by several hundred miles of modern-day Hungary. Though the two North Dakota groups had somewhat similar origins, there was little, if any, early-day commerce between them.

GERMAN-RUSSIANS

Largest of all national groups in the West River country (130 townships and 25 percent of the land area) is a special kind of eastern European German. They are, to be exact, "Black Sea Germans," coming from what is now Russia, specifically the Ukraine. The terms "German-Russians" or "Russian-Germans" (though now in general use) can be misleading, for they have no Russian blood in their heritage. They are the descendants of Germans who migrated to the Ukraine at the invitation of the Czar early in the nineteenth century from the provinces of Baden, Alsace, Wurtemberg, and Pfalz. Loss of privileges caused them to leave the Russian *dorfs* in which they had lived for several generations and to come to America.

A distinction can be made between the Protestants and Catholics of this group. Though both groups "homesteaded" in Russia's Black Sea region at about the same time (the first two decades of the nineteenth century), and both groups underwent much the same experience, they are in some ways quite different. They came from different areas of Germany; they usually lived in separate colonies in Russia; they had different dialects; they avoided intermarriage and generally considered themselves separate entities. There is reason to believe that they differed in small and sometimes major ways in their adjustments to American conditions.

Catholic German-Russians

Most of the German-Russians in the counties north and south and west of Dickinson are Catholic. A few early families came to the Antelope area near Hebron in 1887. Within two years, another group had settled north of Mott. The influx increased and soon two rural communities grew up: St. Placidus parish (Steiner Township) and St. Michael's parish (St. Croix Township). Between 1891 and 1893 there were German Catholic migrations to the Dickinson and Richardton areas. Immigration continued throughout the region until World War I. Heavy concentrations developed in the Schefield vicinity (St. Pius Church and school), and they extended north to Dickinson and southwest into Slope County. St. Helen's Church took care of German-Russians south of New England. Here, and elsewhere in the area west of the Missouri, the Catholic Germans had come primarily from the Beresan colonies in the Ukraine. A small proportion had come from the Kutschurgan and Liebental areas; a few from Bessarabia west of the Dniester River.

Catholics farther to the east (north and south of Hebron and New Salem) settled on what eventually became a solid mass of German farms which spread from St. Anthony, southwest to Fallon (1892), Flasher and Raleigh (1906), and down to the Cannonball River. Another group of Catholic German-Russians first settled northwest of Mandan, centering around St. Vincent's Church, in 1888. Descendants of these settlers live in almost every part of four townships and extend for fifteen miles into Oliver County. A smaller German "colony" is located about fifteen miles southeast of Beulah around St. Benedict's Church.

Another large German Catholic area stretches from Glen Ullin through the Heart Butte vicinity and south to Lake Tschida. SS. Peter and Paul's stone and clay church (T 137-R 90)* served the early settlers, and this thick-walled church is still in use. St. Joseph's Church, however, near Heart Butte (built first in 1898) was and continues to be a center for most of these local farmers. The Katharinental and Karlsruhe colonies of south Russia were the homes of most of their ancestors. The first arrivals came in 1892.

The Raleigh region, mentioned above, is unique in that the early people came from Krassna, the lone major Catholic colony in Bessarabia. These are said to have come by way of Strasburg, North Dakota, across the Missouri.

The Raleigh and Fallon German settlements are, in effect, relatively small rural communities; nevertheless, they had parochial schools. The Fallon Catholic parish erected a school in 1916 which continued until the 1960's. Its enrollment (both boarding and day students) numbered as high as 118 pupils in one year. At Raleigh, St. Gertrude's School continues today, offering grade and high school curricula.

The parochial school was a vehicle for perpetuating both Catholicism and the German community culture in many southwestern North Dakota German-Russian areas. Besides Fallon and Raleigh, schools existed in Schefield, St. Anthony, New England, and Glen Ullin. In these, German was never a classroom language, at least after the First World War; but it was a regular feature of playground and school social life.

Protestant German-Russians

Protestant German-Russians comprise the largest national group in the eastern half of the West River area, residing especially in two sizable regions. The first region includes almost the entire rural portion of Mercer County, with adjacent townships in Dunn and Oliver counties. A second and extensive settlement area runs north of New Leipzig for over twenty miles and south of that village for almost fifteen miles. The stone and clay Hope Lutheran Church near Old Leipzig, built in 1897, was a community center. To the west the German Protestant region embraces the Burt and Odessa area; to the east it includes a considerable amount of land north and south of Elgin and Heil. The *Wasse Kirche*, a sod structure northeast of Heil, and the Bethesda Lutheran Church south of Leith also became community centers. The Elgin, New Leipzig, and Leith territory was settled to a great extent shortly before and after the turn of the century by individuals and families from McIntosh and Logan counties. These German homesteaders left the eastern counties when new land became scarce. Ashley and Wishek family names and house styles can still be found in Grant County neighborhoods.

Within all these areas, loyalties were directed toward rural communities, many of which no longer exist. Some,

---

*In this volume, where possible, townships are indicated by using their popular names. In the absence of such names, the United States Land Survey designations are utilized. Since every part of North Dakota is governed by the same base line and principal meridian, the descriptions use the simple township and range numbers.

such as Krem and Leipzig, were comparatively large; some were just a church and its neighboring farms (*e.g.*, Neu Gleuckstal, Krontal, and Friedenthal in Mercer County). Protestant German-Russians tended to name the earliest churches (and thereby their neighborhoods) after their home colonies in Russia. A complete map of the very early churches would be helpful in determining more precise points of national origin.

In the northern group, the earliest German-Russian Protestants were probably the occupants of a group of wagons which came to Mercer County in 1886 over a series of immigrant trails from Scotland (near Yankton), Dakota Territory. In the south, colonists from Leipzig, Bessarabia, founded Old Leipzig and later New Leipzig in present-day Grant County. These early settlers established a pattern that was to be followed by many Protestant colonists in the first decade of settlement. They arrived from Russia in the Yankton area (towns such as Menno, Tripp, and Freeman), traveled a wagon route north through the Aberdeen-Eureka territory, and then crossed the Missouri to the Mercer and Grant county villages. Later groups came by rail directly to such dispersal points as Glen Ullin and Richardton.

The majority of German Protestants in Grant and Morton counties came from Bessarabia or from the Gleuckstal Ukrainian villages, while a lesser number came from the Crimea and the Grossliebental area. The more northerly group in the Oliver-Mercer-Dunn region traces its origins, for the most part, to Bessarabia and to its neighboring colonies, though a surprisingly large number seem to have migrated from the Crimea (as the name Krem implies).

The German-Russians, whether Protestant or Catholic, were generally not cattle people; rather, they came from a tradition of farms, vineyards, and gardens. They avoided the rough country of the region. As one of their adages puts it, "Every hill was a thorn." Only in the last several decades have they seriously gone into ranching or moved into the ranching areas.

Studies of earlier ownership patterns will probably show, however, that the German-Russians have been more aggressive than other nationalities in acquiring crop land for farming purposes. Farms which were once possessed by Anglo-Americans, Irish, and other minor groups are very often now occupied by Germans, because ownership of land was central to their aspirations and family endeavors.

HOLLANDERS

North Dakota newspapers announced in May, 1910, that at least 10,000 acres of Stark County land had been purchased by a syndicate of "bankers and capitalists" who headquartered in Amsterdam, Holland. It was a "million dollar deal," the accounts said. With great expectations the *Holland-Dakota Landbouw Compagnie* had acquired many of the odd-numbered sections between Belfield and South Heart (particularly at Zenith). The land holdings were especially evident in the township T 139-R 98.

That summer two different contingents of men and women (at least 100 in all) arrived directly from Holland. By fall a large warehouse and office had been erected; a demonstration farm had been set up, and plans were made to try out not only varieties of wheat and corn, but also such things as sugarbeets, potatoes, navy beans and field peas. The next year, farm work got underway with special vigor. Steam plows and farm experts from Europe were on hand. Unfortunately, the summer's returns were not good, nor was the production in any of the following years. By 1914 the warehouse and office buildings in Belfield were sold to an American firm, and the *Landbouw* Company's aims, thereafter, became quite modest. It became a routine type of land-holding company and rented its land to local farmers. Eventually, the Dutch company sold all of its properties; nevertheless, it held title to some land in the South Heart-Belfield region as late as the second World War.

Some of the Dutch settlers were Catholic, and some were of Dutch Reformed background. A Christian Reformed Church existed at Zenith from 1912 to 1921. One report said: "Most of the Dutch returned to Holland." This was probably an exaggeration. Farming conditions were difficult, but many immigrants took American jobs and became citizens: some were store-keepers; some worked for the railroad, and some home-steaded elsewhere. Descendants of several of the original families still farm in the South Heart area.

Seventy miles east of Zenith another influx of Hollander settlers took place at about the same time (1910). A number of Dutch farmers joined homesteaders from a variety of national backgrounds and acquired land near the newly-formed town of Lark in Grant County. A Christian Reformed Church was active at Lark from 1910 to 1929; a minister is said to have come from South Dakota for occasional services. The Dutch community was small in size. Some of their descendants now live in Bismarck; only one or two families are still in the Lark region.

INDIANS (American)

Two Indian reservations exist west of the Missouri. The northernmost is Fort Berthold, which was established when the American Fur Company, after abandoning Fort Clark, moved up the Missouri to a place the Indians called "Like a Fish Hook." There, in 1845, the company built what was to be called Fort St. James. Hidatsa Indians, who had just arrived at the site, assisted in the building project. The following year, the fort was re-named Fort Berthold. Mandan Indians moved to the vicinity shortly afterward, and in 1862 the Arikaras joined them. Members of these three tribes, fearing the Sioux, built lodges nearby in the traditional log-and-earth fashion. In December 1862 the Sioux destroyed the original Fort Berthold, and nearby Fort Atkinson became the company headquarters and was re-named Fort Berthold. President Grant, in 1870, created the Fort Berthold Reservation for Mandan, Arikara, and Hidatsa Indians. Descendants of these people make up the residents of the present-day reservation located on the Missouri to the north of Dunn County and to the east of McKenzie County. Some anthropological studies, many government documents, and a number of travelers' reports and private accounts are available concerning the early Fort Berthold Indian people. In 1965, only a few non-Indian ranchers were listed as residing on the reservation.

Standing Rock is the second reservation, one made up of Sioux Indians and established in 1860. A surprisingly large number of white residents live within the reservation confines. The whole of Sioux County technically is reservation area; yet few, if any, Indians are engaged in agricultural pursuits in much of the county. Those who do farm can most often be found in the areas around Fort Yates. Apparently, tribal policies and historic circumstances made it relatively easy for white settlers to acquire land in Sioux County, at least in earlier decades. The eastern end of Sioux County tends to be farmed by German-Russian Catholics, an extension of the Raleigh and St. Anthony group. The western portion of the county is generally Norwegian or Anglo-American.

IRISH

Although accounts give evidence of some Irish among the earliest homesteaders in the farming regions west of the Missouri, few are on the land today. Most of the Irish were "boomers" who, after taking up land and acquiring titles to their claims, sold them to others and left the farm way of life. The Irish who remain are usually part of the ranching tradition of Anglo-Saxon and Old American origins. They came with the cattle people and are part of that independent culture. Several dozen Irish families still remain, scattered throughout the ranching areas.

JEWS

A number of Jewish individuals, at least fifteen, filed on homestead lands about ten miles north of Flasher between 1902 and 1906. Assisted by a Jewish "back to the land" organization, these early settlers located in DeVaul Township in Morton County (T 136-R 84) and in the township immediately to the east. Within two decades, it seems, almost every family had left the area, although one individual farmed there until his death in the 1940's.

A second and larger cluster of Jewish homesteads was located about fifteen miles southwest of Rhame in Bowman County. Jewish men and women made up the majority of settlers in T 129-R 105, but they were also in the townships to the north and to the west. The Jewish influx started in 1908 and reached its peak years in 1910-1911. Seventy-five Jewish men and women are known to have filed on land in the area. Some relinquished their claims, but most of the newcomers fulfilled the requirements and acquired their acreages. Within a few years the majority left Bowman County; no Jewish farmers are present today.

NORWEGIANS

The most widely dispersed of the national groups in the area, and the second most numerous, are the Norwegians. They were also among the earliest settlers, for some few came to the region with the Anglo-American ranchers as early as 1881. In 1883 and 1884, a small group of Norwegians are said to have come to new land near Stanton; these settlers apparently came from Glenwood, Minnesota. At the same time, a settlement was made at Taylor in Stark County; this concentration presently runs almost twenty miles north and six miles south of that town. The Taylor Lutheran Church first met in 1885.

Bowman County, both south and east of Rhame, is today very much Norwegian. The Spring Creek, Grand River, and Union Prairie Norwegian Lutheran congregations were all organized in 1908. Norwegians are also present in a small area southwest of Daglum (Daglum Lutheran Church was organized in 1907).

Farmlands south of Dunn Center for ten miles, and as far east as Halliday are solidly Norwegian: Normanna congregation (1908), Ridgeway (1915), and Vang Lutheran churches (1909). Adams County's Reeder and Bucyrus vicinities are heavily Norwegian: rural Richland, Immanuel, and North Grand Lutheran churches were organized in the first decade of the twentieth century.

Another sizable concentration exists around Almont in Morton County and extends west of Sims (Sims Church and Heart River Lutheran Church). The Sims Scandinavian Lutheran Church, along the early Northern Pacific route, was organized in 1884 and became the oldest Lutheran church west of the Mandan; it was, in fact, a kind of mother church for the West. Ministers moved out from Sims to found congregations along the Montana border in Golden Valley County, to the south at Flasher, and in the Norwegian areas north of the Northern Pacific railroad.

Norwegian residents are found, sometimes mixed with Anglo-Americans and sometimes in solid concentrations, throughout central and northern McKenzie County. At least twenty Norwegian congregations were organized in that county by World War I. They included the Tobacco Garden Creek area's Garden Valley Church (organized in 1905) and the Keene Church (organized in 1905). There were also the Trinity Church near Schafer (1910), the Clear Creek Church (organized in 1906), the Farland Church (1909), and the Spring Creek Church (1914).

In central Golden Valley County a considerable number of Norwegians are still present. Their forebears built their first church in Beach in 1907. Occasional Lutheran services, however, were held in Beach homes for ranchers and railroad workers as early as 1885.

Norwegians are also found alone, or mixed with Anglo-Americans, along a thirty-mile strip of sometimes rugged land north of the Cannonball River in Grant County. Other Norwegians, mixed with families of a variety of backgrounds, reside south of Sweetbriar and extend in a southerly direction to a point about four miles north of Flasher. The apparent ease with which Norwegians and Anglo-Americans mix together in the hills and broken terrain of western North Dakota is noteworthy. Norwegians seem to have been the first of the immigrants to join the Anglo-Saxon "rough country" ranching enterprises in any significant numbers. The old observation that Norwegians "liked the valley" seems to hold true.

It should be noted, also, that most of the original settlers, though born in Norway, did not come to this part of the country "right off the boat." Rather, they had settled for some months or years in the Norwegian communities of eastern Dakota or Minnesota and were thereby already acclimated to the American social and economic scene. This prior experience gave them a distinct advantage over most other immigrant groups. It may partially explain why Norwegians were more active in politics, valued education more highly, and seemed to have adopted American business and farming practices in a more rapid fashion. A possible cultural disadvantage was that they gave up their language and national customs more readily than their Eastern European neighbors.

POLES

Polish farmers are present in several townships south of Scranton. They, with a handful of Bohemian neighbors, came to Bowman County to work in local mines and to look into the prospect of acquiring land. A few did move onto farms. Some of their descendants remain, though many have left the area.

Scattered Polish farmers live on farms near the Belfield Ukrainians and near Beach and Golva. Among them are Poles whose forebears came with groups of Germans from the Stearns County area of central Minnesota. Some also trace their origins to immigrants from an earlier Polish settlement at Greenbush, Minnesota. St. Stanislaus Polish Catholic Church was built in 1909 in the southern part of T 141-R 99. In the initial settlement decade a Polish priest from Wibaux, Montana, served the congregation; the church was closed in 1954. Close ties were maintained between the Golva and Belfield Poles, and between these groups and a larger Polish settlement at St. Philips Church south of Wibaux in Montana.

SWEDES

Starting in 1882, a group of settlers from Sweden began moving into the Fort Clark locality. Eventually, they might have numbered as high as forty families; a few still reside on the land along the Missouri northwest of Fort Clark; the rest have disappeared. The earliest arrivals came from Pennsylvania; later ones came directly from the old country. The settlement probably had close ties with a much larger group of Swedes who resided in the vicinity of Painted Woods, Wilton, and Coleharbor, immediately across the Missouri.

Very often the earliest Norwegian settlements contained a family of Swedish background. Sometimes a cluster of such families was present. Early Swedish homesteaders in the Norwegian areas of southeastern Bowman County and nearby Adams County attended a Swedish Lutheran church across the line in South Dakota. The Gascoyne community had the Bethesda Lutheran Church (Augustana), which was founded in 1910.

Immediately south of Taylor, a number of Swedish families homesteaded. Here, too, they were part of a larger Norwegian area. Without their own church or organization, they eventually joined the Norwegian social and religious life. If any descendants remain today, they are usually in families of mixed national background.

UKRAINIANS

Living in the area directly north of Belfield (Gorham, Fairfield, and Ukrainia communities), the Ukrainians are a distinct and spectacular people. The region extends northward from the town of Belfield for about 25 miles, and is primarily in Billings County. Local Bohemians had already occupied some of the better homestead lands when the first Ukrainians came in 1896. Great numbers of Ukrainians followed thereafter, coming from Canada or directly by train from New York. Eventually, they occupied almost the entire area between the Bohemians and the Badlands. Most of the early residents of the Belfield area came from Galicia (Borschev, Stanislaw), which was, at that time, under the control of the Austro-Hungarian monarchy. For the most part, the present day descendants are Catholic, of the Byzantine-Ruthenian Rite, though some are Ukrainian Orthodox. Many retain their language, foods, and celebrations. The family names often end in -uk. Traditionally, they have had bonds of friendship and marriage with the Ukrainian people of Wilton, North Dakota.

Through the decades their community life has centered around their unique and picturesque onion-shape-domed churches. In 1906, St. Demetrius Church was built on Section 4, T 141-R 98, in Billings County; and the site became known as Ukrainia. In 1917 the SS. Peter and Paul Ukrainian Orthodox Church was built nearby. Another social and religious center was some fifteen miles northwest at Gorham, where St. Josaphat's Church was built in 1911. In 1939 a residence for nuns was built near St. Demetrius Church. For a number of years the sisters taught catechism and the Ukrainian language during summer and in public school classes during the school year.

The increase in farm sizes has taken its toll in recent decades. The Gorham Church was closed in 1953; St. Demetrius was moved to a more central location along the highway in 1949 (Section 22, T 142-R 99); the SS. Peter and Paul Church in recent years has had no resident pastor. A large and elegant St. John the Baptist Ukrainian Catholic Church flourishes in Belfield. It was established in 1944 by Ukrainian farm folk as they moved "into town."

RUSSIANS

Distinct from the Belfield Ukrainians, another group of farmers from Russia can be found scattered through a U-shaped area starting about seven miles north of Grassy Butte in McKenzie County, continuing south of that city for about eight miles, thence east about twenty miles, and then north to the area west of Killdeer in Dunn County. Mixed with them are Germans, Norwegians, and others. These farmers are called "Russians" and even refer to themselves by that name, although they come from a region within fifty miles of the Ukrainian capital, Kiev, and thus technically should be classed as Ukrainians. Their names, in contrast to the other Ukrainians, often end in -enko. Local farmers have traditional ties of friendship and marriage with the Ukrainians of Kief, Butte, and Ruso, North Dakota. Though many of the original homesteaders were of the Ukrainian Orthodox faith, their present-day descendants tend to adhere to American Protestant denominations. Nevertheless, a small Orthodox church, St. Pokrova, still stands in Section 34 of T 145-R 97. Baptisms and funerals took place in that building in the earlier years, but such things are rare now. As in the Belfield area, occasional adobe-type houses and barns can still be seen in the countryside. The famous Grassy Butte "sod post office" is, in fact, a typical Ukrainian log-clay structure.

SYRIANS (Lebanese)

Several people with Syrian names reside on farms in the southern half of the West River county area. These may be the remnants of Syrian families who worked in the coal mines at Zenith and elsewhere before World War I. There may also have been a cluster of Syrian farms somewhere in the region during homestead days, for other Syrian rural communities sprang up in North Dakota at that time. Specific information, however, is not available.

Ethnic Population Distribution
Northwest Section of North Dakota

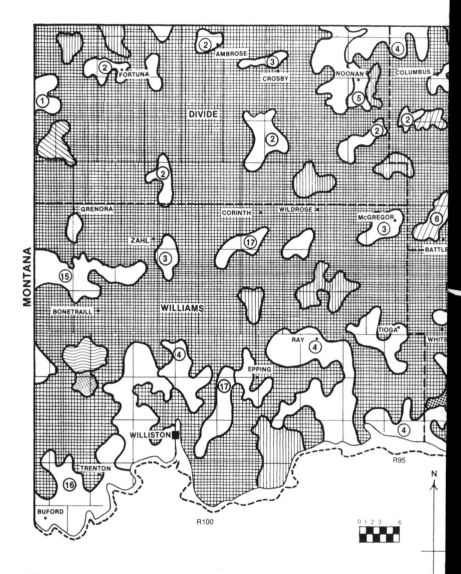

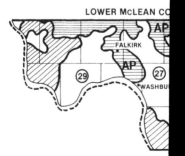

1. Dane 50%; others
2. Anglo-American 50%; others
3. Anglo-American 50%; Norwegian 50%
4. Anglo-American 50%; German 50%
5. Belgian 50%; Anglo-American 50%
6. Swede 50%; Norwegian 50%
7. Bohemian 40%; Norwegian 40%; Anglo-American 20%
8. Hollander 50%; Dane 50%
9. Mixed; Anglo-Ontarian, Anglo-American, Dane
10. German 50%; Norwegian 50%
11. Anglo-American and Anglo-Ontarians
12. Anglo-American 70%; German 30%
13. Dane 50%; other 50%
14. German (Stearns County)
15. Luxemburger and German 75%; Bohemian and others 25%
16. Anglo-American 75%; French, Indian and others 25%
17. Anglo-American 75%; others 25%
18. Anglo-American 70%; German 30%
19. German 70%; Anglo-American 30%
20. Mennonite
21. Mennonite Brethren German-Russian and some other Germans
22. Anglo-American 35%; Norwegian 30%; German, German-Russian, Swede, others 35%
23. German and German-Russian 60%; Ukrainian, Norwegian, Anglo-American 40%
24. Norwegians 60%; German and German-Russian 30%; others 10%
25. Mixed: Norwegian, German-Russian, German, Anglo-American
26. Mixed: Anglo-American, Swede, German, German-Russian, Norwegian
27. Swede 50%; Norwegian 25%; German-Russian 25%
28. Anglo-American 50%; German-Russian, German, Swede, Norwegian 50%
29. Norwegian 50%; Anglo-American, German-Russian, Swede 50%
30. German-Russian 40%; Anglo-American 30%; German 30%

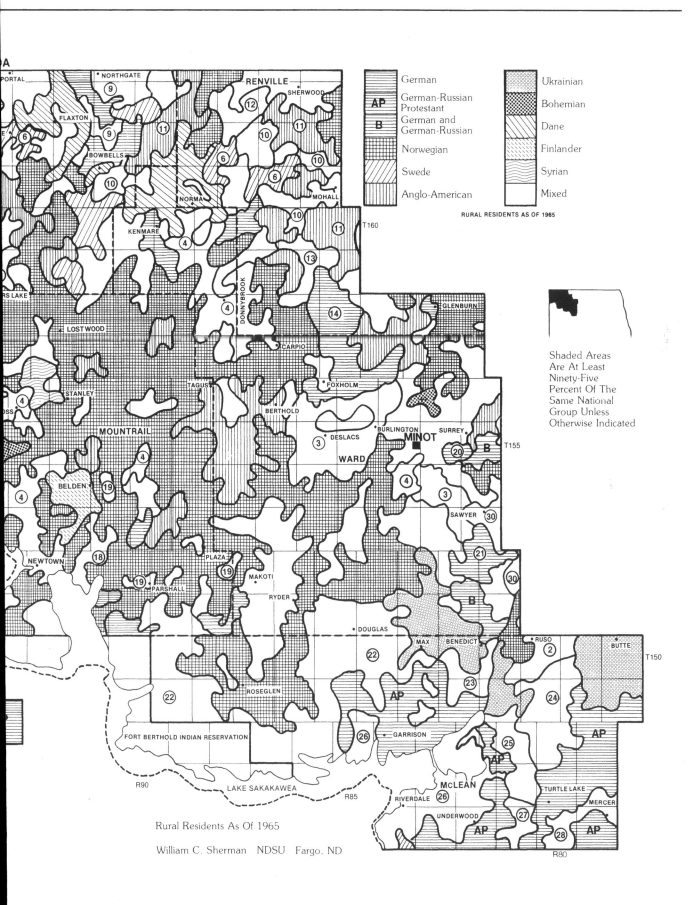

German

German-Russian
Protestant

German and
German-Russian

Norwegian

Swede

Anglo-American

Ukrainian

Bohemian

Dane

Finlander

Syrian

Mixed

RURAL RESIDENTS AS OF 1965

Shaded Areas
Are At Least
Ninety-Five
Percent Of The
Same National
Group Unless
Otherwise Indicated

Rural Residents As Of 1965

William C. Sherman   NDSU   Fargo, ND

Township Names and Descriptions
Northwest Section of North Dakota

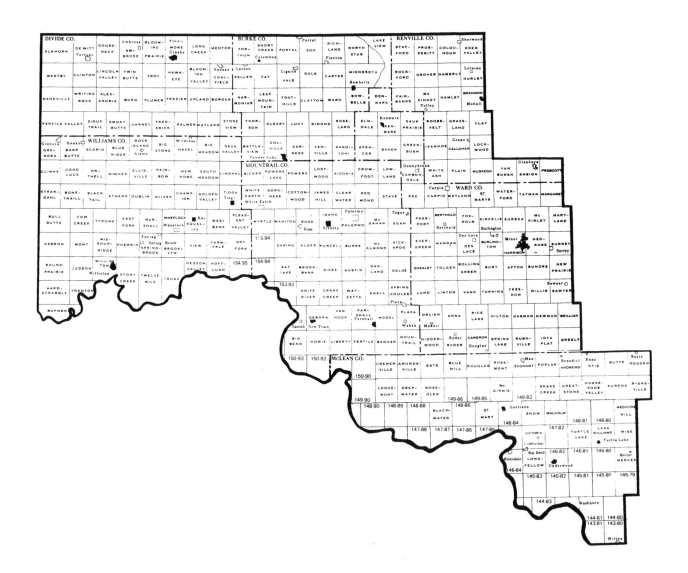

Commentary

ANGLO-AMERICANS

The first permanent white residents of the northwestern counties were, without doubt, Americans whose ancestry extended back to pre-Civil War days and often to Revolutionary times. In the earliest days, such settlers took up bottom land around Fort Buford, Fort Stevenson, and Fort Berthold, raising hay, cattle, and horses for the military garrisons and the Indian tribes nearby. Some non-military settlers established Little Muddy near Fort Buford as early as 1884. Among them were "wood-hawks" who supplied wood for the boilers of Missouri River steamboats. (Wood suppliers probably lived, at least seasonally, on bottom lands throughout the entire Missouri Valley, if not in the late 1860's, at least in the 1870's.) Little Muddy, in Williams County, was a center not only for soldiers, but also for cattlemen who entered the region in the early 1880's. Down river near Fort Stevenson in present-day McLean County, a similar settlement grew up which supplied the needs of soldiers and Indians in the neighboring locale. Fort Stevenson and nearby Fort Berthold were both established in the 1860's; cattle, horses, and fodder became vital necessities. Almost without exception these small agriculturalists and wood cutters were a type of Anglo-American frontiersmen, men who seldom stayed long in one place and eventually moved farther west or returned to their eastern homes.

Some large American ranching enterprises came into existence before homesteading. A sixty-acre stockyard at Spiral in Bowbells Township, Burke County, shipped thousands of cattle each year. The loading facilities could handle eight railroad cars at one time. In 1896, however, the year when the first homesteaders came to the area, the stockyard operations closed down completely. Yet, it was still seven years before the great land rush in that region. Some Montana cattle firms, likewise, were present in Williams and Divide counties during the early "open range" period, well before the homesteaders.

As serious farming became a possibility, Anglo-Americans took up homesteads throughout the northwestern seven-county area, doing so in a sort of scattered fashion. Being fully American, they had little need to settle in colonies; some did come, however, in an organized manner. For example, a group of Missouri settlers came north during homestead times to Ward County, taking land about five miles south of Des Lacs. Their names were most often Anglo-Saxon, but some were of second or third-generation European immigrant background. Kandiyohi Township in Burke County was named for the many Kandiyohi, Minnesota, homesteaders who came as a group to that area in the earliest days. In the same county the Westminster community in North Star Township grew up after the arrival of a great number of Anglo-Americans from Dry Run, Pennsylvania. Such collective ventures were common throughout the North Dakota settlement period. Often the organization was quite informal, just a collection of neighbors who heard of the new opportunities in Dakota and, either in clusters or as individuals, made the journey westward to the designated land area.

In retrospect, it seems that many of the first Anglo homesteaders were "boomers" — opportunists who sold their claims to more durable neighbors after several years of residence. Knowing that better opportunities existed elsewhere, and well aware of the advantages of town living, great numbers of the American settlers soon departed. By the 1930's, and in some places by the time of World War I, only a few remained. Immigrant European ethnic groups had taken over their land. A perceptive observer can still see signs of their presence — a foundation here, an abandoned shanty there, an old barn and a flowing spring.

In the place names, however, their historic presence becomes clearly evident. Divide County has thirty-three townships, and only one seems to have a name of Norwegian background. Williams County has fifty-seven townships; yet, in spite of the preponderance of Norwegian residents only two names are of Norwegian origin and two are Swedish. One does find in Williams County, however, a Brooklyn Township and a Dublin Township. McLean County, with over sixty townships and a number of highly visible and presently intact immigrant national groups, has only four townships whose names are of Scandinavian origin, four of German, and one of Jewish origin. The rest are of English or Anglo-American derivation.

As elsewhere in the state, Anglo-Americans (with their Anglo-Ontarian "cousins") are now seen as the "Founding Fathers" of almost every town in northwestern North Dakota. They established the earliest businesses, were the first professionals, controlled the school boards and, in general, were the knowledgeable and prestigious people of the day. But the departure rate of the Anglo-Americans in the towns, like those on the farms, was very high. The second-generation offspring, seeing local opportunity as limited, abandoned the region in great numbers. Sons and daughters of more durable ethnic groups, especially those from northern Europe, moved into the ensuing political and social vacuum. In most cases, these same people occupy the positions of privilege even today.

The decline of Anglo-American farmers is evident especially in the demise of their churches. Presbyterian, Congregational, and Methodist churches were once present in many towns and in the countryside; in their places today stand, most often, Norwegian Lutheran churches, or sometimes German Catholic or German Lutheran churches. A Divide County historical reference to the Presbyterian Church in Ambrose has this to say: "So many of the Presbyterian crowd had disappeared — died, moved away, young people to college and did not return — that all services were discontinued."

Nevertheless, some few farmers remain; and, interestingly, a certain amount of Anglo-American ranching still continues along the Missouri and in the bottom lands of the Souris River. An occasional family, with a name that dates from territorial times, is still of significance in the present ranching scene.

ANGLO-ONTARIANS

The northern border counties of North Dakota received a sprinkling of Canadian people (mostly from Ontario) in the earliest days. Some came as merchants; many more came as homesteaders. For the most part, they were of English, Scotch and Scotch-Irish origin; but some Irish came, too. Burke and Renville counties received an unusually large number of these pioneer settlers, especially along the Souris and Des Lacs rivers. Some came as ranchers, but most were of farming background. Divide County has a cluster of settlements along its northern townships which seem to be an extension of Anglo-Saxon farming settlements in Saskatchewan. In most cases, whether as ranchers or farmers, the Ontario people were among the very first to arrive. In towns, too, they were found among the early arrivals.

Some of these pioneer settlers, here and elsewhere in North Dakota, may have been the descendants of Tories who left the United States after the Revolution and took up parcels of Ontario land which the British government gave to refugees of loyalist persuasion. After 100 years, their descendants returned to the States to become citizens. For the most part, however, the Anglo-Ontarians along the Canadian border of North Dakota seem to have been the descendants of later British Isles immigrants, second sons or opportunity-seeking farmers, who responded to the Canadian government's own homestead promotional activities; they crossed the American frontier, without political scruples, and found themselves residents of the United States.

Anglo-Ontarian settlers were familiar with the American legal and economic systems and found themselves more at ease in their new country than did their neighbors of European background. Like their cultural kinfolk, the Anglo-Americans, they tended to drift away from the land. They readily took offices in local and state politics, and throughout their stay in Dakota were classed as successful citizens.

BELGIANS

In the vicinity of Noonan in Divide County, a number of Belgian farmers still reside today. They are the descendants of at least a dozen families who are said to have purchased local land in the first two decades of this century. Some worked first in the Noonan area coal fields and then began to farm. Some had roots in the Belgian communities of southern Minnesota, such as Ghent and Marshall. Their religious affiliation was Catholic. The only other Belgian community in the state is the tiny settlement at Joliette on the Red River in Pembina County.

BOHEMIANS

Two settlements of immigrants from Bohemia exist in this part of the state. One is in western Mountrail County and extends over portions of three townships; the other is a smaller group which is located a few miles north of Minot in Eureka and McKinley townships. The Mountrail community, centering in Debing Township, began with perhaps fifty original families and had Ross and Manitou as its trade centers. The Ward County group, which consisted of several dozen families, gravitated to Minot for shopping purposes.

In 1905 the first Bohemian arrived near Ross. This knowledgeable gentleman had previously lived in Nebraska; and because of his letterwriting abilities, ten more families arrived that same year. This closely parallels the origins of the earlier Bohemian settlement at Lidgerwood in Richland County. In both cases, enthusiastic letters published in Bohemian newspapers brought about the foundation of a settlement which exists today.

The Mountrail County and the Ward County settlers never established an exclusively Bohemian Catholic church. As in most North Dakota Bohemian communities, ethnic allegiance centered not just around the church, but also around a national lodge. Rather unusual among Dakota ethnic groups, this particular nationality almost inevitably brought along a divided loyalty. Some were church members, but others who tended to give nominal allegiance to the church were in fact antagonistic to organized religion and focused their social life on the local lodges. A Bohemian ZCBJ lodge (*Západni Česka Bratrská Jednota*) was founded at Ross in 1908, and within a few years a lodge hall was erected tive miles southwest of town. A similar ZCBJ lodge was built in 1910 north of Minot on Section 1, Minot Township; at a later date it was moved three miles farther north. Both lodges were modest in size, numbering around thirty members in 1912 (compared to 121 in Lidgerwood, North Dakota, and 103 in Mandan).

The lodges became community centers, and a rather full program of dances and other social activities took place under their auspices. Members were buried in the lodge cemetery. A certain physical-culture theme was present, and a motif of science and intellectual endeavor was in the background of their thought. The lodge tradition, thus, reflected the anti-clerical rationalist ideas of their central European progressive counterparts.

Although its vigor has diminished, the Minot Lodge is still a community meeting place, and the building is kept in repair. The Ross Lodge Hall, however, was dismantled in 1963, though its cemetery is still intact. Today many Bohemian families find their most lasting ties with the organization through the Western Fraternal Life Association, the modern insurance arm of the ZCBJ national organization. Those Bohemians who affiliated with a religious group, particularly in the second and third generations, joined various local congregations — Lutheran, Catholic, and Methodist.

Neither the Minot nor the Ross people seemed to have much connection with the Walsh County Bohemians. Some early families in Minot came to the region by way of the Lidgerwood Bohemian community in Richland County. Prague, Nebraska is often mentioned as the origin of many Ross families.

Bohemians were not adverse to settling in small two- or three-family groups elsewhere in the area. For example, a cluster of families took up land in Coleville Township, Burke County, in the first decade of the 1900's.

DANES

Burke and Renville counties have, without doubt, the most extensive Danish settlements in all of North Dakota. The largest is north of Kenmare, in Renville County and to a certain extent in Ward County. This community, which centers around Norma, spills over into about five townships, but occupies most of Denmark and Fairbanks townships. The first Danes seem to have arrived around 1889. These newcomers, many of whom came from Iowa, set up the rural Trinity Lutheran congregation in 1896, building a church in 1899 just five miles north of Kenmare in Denmark Township. A few miles northeast, another center of Danish life sprang up; the Bethany Church, which was organized in 1899. A third rural community developed around the Zion Lutheran Church organized farther north in Rockford Township in 1900.

Prior to the formal development of these churches, an itinerant Danish preacher (perhaps a layman) visited his countrymen at isolated settlements, traveling from Renville County as far west as Montana. The Trinity Church, still an active organization, is known as the "Mother Church" of the Danish community. The Bethany Church closed its doors in 1930 and has since been moved away. The Zion Church is still intact, but regular services were discontinued in 1981.

Both the Trinity and Zion churches affiliated with the United Evangelical Lutheran Church (the Danish Synod). Bethany was of a different Danish synod. All three, however, could be classed in the "Sad" or "Singing" Dane tradition. The Nazareth Lutheran Church in Kenmare, originally a mission of the rural Trinity Church, now supplies ministers for the earlier country churches.

A distinction was made between what was popularly called the "Singing Dane" (who had a strong Inner Mission emphasis) and the "Happy Dane" of Grundtvig background. The separation reflected a theological dispute which arose in Denmark before American settlement. One aspect of the division was the seeming willingness of the Grundtvig Danes to accept dances and liquor as part of their family and community life. The

"Singing Danes" were more restrained in their approach to such things.

No "Happy Dane" churches arose in the Kenmare-Norma area. A Danish Brotherhood Lodge hall was constructed in Kenmare, however, and dances took place on its premises. A Flaxton pastor of "Happy Dane" tradition came to Kenmare and held services in various Danish homes.

A second large Danish group exists just a few miles west in Burke County; its activities focused around two little country churches, one of the Grundtvig tradition (two miles north of Flaxton) and the other of "Singing Dane" orientation (five miles northeast of that town). This latter group was called the Ebenezer congregation. Established in 1900, the church later burned down and its members transferred to Flaxton and there merged with a local Norwegian church group. The United Lutheran Church which emerged in Flaxton was for many years associated with the United Evangelical Lutheran Church synod and is still an active organization. The first Danes in the Flaxton area came in 1889. The earliest arrivals originated, very often, from Illinois and Wisconsin.

The Grundtvig or "Happy Dane" church was always a struggling enterprise, having a smaller number of adherents and a tiny church building. Founded shortly before the Ebenezer Congregation, its members did dance and play cards; they also placed a certain emphasis on Danish culture. The little group had a Danish-language lending library and sponsored frequent lectures on Danish literary and historical matters. By the 1940's, the congregation having diminished in numbers, services were no longer held. Its members joined other local congregations.

Perhaps because of the size of the Kenmare and Flaxton Danish communities, their special culture flourished to an extent that exceeded any other place in North Dakota. A memorial to this special kind of immigrant exists in the enduring presence of a Danish wind-driven flour mill which occupies the center of the Kenmare city park. This mill, the only one left in the state, was built on a Danish farmer's open prairie land and serviced farm families for twenty years until its abandonment in 1923. The Hill Township Danes built smaller mills in early Cass County, and a Dane built a large one at Anselm in Ransom County. The Kenmare mill is, perhaps, the only permanent tribute to the dozen or so pioneer Danish North Dakota settlements.

In Divide County several Danish communities were established. In 1905 an initial eleven Danes, led by a Danish missionary, took up land along the Montana border in what is now Daneville Township; the settlement extended southward into Fertile Township. This group came primarily from Kenmare, but some of their number were originally from Hutchinson, Minnesota. The Bethel Lutheran congregation in Fertile Township, organized in 1906, held its services in an unfinished basement and never did complete the proposed church structure; the church community dissolved in 1939. Much more successful was the founding in 1905 of the Daneville Township Church, officially called the Danish Evangelical

Lutheran congregation. A church building was erected in 1907, and that structure became the enduring home of the Danish community until its dissolution in 1963. Families of the original Daneville settlement are still present, although the strong Danish traditions have disappeared.

A group of Danish Baptists came to the Donnybrook area in Ward County at the turn of the century. Apparently these Danes came from Clarks Grove, Minnesota, where their Baptist roots had previously been established. A "Donnybrook Danish-Norwegian Baptist Church" was built in 1906, and this structure was the religious home of thirty-eight adult members. By 1910 the group had no regular pastor; members began moving away, and the congregation soon became defunct.

In McLean County a smaller Danish enclave was formed with the arrival of a dozen families in Medicine Hill Township in 1902. Local people called it "the Dane Settlement." Danish-language religious services were held for some years in farm homes, with occasional visits by pastors from the Kenmare Danish Lutheran churches.

A rarity in North Dakota was the erection of the Brorson Parochial High School, located near the Trinity Lutheran Church five miles north of Kenmare in Denmark Township. The school, probably the only one under North Dakota Danish auspices, opened in 1902. Eventually, a large two-story building was erected, and a gymnasium was added several years later. The school emphasis was on the education of young people from Danish-American homes, and also on the education of immigrants from Denmark. By World War I the institution was in serious trouble from lack of students. A few years later it was sold to the Trinity Church congregation and no longer existed as a formal school.

The short-lived interest in the Brorson High School dramatizes an attribute of the North Dakota Danish community — namely, that a concern for maintaining ethnic traditions was less intense among the Danes than among their Norwegian and German neighbors. Danes tended to enter the mainstream of American life rather quickly. Their interest in prairie farming was often minimal, and they moved rather rapidly to the large urban centers. Norwegian parochial schools flourished in such places as Fargo and in western Minnesota towns such as Fergus Falls through the 1930's; some of these schools continue today. German-language schools were numerous among Catholics and Lutherans. The anti-German sentiment of World War I dampened enthusiasm for them, but the church-school tradition continued among Germans even into the 1950's. It is interesting to note that the small western North Dakota German Lutheran congregations of Zap and Hannover had grade schools well into the 1930's.

DUNKARDS (Brethren) *

A surprisingly large number of German-Americans of Dunkard background came to northwestern North

---

*The word "Dunkard" will occur frequently in this volume, for it was almost the only name in popular use at the time of settlement. Newspaper accounts invariably used it; occasionally church leaders adopted the term.

Dakota. They came in the earliest of times and with high hopes, but in retrospect, they seem to have had great difficulty in adjusting to the prairies, for very few of the original families remain.

The first settlers in the Bowbells community of Burke County were Dunkards who arrived on immigrant cars in 1896, two or three years before Norwegians and other homesteaders found the area. Several dozen families from Indiana made up the settlement. The Bowbells community built a church which existed until 1912. In 1901 and 1906, church records list fifty members. The congregation ceased to exist formally in 1912, but a rural cemetery remains.

Ward County had several Dunkard settlements. One was at Berthold, where a sod church was built in 1901 at a total cost of $150.00. This group numbered seventy-five members in 1910 and declined to ten individuals (three families) in 1927. It had disappeared from the scene by the mid-1940's. Their descendants are now apparently Baptist.

The Kenmare community had a Dunkard congregation which was organized, again at an early date, in 1897. A church was built in Kenmare in 1904; it was one of the largest congregations in the town, but its activities came to an end in the 1940's.

A third Ward County congregation was established a few miles outside of Minot in the Surrey community. This group seemed to have had aggressive adherents from the beginning. It built a large church in 1902 and had a history of strong and consistent leadership. Church membership reached 200 as early as 1908. The congregation flourishes today and has a newly decorated church which serves rural families and some Minot residents. A Minot city congregation was organized in 1912, and it continued until 1949, when it merged with the Surrey church. Its membership probably never exceeded a total of twenty-five families.

In Williams County, a Spring Brook Dunkard settlement church was organized in 1907. This group, halfway between Ray and Williston, flourished in a modest way for a short while. Meetings were held at a school and at a rented Norwegian church. Williston itself had a congregation which was established sometime around 1904. Its membership reached eighty-two by 1907; it had disappeared from the official church roster by 1932.

The term "Dunkard" was becoming obsolete by the time this historic American denomination reached North Dakota. Though members seemed to accept the term and outsiders regularly used it, in most cases the group was referred to officially as the "German Baptist Brethren." In recent decades, as the ethnic dimension has declined, their title has become "The Church of the

Brethren." With their roots in Pennsylvania, these German-speaking Americans moved west with the frontier into Iowa, Minnesota, and the prairie states. Indiana, in particular, seemed to have several towns which were important to their national ethnic and religious life. In North Dakota, Cando became a sort of mother colony, and local records indicate as high as 6,000 Brethren may have come to North Dakota. The Bowbells community arrived on the newly built Soo Line; but this was an exception, for the Great Northern Railroad was responsible for bringing most of the Brethren into the state.

Max Bass, the famous immigration agent for the Great Northern Railroad, was especially active in seeking Brethren settlement along the main line and branch lines of that railroad. He visited the denomination's annual conference in Muncie, Indiana, in 1893, and sought the backing of church authorities for various homesteading ventures. The Great Northern extolled the advantages of North Dakota settlement in Brethren publications. Free trips to North Dakota for investigation purposes were given to specially assigned church leaders. Max Bass later spoke at other Brethren gatherings in Indiana and Ohio; through these efforts almost two dozen Brethren communities came into existence in northcentral and northwestern North Dakota.

Why Max Bass should have felt the Brethren were a particularly apt group for prairie settlement is still not clear. Their German predilection for work and their seriousness of purpose were well known. Their several generations of past American life gave them a certain advantage over other ethnic groups. Unlike some Mennonites, they were not colony people and could live separately on their homestead acreages. Their large families and careful financial practices were certain to be helpful in surviving the hard times and precarious financial circumstances which would necessarily arise in a frontier situation. In any event, Max Bass' work did not produce a spectacular success. In spite of the theoretical advantages, the groups never flourished on the prairies; by the 1920's, most settlements had disappeared. A Brethren church history has this to say about their Dakota experience: "Urge for more land and the militant climate caused many to migrate to the West Coast." Perhaps their lack of strong internal church organization made them less effective in the harsh prairie conditions. Their clergy were elected laymen, and internal controls seem to have been at a minimum. Perhaps their familiarity with the United States was a disadvantage, for they could freely leave the region, while their neighbors from foreign lands, being unaware of opportunities elsewhere, were forced to remain in North Dakota.

FINNS

A Finnish settlement was established in central Mountrail County during homestead times (1903-1910), with Belden as its community center. It seems that most of the original families began to come in 1903 from Minnesota Finnish localities such as New York Mills, the Iron Range, and Duluth. Finns seldom settled among outsiders; they were almost inevitably colony people. "Finlander" is the term used most often by their North Dakota neighbors as they refer to these special immigrants from Scandinavia.

Like the Bohemians, Finns were unusual in that their ethnic allegiance was divided between the Finnish church and the more secular Finnish lodge. In Belden, an Apostolic Lutheran Church and a Finn Hall vied with each other as the center of social and religious life for the first two generations.

The non-religious members of the community seem to have been more aggressive than those who were church oriented. Church gatherings in Belden were sporadic until 1923, when a formal religious organization came into being. This group met in homes and schools until a church building was erected in 1949. The Finn Hall, in contrast, was built two miles south of town in 1913. Dances, lectures, and social gatherings continued regularly through the years.

The Belden Finnish community had the reputation, whether deservedly or not, of being a settlement of strong liberal traditions, In this they reflected the political moods of some northern Minnesota Finnish communities. During the difficult economic times of the twenties and thirties, some Belden citizens assumed western Dakota leadership positions in what might be called "extreme left wing" political movements. The Belden community was the site of socialist and, on occasions, even communist rallies. The Finns in Mountrail County were activists in other ways. They set up several cooperatives. The Belden Shipping Association, which began in 1921, helped Finnish farmers dispose of their products at favorable prices and made possible the purchase of farm supplies in quantity lots. The local Fairview Farmers Club, predominately Finnish, did something of the same thing.

GERMANS (Reichsdeutsch)

Germans from the homeland — some newly arrived and others with a decade of American experience — settled in small communities throughout the northwest counties. Those of Protestant persuasion frequently established Missouri Synod Lutheran churches. Others, for example the Stearns County Germans, set up German Catholic parishes.

A sizable German settlement still exists near Stanley and Epworth in Mountrail County; its roots go back to homestead times. Other Germans settled near Parshall. Farther south, German Catholics occupied land in the same county. Portal and Flaxton in Burke County, and Tolley and Sherwood in Renville County, had German settlers on nearby farmlands. Though the number of residents has declined, descendants of the original farmers remain today. Missouri Synod churches were established in the Burke and Renville County communities between 1901 and 1904 (Tolley began in 1916). Several continue in the present day. St. Paul's Lutheran Church (organized in 1924) at Stanley, the Immanuel Church at Parshall (1917), and the church at Ryder are still active.

In the Bowbells area of Burke County, two Evangelical United Brethren churches, Calvary and Salem, served local homesteading Germans. Their grandchildren still reside on farms and in the town.

Crosby and Fortuna in Divide County also had German Lutheran churches in the earliest days. The Fortuna Missouri Synod congregation was organized in 1913; a church was later built and continues until the present. Palmer Township north of Wildrose had an early-day Missouri Synod congregation.

St. Mary's Township southwest of Garrison in McLean County had a number of German Catholics during settlement times. They were instrumental in setting up St. Nicholas Church in 1906 and a parochial school in 1916. Priests with a German Benedictine background staffed the parish and nearby county churches. The Catholic population of McLean and northern Burleigh counties was of mixed national origin, and the German culture was never a matter of special emphasis.

Germans were taking up land in southern Ward County in homestead days. Many remain in a less concentrated fashion today. Missouri Synod churches were at Ryder, Douglas, and Max. McLean County had earlier congregations at Underwood (1903) and Garrison (1905).

GERMAN MENNONITES

Two very different Mennonite traditions are still present in the northwestern section of North Dakota, the one from Russia and the other of Pennsylvania-American background.

What is now called the Fairview Congregation began with the arrival of a handful of Mennonites in 1902 near Surrey in Ward County. Some families came from Ohio; but the largest number (twenty-two individuals in 1903) came from Mifflin County, Pennsylvania. A meeting house was built in 1905. Though the first church burned in 1959, a new structure has been erected; a small but active congregation still flourishes.

An earlier group of Mennonites of the same background arrived in Kenmare in 1899 and located in Baden Township, Ward County. The group was called the Spring Valley Mennonite Congregation. The earliest members of this group came from Missouri, Iowa, and other midwestern states. The Kenmare group, which may have the distinction of being the earliest American Mennonites in North Dakota, existed for forty years. "Drought and hard times caused them to move away," according to a local Kenmare history book. The church building is now a granary on a local farm; a cemetery remains.

Mennonites of similar origins were at Portal in Burke County, and occasional families were in Williams County in the first decade of the present century. The Surrey congregation is the only one to continue in northwestern North Dakota today. Denominational ties, however, still exist between this congregation and the Munich (Cavalier County) and Arena (Burleigh County) church bodies.

A decidedly different Mennonite group settled a few miles south of Surrey near the town of Sawyer. These are known as the Mennonite Brethren and are Germans of Russian Black Sea origin. They came to Ward County at the turn of the century, during the homestead days, and had close ties with the Wells County Mennonites who reside south of Harvey. In fact, some of the first families were actually of Lutheran background and were converted to the Mennonite faith in North America.

The Sawyer Mennonite community extends almost ten miles south of the town. The Mennonite Brethren Church was first organized in 1909. A small church was constructed eight miles south of Sawyer and it was superseded by another church building a few miles farther north. In 1957 a new church was dedicated in Sawyer itself. The congregation is still active with a full-time pastor in residence.

A late arriving group came to Mountrail County, beginning in 1916. A land company contacted their community in Minnesota and encouraged them to purchase farms in Lostwood Township. Some thirty-one families were present in 1930. A small church was built, but severe drought brought discouragement; many members returned to Minnesota. The last church service was in 1936. Every family, with one exception, was gone by 1940.

None of the Mennonite groups was of the colony tradition; rather, they settled on isolated homestead plots. This may, at times, have lessened their ties to the church. Some descendants of the first settlers are now affiliated with other Protestant denominations. Nevertheless, German was the language of the early religious gatherings; and a distinctive clothing was part of the life of all the women and some of the men. Today, most of the North Dakota Mennonite pioneers' grandchildren seem faithful to their family religious traditions, though special language and garb are things of the past.

There was little, if any, contact between the Mennonites of American background and those of Russian origins. But in Ward County, it seems, relations were free and easy between the Surrey Brethren of Dunker background and the Mennonites of similar early American experience. Both groups had roots in Indiana and in Pennsylvania. In recent years, some shared Sunday School activities between the two groups have taken place in the Surrey community.

The small size of many Mennonite settlements in North Dakota brings identity problems. The church traditions, however, have been kept alive to some extent through the practice of sending children away to Mennonite colleges where the young people mingle with others of their special background.

GERMAN MORAVIANS

A tiny group of Moravian German families settled near Donnybrook in Ward County at the turn of the century. The original families came from Hector, Minnesota. An Aurelia Church congregation was organized in 1903, and a church was built in 1907. Enrollment was always small, and the church closed in 1970.

A second Moravian group of homesteaders took up land some fifteen miles south of Aurelia, near Tagus, on the east edge of Mountrail County. Here, too, a congregation was formed about 1904, and a minister from Aurelia conducted services. A church was built in Tagus in 1916; the diminishing number of affiliates led to its closing and eventual sale in 1940.

The Aurelia and Tagus families are the only organized groups of Moravians known to have settled in the entire central and western part of North Dakota. The Cass County Casselton Moravians, of course, had large and successful settlements, which antedated the Aurelia and Tagus groups by several decades.

GERMAN-RUSSIANS

Germans from Russia (in fact, the Ukraine) are found in McLean County in great numbers. The county population, at least in the southern and eastern regions, is almost half German. This special kind of emigrant left Russia in the late 1800's, after taking up "homesteads" in the Black Sea portion of that country in the first decade of the nineteenth century. The McLean County Germans are part of a massive concentration that extends throughout central North Dakota, starting at the South Dakota border and reaching as far north as Garrison and Rugby.

German-Russians in McLean County are almost exclusively Protestant in background. In Russia they were most often of a Lutheran tradition, but in this country their evangelical and German tendencies led many to ally themselves with non-Lutheran German-speaking denominations. In McLean County, for example, many joined the German Zion Congregational Church of Turtle Lake (organized in 1914); others joined the Turtle Lake Baptist Church (1906). Nevertheless, Lutheran churches were present. The Zion Lutheran Church in McLean County (first organized in 1906) was one of six sister churches which served rural residents in the Mercer area. The Peace Lutheran Church of Turtle Lake, organized first in the country and later moved to town, is still active. The Ohio Synod was a national affiliation which coordinated many of the area's German Lutheran churches in the initial decades of settlement.

The first migrants into the region came by wagon all the way from McIntosh and Logan counties. The first major German store in Turtle Lake was called the Eureka Bazaar, a name which reflected their historical past. The word "Bazaar" indicated the eastern European open market place, and "Eureka" was a sort of American mother colony, the town in South Dakota through which most Germans passed on their journey from Russia. The Turtle Lake-Mercer German settlements are really an extension of an enclave which includes much of Sheridan County and parts of Burleigh and Stutsman counties. The Garrison German-Russians are a further extension of that group, though separated by several townships of Norwegians and Anglo-Americans.

East of Minot a mixed collection of German-Russians and *Reichsdeutsch* is found. These German-Russian families are of Catholic background and represent the western edge of a settlement of Catholic German-Russians who occupy the central portions of McHenry and Pierce counties.

Protestant German-Russians sometimes list their place of origin as Rumania. This is partially correct, for the majority are, in fact, from Bessarabia, the western portion of the Ukraine which between the two World Wars was under the political jurisdiction of Rumania.

Across the Missouri River, Oliver and Mercer counties are almost exclusively Germans from Russia of a similar Protestant Bessarabian (and sometimes Crimean) background.

GERMANS (Stearns County)

Stearns County, Minnesota, is a name that can be found in many North Dakota pioneer chronicles. That part of central Minnesota (St. Cloud and its outlying villages) received a heavy influx of Catholic emigrants from southern Germany during and shortly after the American Civil War. A generation later, sons and daughters of Stearns County farmers sought new land in North Dakota. Groups of Stearns County families can be found in such places as Golva and Richardton along the Northern Pacific line, and also at Bisbee and Cando in central North Dakota.

The northwestern part of the state received three large groups of these same people during the homestead era. A large settlement came to take land northeast of Foxholm, filling at least two townships — one in Ward County and one in Renville County. This could be called the St. Henry's community, for it centered around a large ornate gothic wood frame church (Section 22, Muskego Township), which was dedicated in 1910. Some Burgenland Germans with roots in Fingal, North Dakota, were also present in the settlement. The community still remains, although the church edifice has been destroyed; descendants attend the Catholic Church in Foxholm.

A second cluster of Stearns County Germans settled in Roosevelt Township around SS. Peter and Paul Church not far from Tolley. Farmers of this Renville County settlement still occupy the land in the community, but the church has since been closed.

A third Stearns County group settled in Williams County around St. Boniface Church in the western half of Good Luck Township and spilled over into Climax Township. The parish was established in 1908; the church structure was demolished in 1965. Descendants of these pioneer Germans still reside on the land.

HOLLANDERS

When Divide County was opened to land seekers, a small number of Dutch Catholics came to the Kermit area, west of Noonan (Mentor and Coalfield townships). A few families still remain.

In southern Burke County, a large Hollander family with seven sons came as the first settlers in Garness Township east of Powers Lake. Their grandchildren still occupy much of that township.

ICELANDERS

A group of farmers of Icelandic background homesteaded in Renville County, Eden Valley Township, at the turn of the century. An initial ten families were probably present; none remains today.

INDIANS (American)

The southwestern corner of Williams County was part of the Fort Buford Military Reservation until 1900. Shortly after that date, the area was opened for homesteading. A number of American Indians had been associated with the Fort (abandoned in 1895); some may have been scouts and military personnel. In 1907, parcels of land were allotted to at least twenty Indian men and women in Hardscrabble and Trenton townships. Others received nearby land in later years. Many of the land holders were Métis, with Turtle Mountain backgrounds. Some of their descendants still live in the Trenton area.

Also present in northwestern North Dakota is a portion of the Fort Berthold Indian Reservation. A discussion of that reservation is found in the southwestern area commentary.

JAPANESE

A most unlikely group of homesteaders laid claim to land in western Mountrail County and in nearby Williams County. Federal Land Office ledgers indicate that five Japanese men filed on acreages in the northwestern corner of Manitou Township in Mountrail County, and four more were in the adjoining White Earth Township. Another five individuals sought land near Tioga in Williams County. All of the homestead applications came during the local land boom period, the years 1903 to 1908. Only one Japanese man, Manitou Township's Tighita Nishimura, fulfilled the homestead requirements; the rest abandoned their claim for one reason or another. Mr. Nishimura (Nishemera, in some records) retained his 120 acres for five years and sold it in 1910. The Great Northern Railroad employed Japanese laborers in those same years, and most likely the homesteaders had some association with the railroad extra gangs. (Ten Japanese are buried in the Williston Riverview Cemetery. They were victims of a work train collision in November, 1902).

One of the Mountrail homesteaders, who relinquished his claim in Manitou Township, shortly afterward took up land fifteen miles farther west near Temple in Williams County. This Japanese gentleman lived with his family on the farm for at least ten years and later owned a hotel and restaurant in Minot. In 1969, he died at the age of 93 in Denver, Colorado.

NORWEGIANS

Without question, Norwegians constitute the largest single ethnic group in the region. In fact, the four counties that form the northwestern corner of North Dakota can be described as a Norwegian Sea with islands of other groups interspersed at random inside its boundaries. A venturesome soul could walk (with an occasional detour) from the Garrison Dam to the northwest corner of the state without stepping off Norwegian-owned land.

Divide County has the honor of being the most intensely Norwegian part of the state. In that county some "islands" of non-Norwegians do exist; but they are generally around the towns, particularly in the coal-mining regions. This is also true of northern Williams County. In both areas the towns may be diverse in population, but the hinterland belongs to the Norwegians.

Norwegians, however, were not the first settlers in the region. Early Anglo-Saxon settlements existed around Fort Buford and Fort Stevenson; and in these localities Americans, Swedes, and Germans took up plots of bottomland along the Missouri before extensive systematic homesteading took place. In the same early days, cattle ventures, again dominated by Anglo-Americans, existed in the breaks of the Missouri and in other grass and water areas.

During the northwestern counties' homesteading period (1902 to 1910), Irish, Germans, Poles, Bohemians, Ukrainians, Syrians, and even an occasional Japanese and Black American were taking up land side by side with the Norwegian arrivals. Expectations were often crushed as soil and moisture conditions proved marginal. Indeed, the majority of homesteaders left within the first two decades of settlement. Today, small settlements of Syrians, Finlanders, Bohemians, and Ukrainians remain; but Norwegian farmers seem to have taken over most of the lands vacated by disillusioned or economically distressed outsiders.

The Norwegians who homesteaded in the northwest region represented, for the most part, "second bounce" immigrants. The majority were not "right off the boat." Great numbers, though born in the old country, came from Minnesota Norwegian settlements such as Northfield, Glenwood, and Wheaton. Many came from Norwegian communities on both sides of the Red River: Clay, Wilkin, and Ottertail counties in Minnesota and Richland, Cass, and Traill counties in North Dakota. A few arrived from Wisconsin and Iowa. This gave the Norwegians a special advantage over other immigrant groups in that they were already well acquainted with many American ways. They assumed political offices at an early date and moved readily into educational and business circles.

The political affiliations of the Norwegians in the northwest section of the state tended to be more liberal than that of their fellow countrymen in the eastern portions of North Dakota. Progressive movements, such as the Non-partisan League and the Farmers Union, were popular in the region. This variation in political beliefs has puzzled many. Some have suggested that it may have been due to the more difficult physical surroundings in the West, or perhaps the harsh farming conditions and distances from population centers.

Washburn, in southern McLean County, had Norwegians as early as 1883; the local Sverdrup Norwegian Lutheran Church was organized in that year. Some Norwegians remain, but they are today mixed with other national groups. Perhaps the first Norwegians in the far northwest corner of the state were those who took up land in Williams County at Hofflund (Hofflund Township) in 1887 on the edge of the Missouri. Eventually the Beaver Creek *Skandinavisk Evangelisk Lutherske* congregation was organized in that vicinity.

A dozen years later the area saw its great homestead period begin as Norwegians flooded the region. They homesteaded in a random fashion with other nationalities, but often in clusters. Some townships, therefore, even from the start, were intensely Norwegian in character. In this case early community life, isolated by winter and lack of roads, centered in rural Norwegian Lutheran churches. Within two decades little church steeples dotted the prairies in great numbers. Today some congregations continue to exist, but many have disappeared with the shrinking rural population.

Divide County is, in fact, a classic example of the dispersion of country churches. The county had an average of one Norwegian-oriented church for every two townships. In western Divide County there were the East and West Writing Rock churches (organized about 1911). The eastern part of Divide County had Zion Lutheran (organized in 1905) in Border Township, Glenwood Church in Blooming Valley, and Our Savior's Lutheran (organized in 1909) in Stoneview Township. Central Divide County had Troy Lutheran (organized in 1907) and Blooming Prairie (1911), Zion Lutheran (organized in 1905), Skabo Lutheran (1907) in Frederick Township, Bethlehem (1907) in Plumber Township, and also Trinity Lutheran (1906) in Hayland Township. There were other Norwegian congregations, all of which came into existence within a half decade after the start of homesteading activities.

Being Norwegian and Lutheran was not a simple thing. The early-day believers witnessed an array of Norwegian Lutheran synods which reflected both theological orientation and regional backgrounds. In the countryside a township church would often serve Norwegians of a variety of tastes and origins, for only one congregation was available. In the larger cities, personal preferences could be satisfied. Williston, for example, had three different Norwegian Lutheran groups in 1910: one, a United Norwegian Lutheran Church; another, a Haugean Lutheran Church, and a third church of Norwegian Synod background. An eventual merger was effected, but the early settlers were strong-willed people. When they worshipped, they wanted to be among their own.

Erected between 1905 and 1915 in Williams County were the Plum Creek Church, the East and West Grong churches, St. Olaf's Church, St. Paul's Church, and a dozen others. Burke County had a variety which included the Pleasant Prairie Church, the North and South St. Olaf's Church, the Bethania Church, and the Grand View Church. Mountrail County had a similar array of Lutheran churches: Shell Creek, Spring Valley, Scandia Valley, Bethlehem, and others, all first formed around 1906. In every county the tiny churches were centers of Norwegian pioneer life.

There was also an occasional group of dissenters. In 1901 a Baptist minister homesteaded a dozen miles north

of Powers Lake; the next year he brought a trainload of Norwegian landseekers from the "Bradford Church in Minnesota." These people settled close to Powers Lake and helped each other build their first prairie homes and also a primitive church which, according to early records, was erected in "eight hours." Though the building still had an earthen floor and planks for pews, it was dedicated on June 5, 1903, and was called the "Bethel Norwegian Baptist Church." The thirty-eight charter members were joined by others, and a larger church was constructed one mile south of town in 1908. By 1910, membership had grown to 135, and the Bethel Church had "out stations" as far west as Zahl (Gladys) in Williams County. Descendants of the original Norwegian Baptist migrants are still present in the community.

Minot had Norwegian religious congregations from the first days of settlement. Several Norwegian churches date their origins to the mid-1880's. In 1891 there were five Minot Lutheran churches of Norwegian background. By that same date, Ward County had at least seventeen open-country congregations. The city of Minot has a strategic location, for throughout its entire history it has been an attractive "first step" for Norwegians leaving the villages and farms of the northwestern part of the state. Even today, Minot's *Höstefest* is said to draw 15,000 visitors to its annual celebration of Norwegian heritage.

Norwegians differed from most immigrant groups in that the school, as well as the church, was of key importance. Education was stressed, and early school board membership rosters show the presence of many Norwegians whose experience in America was limited to only a few years. Norwegians were unique in many ways. One Norway-born Williams County gentleman arrived in Big Meadow Township in 1904, and after farming for a few years, became active in politics, serving in the North Dakota House of Representatives and, later, in the state Senate. He eventually sold his farm and returned to Norway. This was a remarkable career — migrating to America, prospering in agriculture, mastering both the English language and the American political system, thereafter serving in relatively high state offices, and finally returning to Norway to die. No other large-sized North Dakota national group seems to have had the ability and the desire to become American so rapidly and, at the same time, remain loyal to its ethnic origins.

SWEDES

In McLean County very early Swedish settlers were seeking land in Conkling Township (T 144-R 83) west of Washburn in territorial days, with some coming as early as 1885. That same year, others arrived as part of an organized group from Stordahn in Sweden and took up farm sites in Satterlund Township (T 145-R 81) east of Washburn. The region is, to this day, a heavily Swedish area. Nearby Grass Lake Township of Burleigh County was also composed of Swedish settlers. This series of settlements is still the largest Swedish community in the state. Through local farm families' efforts Augustana Synod Lutheran churches were built in nearby Wilton (Sunne in 1893), Underwood (Augustana in 1913),

Washburn (Birka in 1906), and Coleharbor (Bethel in 1905).

Swedes in McLean and Burleigh counties very often came before the Norwegians. They seem to have been quite at home with the early Anglo-Americans. In fact, land adjacent to the Missouri River contained many extremely early Swedish settlers who did not wait for the arrival of the railroads, but came by wagon with the earliest Yankees and French. In terms of persisting on the land, however, Swedes compare unfavorably with Norwegians; they were less durable. Perhaps it was their affinity to Anglo-Saxon ways, or their familiarity with the wider American scene, that caused them to go elsewhere. Across the river from McLean County is the Ft. Clark Swedish settlement, which had at one time some forty families and now contains only a handful of their descendants.

West of Kenmare in Roseland Township of Burke County, a moderately large Swedish settlement grew up in homestead times. Eventually, the group formed the Elmdale Lutheran Church (Augustana Synod) which became its religious and social center. The congregation began in 1902; its church, which exists today, was built in 1907. The Swedish language was used in services until 1936.

Renville County had a Swedish area north of Tolley; and Burke County had Swedish settlements near Battleview, Lignite, and Niobe. These communities are now composed of Swedish and Norwegian families. Both the Tolley and the nearby Green communities had Augustana Synod churches. The Tolley congregation began in 1903, and the Messiah congregation at Green first met in 1913. Niobe had, in 1925, two Swedish churches: one of the Lutheran background and another of the Baptist tradition. The Niobe Lutheran congregation began in 1903. A Lignite Lutheran group started two years later.

A Swedish Lutheran church located at McGregor in Williams County took care of settlers in the northeast corner of that county and across the line in Burke. Some local farmers trace their ancestry to these first immigrants. The McGregor Swedish congregation was organized in 1916; in 1941 it merged with a local Norwegian Lutheran church group.

Scattered individual Swedish families settled in almost every portion of the various northwestern counties. One estimate has it that the Norwegian areas contained an average of one Swedish family for every fifteen families of Norwegian background. Intermarriage with Norwegians through the years has made the Swedish portion of their heritage rather minimal.

SYRIANS (Lebanese)

Two highly visible settlements of Lebanese are located in the northwest section of the state — one in western Williams County not far from the Montana border, and the other between Stanley and Ross in Mountrail County.

The Williams County Lebanese occupy the eastern part of the Bull Butte Township and extend into Cow

Creek Township. Coming to the state in homestead times, particularly during the first decade of the twentieth century, they were attracted by railroad and land-company advertising. Some, in fact, may have worked on the railroad as section hands. Census designation called them Syrian; but they were, for the most part, Lebanese Christians of the Catholic Maronite and Melkite rites. Some few were Orthodox Christians; a rare early settler was Moslem.

After an initial settlement was made, word-of-mouth information brought additional farmers from Syrian colonies in eastern Dakota counties. Some came from Pierce and Towner counties, and some from northern Minnesota. As the decades passed, wives or husbands were frequently obtained in other state settlements (and occasionally from Syria itself). A Syrian priest sometimes visited the pioneer families, making his way across the Dakota prairie from one settlement to another. No national church seems to have been erected, although a Syrian hall was built in Cow Creek Township.

A Williams County history says, "The Syrians who settled here were not farmers by nature. They had come mostly from families who had been merchants for generations." Plat maps, published when homesteading was completed in 1910, show a Syrian settlement almost twice its present size. Indeed, Syrian farmers did not seem to have the steadfast and aggressive agricultural traits of their Norwegian and Ukrainian fellow homesteaders. They moved from land to town in large numbers; many today are prominent in the professional life of Williston.

The term "Syrian" may have negative connotations for the people in Williams County, but technically their villages in the old country were under Syrian jurisdiction when they left to come to America. Today, this region has separated from Syria and is in modern-day Lebanon. Many local residents prefer the name "Lebanese," which has a Christian connotation, while "Syrian" tends to be a Moslem term.

The Syrian settlement near Ross in Mountrail County is a different situation. Here homesteading took place several years earlier, and under much the same circumstances; railroads, land advertising, and ties in eastern America enticed settlers to the area. But, unlike the Williams County group, the residents were usually Moslem in background. Indeed, in 1929 a small half-basement structure, which was erected two miles east and one mile south of town, served as a mosque. Here Islamic services, which had previously taken place in homes, continued for another generation. Community elders conducted services in most cases, but at times an iman would come from Canada. The mosque was destroyed in the mid-1970's, but an adjoining cemetery is still in good repair.

The earliest Ross settlers, arriving in 1902, numbered about twenty households. Other Syrians arrived within a short time; a hundred were said to have eventually come. Movement to North Dakota was apparently encouraged by letters from two earlier Syrian homesteaders. As the years passed, however, farm conditions became such that settlers had to move away for better opportunities. Today some of the original families remain, especially in Ross and James Hill townships. Many early families settled south of Ross in Alger Township; few, if any, Syrians reside in that area today.

The first Ross arrivals are said to have come from an area which centers around the Syrian (now Lebanese) town of Berrie (Bardje or Barje), which is about fifteen miles south of Beirut. Some of the Syrian descendants are today Christian, but a number of "old timers" are still faithful to the beliefs and practices of Islam.

Today the Williams and Mountrail county Syrian residents are capable and highly Americanized individuals. Nevertheless, a certain number of "old country" traditions continue, especially in terms of foods and family festivals. On occasion, the Lebanese garb and special dances become a part of civic events. The members of the two Syrian groups join with others of their national background throughout North Dakota in an annual Arabic social gathering. The Lebanese heritage, even though it was decidedly different from the general western European culture of most North Dakota immigrants, played a genuinely historic role in North Dakota's pioneer past.

UKRAINIANS

Three distinct Ukrainian settlements sprang up and are still clearly evident in the northwestern section of the state: one is near Wilton, a second is in the Max-Butte-Kief area, and a third is in Williams County.

The Wilton Ukrainian community, an eastern rite Catholic group, is located in the McLean County township immediately north of that town. Their first religious structure, the SS. Peter and Paul Ukrainian Church, was built in 1907 and was located a few miles northeast of Wilton; the church was moved into town in 1911. It served the earliest Ukrainian families who homesteaded the region and others who came to work in the coal mines in the early 1900's. Also present in Wilton is the Ukrainian Greek Orthodox Church (1915), whose early members, likewise, both farmed and worked in the lignite mines. Originally called the St. Nicholas Church, the cruciform structure has three elegant steeples, topped with Greek crosses.

Coming from the steppe of the Ukraine, the new immigrants were attracted to the similar prairies of Dakota. The first settlers who came to the Wilton community in 1897 are said to have been directed to the region after a temporary stay in Canada. The Wilton people are from the western Ukraine, and many call Galicia their place of origin. Ukrainian settlers came over a period of at least one decade, perhaps two; later arrivals came directly from railroad centers in eastern American cities.

Today only one church, the SS. Peter and Paul Ukrainian Church, has a resident pastor. Close bonds of friendship (and kinship) have existed, from the earliest days, between the Wilton Ukrainians and the Belfield Ukrainian community of Stark and Billings counties. Neither group will accept the descriptive term "Russian."

In fact, January 22 is sometimes celebrated as Ukrainian "Independence Day," in remembrance of the short-lived National Republic which broke away from the Czars.

A second and larger group of Ukrainians from different villages in the Cherkassy region of Russia settled in a forty-mile strip of land in northern McLean County and spilled over into Ward and Sheridan counties. Butte and its environs are solidly Ukrainian. The Ruso area farther west contains scattered Ukrainian families. The villages of Max and Benedict are on the southern extremities of a large group of Ukrainians who occupy the greater part of three townships. A further extension of this group is found north and east of Makoti in Ward County. These farm families, however, live among neighbors who come from a variety of ethnic groups. Residents of these McLean, Ward and Sheridan county villages do not object to an occasional use of the label "Russian." Perhaps it helped outsiders distinguish them from the "Catholic" Ukrainians elsewhere. Perhaps it was a more comfortable term, since their home provinces were closer to the Russian heartlands.

The third and smallest of all the Ukrainian groups in northwestern North Dakota can be found in Williams County. This cluster of farms is related to the Max and Kief people in that the first settlers most often came from those earlier communities. The Williams County colony is a few miles south of Bonetrail and is immediately south of the local Syrian community. Settlement there took place about 1905. The parent group in McLean County came to Dakota the previous decade, at least by 1899, perhaps earlier.

The Max-Butte-Kief settlers were unique in that many, perhaps most, were Protestant before they arrived in America. Many, indeed, were seeking religious freedom from the Orthodox Church of Russia. Some early settlers came from Louisville, Kentucky, by way of Yale, Virginia, where a Ukrainian agricultural colony was attempted. The story is told that a Ukrainian immigrant, bound for the Virginia settlement, met a Black Sea German on a steamer from Europe, who suggested that the Great Plains had more land to offer than Virginia. The German-Russian described the Dakotas as similar to the Russian steppe and offered to take his Ukrainian friend to South Dakota to investigate the possibility of prairie settlement. According to another report, some Ukrainian families did, in fact, go to the German-Russian settlement of Tripp, South Dakota, in the winter of 1898 and, with German-Russian guidance, migrated along the wagon route to Harvey, North Dakota, and thence to the new land in McHenry County. If the stories are true, it is appropriate that the German settlers of the Ukraine, who set up their Russian colonies with the assistance of Ukrainian farmers in the first decade of the nineteenth century, should, a hundred years later, assist their Ukrainian neighbors in a similar homestead venture in the broad prairies of North America.

The Ukrainian settlements in northern McLean County and in Williams County continued to be Protestant in orientation through the various generations; Baptist, Congregational, and Seventh Day Adventist congregations are still present. The Russian Baptist Conference had churches in Max, Kief, Butte, Greatstone, and Killdeer, North Dakota. An occasional migrant of Orthodox background is said to have come to the area and to have affiliated with the Ukrainian Protestant groups. The absence of the rich pageantry of the Orthodox church tradition has probably diminished the vigor of the local ethnic heritage. Language and customs had to be preserved almost exclusively in the home. Many of the colorful community festivals of the Ukraine were absent. Ukrainian dances, costumes, and social events are today much more visible in Belfield than in the Butte and Kief communities, though the Ukrainian populations of the two centers are probably of equal size.

Ethnic Population Distribution
Southcentral Section of North Dakota

1. Ukrainian
2. Swede 50%: Anglo-American 20%: Others 30%
3. Mixed: Anglo-American, German, Swede, Norwegian, Others
4. Norwegian 50%: Anglo-American 50%
5. Norwegian 50%: German and German-Russian 50%
6. German 50%: Anglo-American 50%
7. Anglo-American 40%: German-Russian 40%: German 20%
8. German 40%: German-Russian: Anglo-American 25%: Norwegian 10%
9. German 40%: German-Russian 30%: Norwegian 30%
10. Anglo-American 90%: German and Others 10%
11. Anglo-American and Anglo-Ontarian 50%: German 45%: Others 5%
12. Mixed: Norwegian, German-Russian, Anglo-American
13. Norwegian 50%: German: Anglo-American: Swede
14. Mixed: Anglo-American, German, Swede and Norwegian
15. Polish (Silesia) 80%: Polish 20%
16. German (Marienburg region of Poland)
17. German 90%: Others 10%
18. Anglo-American 50%: German-Russian 50%
19. Norwegian 50%: German-Russian 30%: Others 20%
20. German-Russian Mennonite
21. German-Russian Protestant: Occasional German-Russian Catholic
22. Polish 70%: Others 30%
23. Anglo-American (occasional Anglo-Ontarian) 70%: Norwegian 30%
24. Norwegian 60%: German 20%: Anglo-American 20%
25. Anglo-American 50%: German and German-Russian 25%: Hollanders & Others
26. Norwegian 75%: Anglo-American 25%
27. Finlander 65%: Norwegian 35%
28. Norwegian
29. German-Russian Catholic 50%: German-Russian Protestant 50%
30. Norwegian 50%: German-Russian 50%
31. German-Russian 50%: Norwegian and Others
32. Finlander 50%: German-Russian 50%
33. Anglo-American 50%: Anglo-Ontarian 50%

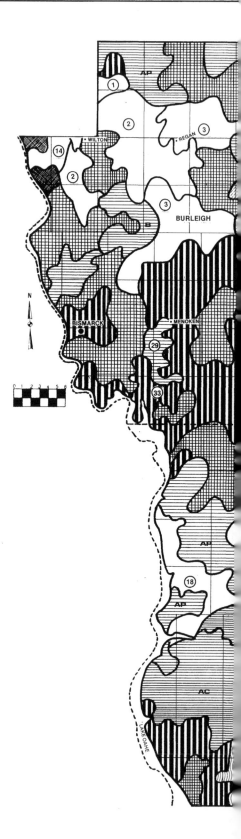

Shaded Areas
Are At Least
Ninety-Five
Percent Of The
Same National
Group Unless
Otherwise Indicated

Rural Residents As Of 1965

William C. Sherman   NDSU   Fargo, ND

German

German-Russian

German-Russian Protestant

German-Russian Catholic

German and German-Russian

Anglo-American

Finlander

Hollander

Swede

Mixed

Township Names and Descriptions
Southcentral Section of North Dakota

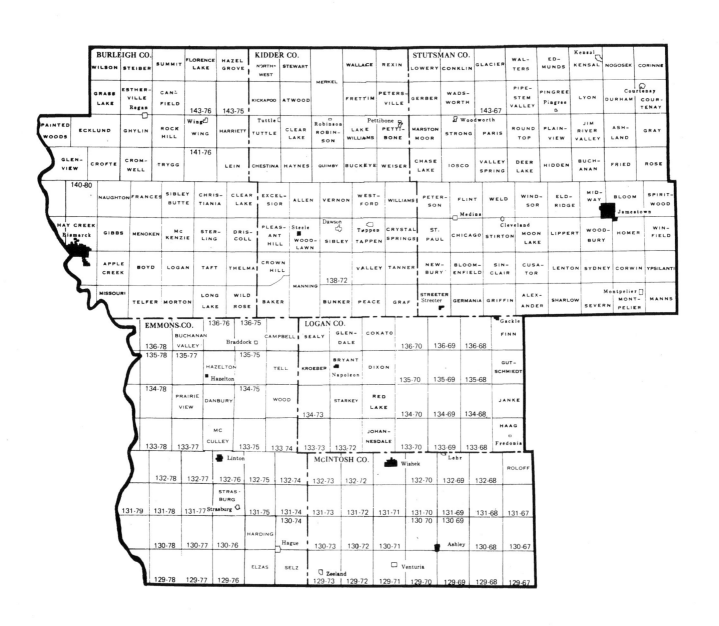

Commentary

ANGLO-AMERICANS

As in most of North Dakota, settlers of early American ancestry were the first to occupy land in the southcentral portion of the state. Some worked on the Missouri as riverboat hands and subsequently acquired acreage in the wood and meadow regions adjacent to the river. Some were "wood hawks" who sold logs for fuel to passing steamboats. A few had military pasts; some had previously been garrisoned in early Fort Rice (1864-1878), Fort Yates (1874-1903), Fort Abraham Lincoln (1872-1891), and Fort Stevenson (1867-1883). A Civil War veteran named Dan Manning, after working on river flatboats, took up land in Section 8 of Missouri Township, Burleigh County, in 1873; thereafter, he sold hay and cattle to the army. William Ward, another Civil War veteran from Pennsylvania, came from the early Owego Settlement (Ransom County) in 1873 and arrived at Bismarck just before the Northern Pacific Railroad. He settled nearby, ran cattle, had a dairy, and hauled freight. Up and down the river such settlers chose the earliest land.

In the winter of 1875 several Irish-Americans squatted at the "Devils Colony," near the future town of Winona, across the Missouri from the Standing Rock Indian Agency. Other clusters of "temporary" settlers grew up and disappeared. They came before the surveyors, and no official documents record their presence.

A handful of early American soldiers stationed with Dakota military units, after leaving the Army, married local Indian women and settled on small parcels of prairie. Their descendants may still reside in central North Dakota, some on modern reservation land. Some ex-soldiers brought wives from eastern states; they, too, were part of the frontier homestead scene.

These first American inhabitants raised hay, cattle, and horses for use at military posts and Indian Agencies. Sale of commodities to eastern America was limited, but river trade and railroad construction brought an additional need for local supplies. Hay Creek Township, site of much of today's Bismarck, is aptly named. Many of its first settlers were Anglo-Americans who came in the 1870's and sold fodder to local consumers.

Ranching operations, which came later, were also primarily Anglo-American enterprises. Large-scale ranching was beyond the reach of the ordinary European immigrant, who understood dairy farming and was familiar with pork but not beef production. Furthermore, the sizable cash investment and vast acreages needed for cattle were beyond his comprehension.

Many relatively wealthy Anglo-American opportunists took up open-range territory before homesteaders arrived; for example, the 6,000-acre Campbell Ranch was established by a Scotchman near present Kintyre in 1882. Others acquired land from the railroad. In the case of the Patterson Ranch in Burleigh County, five gentlemen purchased over a million acres of Northern Pacific Grant Lands in 1901; odd-numbered sections lying north and south of the railway between Bismarck and Jamestown were their preserve. Not all this land was used for ranching, but some large operations did emerge. The Patterson Ranches continue to this day, but on a more limited scale. Special railroad cars brought many Minnesota land seekers to the Patterson acreages, and their descendants can still be found in the area.

Emmons, Burleigh, Kidder, and Stutsman counties all had early-day ranchers. In fact, sizable cattle spreads existed in the rugged areas throughout central and western North Dakota, along the rivers and in the various glacial moraines. The Anglo-American was everywhere present. Ranch owners and managers were of English, Scottish, or Irish origin, or at least of a second- and third-generation American background.

Soon the "dirt farmer" settler began to appear. In fact, the farm and ranch periods often overlapped. The farmer was on the prairie and the rancher was in the "hills." But the very first farmer-homesteaders also tended to have Anglo-American backgrounds. This was especially true in areas adjacent to the land-grant railroad. Such a thing was not surprising, however, for the railroad encouraged English-speaking settlers from eastern states by advertisements in eastern newspapers. Often free transportation for "scouting" purposes was given to prospective parties, and special immigrant trains were provided. Sometimes a large group of immigrants undertook one settlement venture. For example, a colony of settlers from Ashbury Park, New York, arrived in Kidder county in 1883 and settled in what are now Buckeye and Lake Williams townships, putting together a settlement called "New York Town." Only one family seems to be still present in the area.

In 1878 several wealthy men from Troy, New York, purchased approximately 10,000 acres near what is now Tappen and began the Troy Farms in Kidder County. A special manager was employed; and large barns, granaries, and housing for a rancher were erected. This was part of the bonanza-farm tradition. Another such enterprise was the Spiritwood Farm, a large commercial operation started in 1879. Both the name and the population makeup of Spiritwood Village and Township, east of Jamestown, still reflect this settlement venture.

Other groups of settlers from eastern states came with little or no assistance. A number of settlers from Ashland, Ohio, set up the town of Williamsport in 1883 along the Missouri in Emmons County. A colony from Toledo, Ohio, established themselves in Gray Township, a dozen miles north of Jamestown in 1879. Settlers from Lowell, Michigan, named Lowell Post Office south of Ashley in McIntosh County. An immigration agent brought a party of one hundred people to the Napoleon area in the spring of 1886. This became known as the "Pennsylvania Colony." Most of the group left before the year was complete.

Though group ventures were frequent, Anglo-Americans most often tended to settle in scattered patterns. Knowing the ways of America very well, they had little need to cluster in colonies. They came early and sought what they considered to be good land with abundant water and fuel and accessibility to transportation. Americans with their Irish-American friends were found over the entire landscape. Today the farm land of northern Emmons County and southern Burleigh County is heavily Anglo-American. Portions of Kidder County, within reach of the railroad, still contain numerous farmers of this early background.

The Anglo-Americans' familiarity with America gave them an initial advantage; but it proved to be their undoing in many cases, as far as Dakota was concerned, for they readily sold their farms and moved away. Often they went farther west; sometimes they moved to nearby urban centers. Often, with the farm-sale money in their pockets, they moved "back East." A history of Bismarck speaks of the "inherent Scotch-Irish urge to move if they took exception to things where they were and were unable to change them."

The institutions around which they formed their social life were their churches — Congregational, Methodist, and sometimes Episcopal and Presbyterian — and also their lodges, especially the Masonic groups. The town gentry were usually "Yankee"; and, as a result, most of the Anglo-American churches were in the town. Yet sometimes they were in the country; the Dale Methodist Church (1900) in the southwestern corner of Emmons County and the cut-stone McCabe Methodist Church (1908) northeast of Linton were located in rural areas which were and still are Anglo-American in background. As times changed and Americans moved away, the churches and lodges suffered seriously. Many a town in the region has an early Masonic building (whose second story was the lodge home), or a weathered white-frame church, both of which are now unused.

BOHEMIANS

At least fifteen homesteaders of Bohemian background settled in Burleigh County's Summit Township. They came in 1902 and 1903. Only three of the farm families are evident in the area today. The community was never a compact thing; homesteaders occupied only the odd numbered sections, and the Bohemian farmers were scattered throughout the region. No church or lodge was erected to serve their needs.

BULGARIANS

Coming with the first settlers in Kidder County was a handful of Bulgarian families, perhaps twenty in all, who settled in a dispersed fashion some ten to fifteen miles north of Steele. This group represents the only Bulgarian settlement in North Dakota. Neighbors still call them "the Bulgarians," and seven or eight families continue to reside in the county. Their history is an unusual one in that they migrated from Bulgaria to Bessarabia and took up land near the Danube. Ismail is still remembered as their major trading center in the "old country." Their family names almost invariably ended in -ov. The forefathers of this Dakota group, after spending two generations in Bessarabia, probably came directly to Dakota without a stop elsewhere. Homesteading was completed by the time they arrived in Kidder County (several years before World War I), so they were forced to purchase their parcels of land.

The first Bulgarians were Eastern Orthodox Christians and could speak both Bulgarian and Russian. Church services were held in their homes in the 1920's, with an occasional clergyman coming from Granite City, Illinois, and Chicago, Illinois. In the 1930's they had a small church in Steele. Most of their present-day descendants are Lutheran.

Some Bulgarians are also said to have settled for a few years south of Medina. None remains in Stutsman County, but the Bulgarians formerly in this area may have had some relation to the Kidder County group.

FINNS

The southcentral portion of the state contains three Finnish communities: one near Gackle, a second south of Kintyre, and a third near Wing.

The Wing community is the largest. Coming during settlement times in northern Burleigh County (from 1900 to 1905 with some as early as 1898), the earliest Finns arrived from Michigan, Canada, Minnesota, and Dickey County, North Dakota. Apparently two centers of Finnish religious activity were established in the region. The Finnish Evangelical Lutheran Church (Suomi Synod), six miles south of Wing, was incorporated in 1908; it flourished as a rural center until it moved to the town of Wing in 1948. A cemetery still remains near the site of the original church. Today the congregation is called the Bethlehem Lutheran Church and has a Lutheran Church of America (LCA) affiliation. The original Finnish families now worship with Lutherans of German and Norwegian backgrounds. A second center was the Finnish Apostolic Church, some seven miles south and one mile west of Wing. This church is still present on the countryside and has services occasionally. The Ahola Cemetery is located one mile south and one-half mile east of the church.

Some residents affiliated with what was known as the Finn Hall, erected a mile and a half from the rural Apostolic Church. This group tended to be of non-religious background; and the hall became a social center where dancing, Finnish festivals, and some political and educational programs took place. The divisions within the Finnish community have gradually softened, and most social activities take place now in the village of Wing. No Finnish hall existed in that town.

Like their countrymen in other parts of the state, the Finns at Wing set up a nationality-centered lending library. It consisted of approximately 300 volumes and was housed in two family homes. The long winter nights of the first decades of this century were often spent in the study of Finnish history, folklore, poetry, and fiction. Eventually, fluency in the Finnish language declined; and in the thirties the library was transferred to New York Mills, Minnesota.

A second group of Finnish settlers came into Tell Township south of Kintyre in Emmons County in the early 1890's. A Finnish Independent Lutheran Church was organized in 1913, and a church building was completed several years later. The Tell settlement still exists and is bordered by German-Russians to the south and Swedes to the north. The Finnish church continues, but is now used mainly for funerals. Norwegians are interspersed throughout the community and make up thirty percent of the population. Departures in the 1930's left vacant land which was occupied by Norwegian and German neighbors. Early Finnish homesteaders came particularly from the Ellendale and Ludden communities in Dickey County.

The third settlement began at the same time, and its residents came from both Ellendale and Finnish colonies in Michigan state. Some, too, came from the Iron Range and other central Minnesota villages. Together, they formed the Gackle community in northeastern Logan County. Here, almost a whole township (eventually called Finn) was of that background. The farmland west of Finn Township was also settled by similar immigrants. Here, too, the church and the lodge were centers of national life. In the 1930's about half of the Finnish residents left the area, many returning to Minnesota or to Michigan. Two cemeteries remain, the Homola and the Saari; both are south of Gackle. A Finnish library was also established, and a Finnish Creamery Company was founded.

The Finnish colonies throughout the state seem to have had a lively information network. Early settlers moved from one community to another in search of free land. Contacts with Michigan's Upper Peninsula, with Frederick in South Dakota, and with New York Mills and Menahga in Minnesota were much in evidence. Often wives and husbands were procured from other Dakota and Minnesota settlement areas. The Depression and Dust Bowl years brought disillusionment and a corresponding exodus of families. Finnish movement to the West Coast, for example, was made easier by the already existing ties with Finnish communities in Oregon and Washington.

Finnish colonies were for a long time almost completely homogenous. Non-Finns seldom were at home in their midst. "Clannish" was the word most often used by outsiders when describing Finnish settlements. The term, however, was usually free of negative connotations; it meant, "You have to win their trust."

To their eventual discomfort, Finnish families sometimes chose land which was marginal in terms of wheat farming. Stands of timber and hillside areas were often preferred. This frequently meant poor quality soil, and prairie survival was made difficult. The German-Russian neighbors in the Gackle region now occupy half of the land which was once an exclusive Finnish preserve.

GERMANS (Reichsdeutsch)

Coming with the Anglo-American homesteaders in the early days were occasional Germans of American background, sometimes long-term first-generation residents, but often second-generation people. Usually from Wisconsin, Illinois, and Minnesota, they felt comfortable in the United States and moved easily among the Yankee gentry. This special kind of German took up farms without much concern for ethnic surroundings. Some prospered, building large farm homes and barns; many moved elsewhere in search of better opportunities. In the

southcentral portion of the state (except for parts of Stutsman County) their descendants are not numerous; where they remain they are often mixed with German-Russians. They are present, however, north of Woodworth and also between Fried and Courtenay in Stutsman County. The Protestants among these farmers often attended the Missouri Synod churches at Wimbledon (St. Paul's) and at Courtenay (Zion, organized in 1892). Germans in the Kensal vicinity had the St. Paul's Church, organized in 1905. Some Germans are mixed with German-Russians southwest of Jamestown and between Jamestown and Cleveland.

Reichsdeutsch Germans were in the towns as well as the country. Two outstanding Germans were extremely active in early settlement times. One was Anton Klaus, sometimes called the "Father of Jamestown." This venturesome individual was born in the old country, and as a young man acquired a good knowledge of America in Wisconsin. In 1879 he came to Jamestown and set up a general merchandise store; later he established a hotel, a mill and elevator, and several other businesses. Involved in real estate and being civic minded, he gave land and money for the erection of seven churches and provided land for a 26-acre park.

John H. Wishek, the son of German-born parents, was born in Pennsylvania and received a law degree from the University of Michigan. In 1884 he moved to the new town of Hoskins, in southern McIntosh County. There, in partnership with others, he set about developing the new territory. Soon the name Wishek became synonymous with the area. He set up the first local bank, helped the railroad come to the region, and acquired the townsites of Ashley, Wishek, Artas, and Pollock. He organized some thirty-five separate corporations, donated the land for churches in every nearby town, and was a powerful figure in local and state politics. Above all, he was a great advocate and defender of the Germans from Russia. With contacts in Russia and Eureka, he encouraged Germans to take land in the southcentral part of the state. His efforts were obviously successful: the Wishek area is surrounded by America's largest German-Russian settlement.

MARIENBURG GERMANS

An unusual group of settlers came to the country around Courtenay in Stutsman County. This was a group of Germans who often had Polish names. They began arriving as early as 1893 from the area of northern Germany near Danzig on the North Sea (West Prussia). This territory had once belonged to Poland (thus the Polish names), but had been part of Germany for two or three hundred years. The large towns in their home region were Marburg (Marienburg) and Elbing, some fifty kilometers southeast of Gdansk in the Danzig delta area. Among the first families were such names as Kouchkouwski and Stachlowski, but there was also a Falk, a Schwalk, and a Ligmen. This group was unique in that they went to Russia in the 1850's, going to the Black Sea region and settling not far from earlier German colonies to the north of the city of Berdyansk. Being Catholic, they were part of the German-Russian diocese of Tiraspol. The parish center for many of the settlers was the Mariupol colony of Eichwald.

These Germans, it seems, were not settlers in southern Russia, but were "renters," and they worked on large estates. Land in the Ukraine was scarce by the time of their arrival; they did not become Russian citizens, for citizenship and land holding were tied together. Finding themselves dreadfully poor, they were dissatisfied with their situation and eventually joined the many other groups who were leaving Russia.

Apparently, as German citizens, they dealt primarily with the German consul, not the Russian officials, as they made their departure. Despite their short stay in the Ukraine, the "renter" Germans did take on some eastern European characteristics. When they arrived in America, they had Russian sheepskin coats; they ate *borsch* and *kase knepla*. They also built a Russian-style house with home and barn connected. Many of these Marienburg renter-Germans came directly to the United States, but others went from Russia back to their German homeland and then came to the states. They say that there are "hundreds" of their fellow countrymen in Canada north of Montana.

After their experience on the Russian steppe, the Stutsman County prairies looked most attractive. They became independent and very durable farmers. Apparently a small St. Mary's Church was built west of Courtenay in settlement days, and this provided a community center for the newly arrived group. In 1904 the parish was moved into the town, and it continues active at the present time.

GERMAN MENNONITES

Two clusters of Mennonite farmers were in the northern part of Burleigh County in the early decades of this century. One group resided on a series of farms in Schrunk (Summit) Township, and their settlement extended into Sheridan County as far north as John's Lake. The settlers were Germans of Russian background who came during the homestead era, especially in 1901 and 1902. They organized the John's Lake congregation in 1904, calling it the Johannestal Mennonite Community. On October 1, 1916, a small church structure was dedicated; the congregation flourished for several decades. The years took their toll, however, and regular meetings ended in the late 1940's. The remaining members attended a church of the same Mennonite Brethren background in nearby McClusky. The country church reopened a decade later, but only a few original families remained.

A second group of Mennonites homesteaded in Burleigh County, south of Arena, particularly in Harriet and Lien townships. The first settlers came north from South Dakota in the early 1900's. Some families came alone from such places as Mountain Lake, Minnesota, and the Cavalier County Mennonite communities. But some came as a group, for on April 4, 1904, seven carloads of families and implements left Marion, South Dakota, for new lands in Burleigh County. The Zion Mennonite

Church, erected in the mid-1920's four miles south of Arena, was their religious home. This church was of General Conference affiliation, even though most of its members were of German-Russian origin.

There was no true Mennonite colony in Burleigh County, at least in the sense that the farms were adjacent to each other. Rather, the early settlers had non-Mennonites dispersed among them. Relatively few Mennonite families still remain in the area today. The John's Lake Church, especially, has had to struggle to keep alive.

Mennonite families, perhaps a dozen, settled in Lowery Township in the northwest corner of Stutsman County. These early settlers took land in the central and northeast portion of the township and built a church on what was the old New Home townsite (section 12). Most, but not all, of the first German farmers came from southern Russia. Time has been hard on the settlement, and many Mennonites have moved away. Their descendants are now Seventh Day Adventists, and the New Home Church is still their religious and social center.

GERMAN-RUSSIANS

German-Russians are the largest national group in the southcentral counties, occupying over fifty percent of the land area and making up the majority of the residents of Logan and Emmons counties, and over ninety percent of the rural residents of McIntosh County. This strong and steady people first entered what is now the state of North Dakota in 1884. The first of their countrymen to reach Dakota Territory arrived in Yankton in 1874 and settled thereafter in such towns as Tripp, Scotland, and Menno. Later arrivals moved by wagon (in the 1880's) northward from the southern towns and took up land along the northern tier of South Dakota's counties. The Chicago, Milwaukee and St. Paul Railroad apparently did extensive advertising in the Ukraine, for it quickly became the favorite transportation route to the Dakotas. Hundreds of German families arrived in St. Paul, Minnesota, took immigrant trains to the rail end at Aberdeen (South Dakota), and settled in the nearby townships. When the railroad was built to Ipswich, that village, too, became a hub of German settlement. When a branch line was built to Eureka, that city became *the* major dispersal point for German-Russians who then spread northward throughout the Dakota prairies, from the Missouri River north to Medina in Stutsman County and eastward to Monango in Dickey County. A decade later long lines of German wagons moved farther north into Kidder, Burleigh, Sheridan, Pierce, and McHenry counties.

A unique and possibly significant aspect of the German-Russian movement into North Dakota is the fact that it was mostly a family affair. Germans usually came as a group: father, mother, and children. Other ethnic concentrations such as French, Americans, Irish, and Norwegians seem to have had a great many single men and even a certain number of unattached women. The "mail order bride" and the "Swedish domestic" phenomena were rarely, if ever, seen among German-Russians. This characteristic may help explain why German-Russians seldom had the adventuring characteristics of the classic frontiersmen who went avidly ahead of the pack and squatted on lonely acreages at the very edge of civilization. A sense of caution and planning was evident in almost every German move. That the Germans were people of great mobility is undeniable. They had previously leapt from one continent to another. They were known to shift from country to country and, in America, from county to county. But always there were advance scouts and reports, and then a massive and decisive movement of people and goods.

Entering what is now North Dakota in 1884, the German farmers took up new land at a fast pace. By 1885 they were established in the Zeeland and Venturia area; a year later they were approaching what is now Wishek and Fredonia in northern McIntosh County. In 1891 the first arrivals were in western Dickey county. To the west, scouts had already had a good look at Emmons County; and a settlement had been made at Strasburg in 1889. Within several years, scouts were checking out Pierce County, one hundred fifty airline miles north of Eureka; the Odessa Colony began in that county in 1895. This was, indeed, a remarkable migration — one which went northward, "across the grain" of the normal east-west railway routes. Outward expansion of Germans from Eureka averaged almost ten miles a year for the first decade of North Dakota settlement.

Throughout this whole period, land seekers were literally pouring into Eureka. They were coming north by wagon from the Yankton region, or were disembarking from immigrant trains at the local station. Eureka, it seems, became a sort of "mother colony." In the fall, wagons came to that town with harvest grain from a large part of the German-Russian settlement area — sometimes fifty miles away. Eureka was known as the "world's largest primary wheat market" from 1887 to 1902. In 1892, for example, an estimated 165 trains were required to carry away the wheat that arrived in Eureka during the harvest season. In some years, two hundred men worked alternating day and night shifts, handling three to four million bushels of grain. At the peak of immigration, special trains of twenty and thirty cars of immigrants arrived at regular intervals at the Eureka station. This "end of the line" phenomenon declined as the railroad built farther into North Dakota, and other small towns arose. Nevertheless, for several generations Eureka was a kind of retirement center, to which hundreds of German-Russian couples returned to live out their elderly years "among their own people."

Settlement days found many non-German homesteaders occupying land in today's exclusively German regions. Nina Farley Wishek's account of pioneer life in McIntosh County refers to a number of Anglo-Saxon,

Norwegian, and *Reichsdeutsch* settlements in that county. All of these settlements have disappeared, and Germans from Russia now occupy the land. Knowledgeable Anglo-Americans made up the first contingent of business and professional leaders in that same county. The entire slate of McIntosh County officials prior to 1900 was Anglo-Saxon or *Reichsdeutsch*, with the exception of a German-Russian sheriff who took office in 1895. Today, non-German-Russians are a rarity whether in politics or in business life.

The southcentral German-Russian counties divide into two distinct religious communities. McIntosh County is almost entirely Protestant. The Catholic group begins with the Emmons County line and extends westward. Protestant Germans live in the eastern two-thirds of Logan County and are scattered throughout the lower parts of Stutsman and Kidder counties. Catholics occupy the western one-third of Logan County, centering around Napoleon. A Protestant German-Russian community exists south and west of Hazelton. The Tuttle and Wing areas in northern Burleigh and Kidder counties are the southern portions of an extensive Protestant German-Russian district which extends northward, embracing almost all of Sheridan County.

The distinct division between the Catholic and Protestant communities is not an accidental thing, for the colonies in Russia were, in most cases, exclusively Catholic or Protestant, and their origins in Germany were from provinces which were often Catholic or Protestant in character. The dialects of the two groups differed in minor ways, and the differences were enough to identify immediately an individual as to background and religious category. Surprisingly, their food, clothing, and early housing traditions were quite similar. Small variations existed in these more material matters; but, on the whole, the separate groups were almost identical when contrasted to settlers of other national origins.

The Protestant groups, for the most part, came from Bessarabia on the western edge of the Ukraine. Catholic Emmons and Logan county settlers were mainly from the Kutchurgan cluster of villages, thirty miles northwest of the Black Sea port of Odessa; but some few came from the Catholic Beresan villages to the north of Odessa. Whether Catholic or Protestant, these Germans were part of the Black Sea migrations which came to Russia at the invitation of Czar Alexander I in the first decade of the nineteenth century. The good record of a previous German settlement on the Volga in the 1770's under Catherine the Great led her grandson, Czar Alexander, to invite other Germans to occupy Black Sea territories which had been taken from the Turkish empire.

The first decades in Russia were filled with difficulty. Where previously they had been people of the hills and forests of western Germany, they were forced to become colonists on the wide-open Ukrainian steppe. But they were successful. Their villages prospered, and they were recognized as model farmers. They eventually left Russia, but with reluctance. Forced Russification in educational and community affairs, a military draft, and an increasing resentment by local people turned their attention to the American homestead possibilities. Encouraged by railroad advertising and the reports of early immigrants, the Germans flooded into the central Dakotas, occupying the last of America's free land. They were, therefore, not strangers to their new environment, for their experiences on the steppe had made them suspicious of mountains and uniquely comfortable in the northern prairie landscapes.

For the Germans, the century of life in Russia had meant a constant struggle to maintain their national traditions. When they arrived in America, they were equipped to live in a self-contained manner, if they so wished. Special traits of family and community life, of religion and language, all combined to insure their independence. And, in fact, they did preserve their way of life longer than any other North Dakota group. One can still hear German spoken with fluency in the taverns and on the street corners of many villages in the southcentral part of the state.

This ingrained German loyalty to family, friends, and traditions can, to some extent, explain why the numerous non-German homesteaders who lived among them left the German townships and counties. They were "outsiders" in an environment whose ethnic intensity had been fashioned over many generations. The countryside in the German portions of the southcentral counties is today almost completely German-Russian. No other North Dakota national group exists in such exclusively homogeneous settlement situations.

The tight-knit and local character of the typical North Dakota German communities tended to limit the horizons of their residents. In fact, until the Second World War, German-Russians generally avoided higher education, state and national political office, and leadership in regional affairs. It can be said with a degree of accuracy that the Germans from Russia did not want to become Americans; rather, they wanted to be Germans in America.

Rural churches formed the center of early day German-Russian prairie life. Homestead life was necessarily an isolated existence, with mud, snow, and primitive road conditions limiting contact with larger villages. Furthermore, the early towns "belonged" to someone else, usually the Anglo-Americans. Their educational and social advantages made these "other people" an elite class of citizens, a class which controlled businesses, city governments, and school boards. The countryside, however, could belong to the Germans; and for them the church became a particularly strong center of life. Of all the social institutions, this one alone could be exclusively theirs.

Though exact totals are lacking, a good estimate has it that fifty-five percent of the German-Russians who came to the Dakotas were of Lutheran background; thirty-five percent were Catholic; and ten percent were Mennonite, Reformed, or Baptist. Catholics, with their well-defined traditions and organizational procedures, set up their own German parishes and generally remained Catholic. (Adjustment problems were frequent: priests were forced out of town, and bishops used excommunication and interdict.) Mennonites, bringing their ministers with them, rather easily re-established their religious structures.

Lutherans, however, had serious troubles. In Russia a certain ferment had already been at work: pietism, lay leadership, a sense of autonomy, and revivalism. Starting in South Dakota, in the Yankton area villages and in Eureka, a dozen German-speaking American churches captured the allegiances of the incoming Protestants; and the new affiliations spread north along the wagon trails to every part of North Dakota: German Baptists, German Congregationalists, Methodists, the Reformed Church, the German Evangelical Church, and Lutherans of the Missouri, Iowa, and Wisconsin synods and even the Manitoba Synod. Later, the Seventh Day Adventists, the Church of God, and the Assembly of God joined the scene in northcentral North Dakota.

In the confusion of New World adjustment, certain criteria seemed necessary for survival or success: services had to be in German, local autonomy and a degree of lay control had to be present, and a simple biblical faith had to be possible. Within this framework, several hundred German congregations blossomed forth on the Dakota prairies.

For the Protestants, the church was often named after the village in Russia from whence most of the local residents came: thus, the Neudorf Church near Gackle; the Johannestal congregation six miles northwest of Wishek; the Kassel congregation near Zeeland; the *Hoffnungstal Gemeinde* at Venturia, and the Glueckstal Church south of Tappen.

For Catholics, saints' names prevailed. Rural social and religious centers grew up almost everywhere; some flourish today. Thus, we see St. Anthony Church south of Napoleon, St. Boniface southeast of Kintyre, St. Aloysius east of Linton, St. Michael's east of Strasburg, St. Bernard's in the Katzbach community west of Linton, and Holy Trinity Church in the Grassna community west of Strasburg. Grassna (Krassna) and Katzbach are unique in that they were the only significant Catholic villages in Bessarabia.

Of particular interest, however, was the St. John's parish five miles north of Zeeland. Here a small church was erected in 1885; a later one, built in 1906, exists today. This St. John's Church was the pioneer German-Russian Catholic congregation in the state. Immigrants spread from Eureka into North Dakota through a kind of "Zeeland corridor," and St. John's was remembered as the "home" church by thousands of German Catholics.

In the multiplicity of the Protestant world, no such mother churches were present. Rather, a great number of itinerant ministers set up independent churches as they moved across the wide prairies. There seemed to be little coordination or design in their efforts.

GYPSIES

Gypsies were a part of the North Dakota scene for several generations (until World War II), but they were always a "wandering" people. Every village had its moments when a gypsy caravan would camp nearby.

Many old-time residents recall gypsy wagons stopping at the farm for water or a chicken.

A small gypsy agricultural colony, however, once did take root in the state. Sometime around the turn of the century, gypsy leaders purchased five or six farms in Homer Township, Stutsman County. The gypsy farmers remained only a half dozen years and left. They are remembered for having purchased the land with gold coins and for having treated their horses "badly."

HOLLANDERS

In 1885 the first group of Hollander settlers (at least thirty-five) arrived in southern Emmons County, taking up timber claims and homesteads. Another large influx took place the next year, and by 1890, approximately 500 Dutch newcomers (adults and children) were in the area. Their present-day descendants occupy several townships in North Dakota, centering around Westfield and Hull. To the south, this Dutch area extends into South Dakota as far as Pollock. Many of the earliest land seekers came to Dakota after spending several years elsewhere in Americ~ .. often in Michigan, but sometimes in Iowa (Westfield was named after Westfield, Iowa). South Dakota ties seem to have been important, too, for historical accounts often mention settlements such as New Holland in the southeastern corner of that state. An energetic land agent of Dutch background, one affiliated with the Chicago, Milwaukee and St. Paul Railroad, extolled this portion of Dakota Territory in a prominent Dutch-language newspaper and encouraged settlers to choose the area for their future homes.

The earliest church organization in Emmons County may have been the Hope Reformed Congregation at Westfield. This group built its first church in 1887, and for many years it was known locally as the "Cottonwood Church." Nearby at Hull, a group of immigrants with different religious loyalties organized the Holland Christian Reformed congregation in 1887. They started their church building in that same year, completing it finally in 1894. As farm folk moved into town, a Reformed church was built in Strasburg in 1917. The Westfield and Hull churches are now modern brick structures, and their church congregations still have resident pastors and are strong community centers.

Local social life and ethnic loyalty must have been an intense feature of the Emmons County Dutch community, for little mingling has taken place with the Catholic German-Russians to the north. This is remarkable, considering the fact that the Germans' desire for land led them elsewhere in the state to expand into nearby non-German regions. The line between the Hollanders and the German-Russians has remained stable for several generations.

IRISH

Coming with the first Anglo-Americans were the American Irish. Many were Civil War Veterans; some were employees of the railroad, and some had prior gold-mining or frontier military experience. All spoke English and, almost without exception, had been residents of eastern states for a generation. All felt at home in an American or, at least, a British environment. Early Bismarck had an Irish section called the Kerry Patch. Almost every township had its very early Irish homesteaders (often mingled with the Anglo-Americans). They made up a great portion of the pioneer police and fire departments, county officials, and city councils. In fact, the Irish identified with the Yankees to the extent that they often saw themselves as Old Americans; to them, other groups were "immigrants" and "foreigners."

The Irish formed many of the present-day Catholic congregations. In this they were assisted by Irish priests, who were present in great numbers during frontier times. Some Catholic parishes such as Pingree and Buchanan in Stutsman County were considered by outsiders to be almost exclusively Irish congregations. Even some parishes which now have a Germanic tone in Emmons, Burleigh, and Kidder counties were established and maintained by Irish settlers for the first several generations.

The early day Dakota Irish, however, tended to move to better fortunes. Gregarious people, the Irish found the loneliness and drudgery of prairie farm life unattractive. Those who did not leave the state moved into towns and established small businesses such as hotels, saloons, and dray services. Some few moved into professional life. Many went to normal schools and (with their Anglo-Saxon neighbors) became, very often, the first instructors in the state's burgeoning number of one-room schools. Throughout present-day rural North Dakota relatively few of the original Irish families remain; the great majority have long since departed.

JEWS

In June of 1882 an initial eleven Jewish families arrived by steamboat at the mouth of the Painted Woods Creek in Burleigh County (now McLean County). This was the start of North Dakota's first and most ill-fated Jewish settlement. The early settlers' trip to Dakota and up the Missouri from Bismarck was accomplished with the help of Jewish aid societies and prominent Jewish individuals. The newcomers, mainly from Russia, homesteaded and took tree claims* on land a few miles south of Washburn (T 143-R 81). They established a small village (a cluster of cabins and dugouts) on Section 16 which was land designated for school purposes. Neighbors began to protest their presence on the school section, and legal battles began. Rabbi Judah Wechsler of St. Paul seems to have been a leading figure in the colony history. Through his strenuous efforts a series of subsidies came to the group, and the land-settlement dispute was resolved. Colonists continued to arrive, some purchasing railroad acreage in the odd-numbered sections, and the community eventually contained over fifty families.

Crop failure and prairie fires came in 1885; and, in spite of the best efforts of Rabbi Wechsler and various benevolent groups, the settlement seemed to be doomed. By 1901 only three families remained. A cemetery, with stones marked in Hebraic letters, stood for many years as a testimony to the Jewish pioneers' presence. Now, apparently, the graves are unrecognizable. An Anglo-Jewish name stands as a solitary reminder of the colony's past: Montefiore Township (on older maps) and Montefiore School District.

Some ten or fifteen years after the demise of the Painted Woods settlement in McLean County, another homestead community came into existence fifteen miles farther east in Andrews (now Canfield), Rock Hill, and Richmond (T 143-R 76) townships. In 1901 or 1902 the first Jewish settlers came to that region and settled on a scattered series of farms among great numbers of gentile land seekers. No compact colony formed, but the series of farmsteads made up a community of Jews who had their own special religious and social interrelationships. For the most part the Jews came from Russia or Hungary. Very few, if any, spent time in Eastern cities; most came almost directly by rail from immigration ports to North Dakota.

This second group of Burleigh County Jewish farmers has also left the area, but a cemetery does remain. It is located on Section 30 of Canfield Township, three miles northeast of Regan. The cemetery, whose first tombstone is dated 1903, was not in the center of the Jewish settlement area, but must have been established as an early need required. It then became a community burial place.

Some Jewish settlers were found not only in the four above mentioned townships but also in adjoining areas as well. Jewish settlers were also present in local towns; for example, in Wing Jewish merchants are said to have

established the first store, the first cream station, the first meat market, and the first harness shop. Other Jewish shopkeepers were present in Tuttle, Arena, and Denhoff.

Whether a synagogue was ever established at Wing is not known. A local newspaper reported that one hundred Jewish people gathered at a farm home for Yom Kippur in 1916, and plans for erecting a synagogue were discussed at that occasion. Rabbi J. Hess, a "traveling" sort of clergyman who resided in McIntosh County, often visited the families in the Wing area. At times he would stay for several weeks, instructing the young people in "the Hebrew language and the Jewish faith."

Like their counterparts in Jewish settlements elsewhere in the state, the homesteaders around Wing and Regan generally found the Dakota prairies an unsatisfactory environment. Conditions, however, in the first two decades of the twentieth century were more gentle than those which faced the earlier Painted Woods people. The Wing farmers showed no signs of desperation. Contact with the "outside world" was relatively easy; railroads and good communication systems were fairly well developed. The amenities of civilization were already present.

The number of Jews present, at one time or another, must have been quite large; over seventy are known to have filed on land. An early Canfield Township resident from Illinois said there were two obstacles she could not overcome when she tried to start a Sunday School: ". . .the Norwegian language and Judaism. It seems in that area you were either Norwegian or Jewish."

It turned out that many, if not most, Jews stayed for only five years or until their land was "proved up." After acquiring knowledge of English and the American way of life, they went elsewhere and generally became quite successful. Even though they are gone, their cemetery is kept in good repair by a gentile farmer.

A third Jewish homestead community, perhaps the largest in the state, was founded near Ashley in McIntosh County in 1903. Individual Jewish farmers are said to have settled north of that town as early as 1900. Jews from Russia predominated, but land seekers from Minneapolis and New York were among the early residents. In 1911 some sixty families are reported to have been present in the Ashley-Wishek region.

The term "colony," applied to this group, can be misleading, for the settlement consisted of homesteaders and farmers scattered over four different McIntosh townships. They were, for example, in the townships adjacent to the Ashley village, namely, Ashley (T 130-R 69) and Hoskins (T 130-R 70). They were also in the two townships immediately to the north of that town. The major influx came from 1903 to 1908; during these years almost 100 Jewish individuals, men and women, applied for land ownership. In this they seem to have been at a disadvantage, for their German-Russian neighbors had come earlier, some arriving in 1888. The settlers left the land rapidly; on the 1912 land maps, fewer than a dozen farm owners had identifiable Jewish names. By that time, however, Ashley and Wishek must have had a considerable number of Jewish townspeople, for a rabbi was

*The Timber-Culture Act allowed a settler to acquire a quarter section of land by planting forty acres of trees and tending them for a number of years.

active in the area (part-time and often full-time) for at least two decades.

Jewish settlers worshipped in their farm and town homes during their first few years of McIntosh County life. In 1913 Rabbi J. Hess was in residence in Ashley; he served both the Ashley and Wing (Burleigh County) communities. By 1917, synagogues existed in both Ashley and Wishek. Rabbi Ostrowsky was active in Ashley in 1918. The congregations were never large; Wishek had "twelve to fourteen" adult members in 1917. But the groups were big enough to celebrate the major religious holidays and to have adult and young people's associations.

Although most Jewish homesteaders left the land and the area rather quickly, some rare individuals stayed and flourished. In 1926 one gentleman owned twelve farms in North Dakota and Canada. This phenomenon occurred elsewhere in the state. An occasional Jewish homesteader would move to town, retain his land holdings, and become a successful real-estate agent and farm owner.

The two McIntosh County synagogues have long since disappeared, and their congregations have been dissolved. The ruins, however, of an impressive eighty-year-old stone Jewish farm house and a well-kept cemetery, filled with Hebrew inscriptions, still stand a few miles north of Ashley.

NORWEGIANS

The southcentral counties of North Dakota contain proportionately fewer rural Norwegians than any other part of the state. Some very early arrivals are said to have come to Painted Woods in 1878. They must have been few in number, for no recognizable colony ever seems to have developed. Of more lasting significance, however, was a small and compact Norwegian community which still exists three or four miles southeast of Kintyre in Emmons County. The Tell Norwegian Lutheran Church was established there in Tell Township in 1905. Not far away an earlier Maria Lutheran Congregation was founded in 1890; Swedes as well as Norwegians were active in this group. They built a church in 1900. By the 1940's both groups had dissolved, and the Kintyre Lutheran Church served their needs.

Generally, the Norwegians of the southcentral counties reside today in areas of multiple ethnic backgrounds. North of the Burlington Northern Railroad, Norwegians live among farmers of a variety of backgrounds in Burleigh County's Driscoll, Lein, and Clear Lake townships. In nearby Kidder County, they live alongside Anglo-Americans in Robinson and Buckeye townships. Also, north of Tuttle, Norwegians are found mixed with German-Russians in Atwood Township; St. Peter's Church, established in 1907, served these farm families. South of Tuttle and Robinson the Skudesnes Church was organized in 1890. In these areas, some Norwegians are engaged in ranching ventures.

The main concentration of Norwegians in the southcentral counties is in the townships adjacent to the James River in Stutsman County. The central part of Manns Township in the southeast corner of the county is seventy-five percent Norwegian. Farther north along the river, Ypsilanti, Winfield, and Spiritwood townships have a sizable mixture of Norwegians. The James River Valley Church at Montpelier (organized in 1905) and the North James River Church at Ypsilanti (organized in 1914) served many of these rural and village Norwegians. In the northern part of the county, Norwegians are found in James River townships such as Plainview, Pingree, and Lyon. These Stutsman County areas represent the remote western edge of the extensively Norwegian parts of Barnes and Ransom counties which border the Sheyenne River.

Elsewhere in the region, early clusters of immigrants from Norway (and sometimes lone individuals) settled in what was to become the solidly German-Russian areas of McIntosh, Logan, Stutsman, and Emmons counties. An Emmons County history states that "there was a big Norwegian settlement near Pursian [sic] Lake, now all moved away." Another group of Norwegians is said to have come to McIntosh County, beginning in 1884. They are supposed to have centered at Ashley and extended northward from that town. This is probably true, for a post office named "Norwegian" was set up in a sod farm house in that vicinity in 1890; the location was near the present town of Danzig. In any event, the settlement no longer exists; the area is German-Russian today. Norwegians also settled, according to some reports, in Emmons County near a rural post office called Larvik on Little Beaver Creek; this locality is now completely German-Russian.

SILESIAN POLES

A most interesting group of settlers arrived in Stutsman County's Fried and Kensal areas, starting first in 1879. These were what might be called "Poles from Silesia," although they included a few families of non-Silesian origin. After spending a short time in Polish settlements at Independence and Arcadia, Wisconsin, and nearby Winona, Minnesota, they came by railroad to the developing land north of Jamestown. They were, in fact, people of Polish ancestry who had lived in the German province of Silesia. (Oppeln is remembered as the largest town in their homeland.) The Stutsman homesteaders were Polish in language and in culture. Polish names are found throughout the area today in Fried and Ashland townships, and also in southern Kensal Township; but among them are some remarkably German names like Kaiser and Skroch and Schultz. The original Stutsman settlers, though they could speak some German, felt that Germans had taken their land unjustly. The nationality confusion had an ancient origin; it came about in the 1770's when Germany annexed that part of Poland.

The Silesian Poles were Catholic in background, and the first Mass in the Fried locality took place in 1882. A church was erected in 1887; a parish school was built in 1912. The less numerous Silesian Poles of the Kensal area joined with Germans and Irish in building a church in 1904. Religious services had been held in homes as early as 1898.

POLES

Another cluster of Polish families settled immediately south and west of Windsor, beginning in 1905. Many of these people also came, it seems, from Silesia. These farmers did not consider themselves part of the Fried group; they may well have come from a different part of the province. Reniszowka had been their home in Poland; Richthal Province is also mentioned as a place of origin. In the 1880's, perhaps later, members of this group came to the little town of Wells near Albert Lea, Minnesota. A certain Father Cieszynski, traveling through North Dakota in 1900, saw the good land around Jamestown; returning to Minnesota, he encouraged local Poles to come to the new territory and to purchase farms. This they did. Among the early families were Wanzeks, Kensoks, and Zimneys, but also names such as Schultz. The priest himself owned land in Stutsman County and often visited the Windsor people until his death some few years later. This group spoke Polish and considered themselves Polish, but they also spoke some German.

SWEDES

A very early Swedish community was established in Eckland Township in northern Burleigh County east of Wilton. This group centered around the Sunne Church, which was organized in 1893. Some of the initial settlers came from Wisconsin and Minnesota, but some migrated directly from Sweden. First arrivals came to Burleigh County in 1882; nearby Painted Woods and Ghylin townships also saw a great number of Swedish settlers in territorial days. In fact, they antedated the influx of Norwegians by almost a decade. Swedish homesteaders were often individualists, and throughout the 1880's took land alongside the pioneer Anglo-Americans in many places along the Missouri Valley north of Bismarck. The northern Burleigh County community was probably related to the very sizable Swedish farm region which developed in several townships between Wilton and Coleharbor.

Another collection of Swedish farmers settled in the Kintyre area of Emmons County, and some of their descendants are present today. Some residents came in the early 1880's and settled both around Goose Lake in Campbell Township and also farther south along the creek which runs down the west edge of Tell and Wood townships. The Maria Lutheran Church was built to serve local needs; it flourished for at least forty years. As elsewhere in the state, Swedes tended to leave farming in proportionately large numbers; and the Maria church merged with non-Swede Lutheran congregations. The Burleigh and Emmons county groups are now diluted with non-Swedish farmers who were more eager to stay on the land.

UKRAINIANS

A tiny portion of the Wilton area Ukrainians extends into Burleigh County. The first families settled on homestead land north of the present city of Wilton around 1897. The settlement was and still is a sizable one, containing Ukrainians whose allegiance was divided between the Ukrainian Catholic and Ukrainian Greek Orthodox churches in Wilton.

The Ukrainian settlers often list "Galicia in Austria" as their place of origin. The Galician section of the Ukraine was, indeed, under the control of the Austro-Hungarian empire at the time of their migration to the United States. For further details, see the discussion of the Wilton Ukrainians in the commentary on the northwestern part of the state.

Northcentral North Dakota

Ethnic Population Distribution
Northcentral Section of North Dakota

1. Anglo-American with some Anglo-Ontarian
2. French 50%: Others
3. Norwegian 50%: Anglo-American 50%
4. Swede 50%: Norwegian 50%
5. Anglo-American 50%: German 50%
6. Anglo-Ontarian 60%: Anglo-American 40%
7. Norwegian 70%: Anglo-American 30%
8. German 40%: German-Russian 25%: Anglo-American 25%: Norwegian 10%
9. French and French-Indian
10. Mennonite
11. German 50%: Norwegian 50%
12. Finlander 50%: Others 50%
13. German 50%: Brethren (Dunker) 50%
14. Mixed: German, German-Russian, Anglo-American
15. Icelander 50%: Norwegian 50%
16. German-Russian 40%: Anglo-American 30%: Norwegian 30%
17. German-Russian 40%: Anglo-American 30%: German 30%
18. Anglo-American 50%: Others
19. German-Russian Catholic 50%: Norwegian 50%
20. Anglo-American 40%: Norwegian 30%: German 30%
21. Brethren (Dunker) 40%: Anglo-American 40%: Others 20%
22. Norwegian with occasional Swede
23. Anglo-American 60%: German-Russian 40%
24. Anglo-American 60%: Norwegian 40%
25. Mixed: Anglo-American, German and Brethren (Dunker)
26. Anglo-American, occasional Other
27. American Indian and Others
28. German-Russian Protestant (Dobrudja)
29. Anglo-American 50%: Mixed 50%
30. German-Russian Mennonite and German-Russian
31. German-Russian Mennonite and occasional German-Russian
32. Anglo-American 50%: German-Russian Protestant 50%
33. German 40%: German-Russian 30%: Norwegian 30%
34. German-Russian (Dobrudja) and German
35. Hungarian-German (Burgenland) and other Germans
36. Luxemburger and German
37. Anglo-American (many Irish)
38. Polish and Bohemian
39. German 50% (some Dunkers): Norwegian 50%
40. Syrian and Norwegian

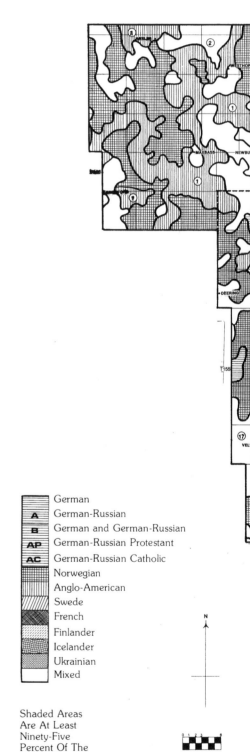

German
A   German-Russian
B   German and German-Russian
AP German-Russian Protestant
AC German-Russian Catholic
Norwegian
Anglo-American
Swede
French
Finlander
Icelander
Ukrainian
Mixed

N

Shaded Areas
Are At Least
Ninety-Five
Percent Of The
Same National
Group Unless
Otherwise
Indicated

Rural Residents as of 1965

William C. Sherman   NDSU   Fargo, ND

Township Names and Descriptions
Northcentral Section of North Dakota

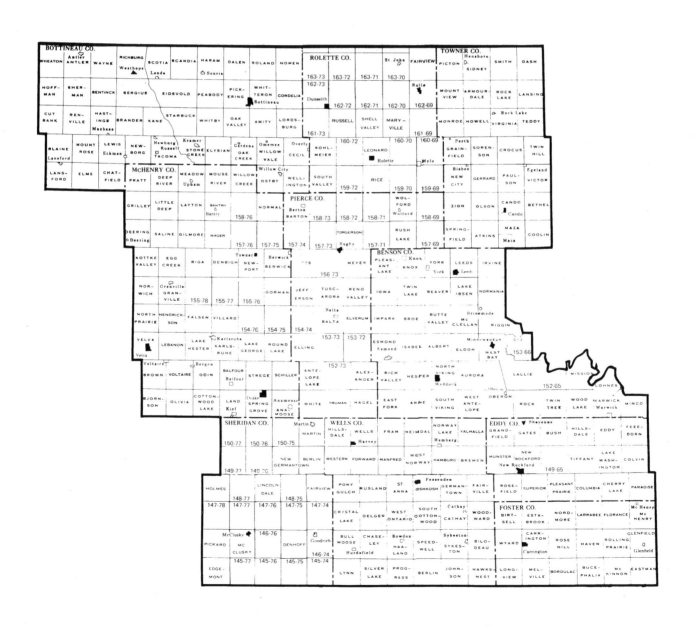

Commentary

AMISH AND AMERICAN MENNONITES

Scouts from an Amish settlement at Goshen, Indiana, looked over land in Rolette County in 1893. The next year the first Amish settlers arrived in Island Lake Township (T 159-R 70) along the Pierce County border. A *Grand Forks Herald* report of April 3, 1897, said three carloads of Amish passed through that city on the way to "the Island Lake vicinity." The report further stated that the settlers were accompanying a contingent of Dunkard and Mennonite immigrants. By 1903, fifty families, some of Old Order Amish and some of Amish Mennonite tradition, were living in Rolette and Pierce counties. The Old Order settlers established two church districts, and the Mennonites had their own religious communities. Both groups had been in America for several generations, having come from Pennsylvania backgrounds.

Despite their dedication to work and their strong interfamily bonds, most of the early settlers (particularly the Old Order people) found Dakota prairie life unsatisfactory. Apparently no Amish Church was built; religious services were usually held in farm homes, although an Amish Sunday School House, in which services were often held, once existed a mile east of Island Lake. Within a few years the majority of Amish settlers left Dakota, many going to Colorado, and some later going to Indiana and Illinois. The group that remained eventually affiliated with the Mennonites and centered their life around the Lakeview Mennonite Church in Section 35 of Island Lake Township. This Rolette County group extended as far south into Pierce County as the village of Wolford.

The Lakeview Mennonite Church is still active, and a new Salem Mennonite Church (organized in 1966) exists four miles northeast of the Lakeview Church in Rolette County. This new congregation is of a more strict orientation — the women wear white caps — and it operates a thriving twelve-grade school in the church basement. No "Amish" family lives in the area today; the last was said to have left in the mid-1940's. Many local residents, however, can name an Amish individual who occupies an honored place in their family ancestry.

ANGLO-AMERICANS

Thousands of English-speaking settlers came to the northcentral part of North Dakota during the homestead days. They came not with the timidity of recent European immigrants, but with a self-confidence that was the product of several generations of American living. They were, quite simply, citizens from eastern states who decided to "move west." Their names, usually of British Isles origin, are prominent on the lists of early squatters — those people who came to the region before surveyors and railroad agents entered the scene. Often in lonely cabins near a spring or grove of cottonwoods, they were in every county and township. Their stay in North Dakota, however, was usually short-lived; their land probably now belongs to Norwegians and Germans. In fact, many of the Anglo-Americans left the very moment they acquired clear titles to their properties. Like tumbleweeds, they bounced along the frontier. Some continued westward; some took

up employment in nearby villages, and many returned to eastern America with farm-sale money in their pockets.

Sometimes their arrival was in an organized fashion. A very early "Missouri Settlement" began near Towner in the mid-1880's. Seventy carloads of livestock and equipment accompanied the incoming group. Another "Missouri Colony" is said to have settled fifteen miles northwest of Granville in 1900 in McHenry County. An "Ohio Settlement" was established twelve miles northeast of Granville at the same time. Pennsylvania Yankees settled in Juniata Township (T 158-R 71) in Pierce County, and an Oshkosh Settlement was founded in Wells County in 1886. A "Michigan Settlement" was also present in that county.

Anglo-Americans who engaged in ranching ventures were in the area at an even earlier date. Anglo-American cattlemen took up land in the southern Pierce County sandhills in 1882, some three years before the first homesteader arrived in that region. In that rough terrain, Abner Hanscom from Maine and other Yankees set up a horse and cattle ranch near Antelope and Buffalo Lakes. Eastern financial backing assisted them; and their operation had, like so many others, a "bonanza" quality about it. This particular Pierce County ranch was not highly successful, though it did continue for some years in a limited fashion.

Ranches, some small and some occasionally large, were also located elsewhere in the region. The southern Benson County and northern Eddy County areas along the Sheyenne had their pioneer "spreads" in earliest times. Northern McHenry County, on both sides of the Souris River, still has a number of Anglo-American families who engage in ranching. This area saw a number of moderate-sized cattle concerns in the first part of the 1880's. Texas cattle were present, but so were Shorthorn cows from Illinois. The Towne, Nohle, and Stevens ranches were among early land holdings. The White House ranch was run by a "southern gentleman" named Colonel Ely. The son of a Scottish nobleman owned the Majoribank Ranch near Hackett's Crossing.

Sometimes homesteading activity came about as a by-product of the ranching enterprises. For example, in 1899 Warren Hurd purchased 6,400 acres of railroad land in southern Wells County. This venture included a large cattle operation which extended throughout the hills of southern Wells and southeastern Sheridan counties. Some American settlers got their start by coming to the region as ranch employees and then setting out on their own.

Land companies were particularly active in the area. The Carrington and Casey Land Company purchased 39,640 acres in Foster and Wells counties in 1882 and set about selling the property to incoming farmers through various promotional activities. At the same time, the Sykes land syndicate took an option on 45,000 acres of Northern Pacific Railroad land; and the Sykes-Hughes farm came into existence. Richard Sykes, the promoter, would plow up a portion of the land, build a house and barn, and sell it as "improved" acreage. Often he would sell a 160-acre plot which adjoined homestead land. The purchaser could, thus, acquire two quarters: one from Sykes and one from the United States government. Some of the Sykes employees filed on nearby land and thereby became permanent residents.

Extensive advertising was done in American large-city newspapers, and Sykeston and Carrington became jump-off points for hundreds of "Easterners" as they took possession of their new farms. Clement Lounsberry in his *History of North Dakota* says that in 1880 there were no farms in the Foster, Wells, and Eddy county areas. In 1885 there were 392. Lounsberry mentions particularly Pennsylvania, Illinois, Michigan, Wisconsin, and Iowa as furnishing a "good share" of the newly arrived settlers. These three counties, even today, reflect the scattered presence of the earliest American land seekers. The area north and south of Sykeston, Fessenden, Carrington, and Glenfield is still half Anglo-American.

DUNKARDS (Brethren)

Max Bass, the German-born immigration agent for the Great Northern Railroad, was responsible for bringing to North Dakota a surprisingly large number of Dunkard colonization groups. Bass attended the annual conference of the church in Muncie, Indiana, in 1893; and a few months later personally escorted church leaders to Mayville, Lakota, and Cando. Through his efforts, land in Towner County west of Cando was selected and filed upon during that same year. The Cando Dunkard settlement thereby came into existence. In 1894, the church members began arriving from Indiana, Ohio, and Virginia. Some came by special train, accompanied along the way by generous amounts of railroad publicity activity: banners, photographs, and newspaper accounts. The initial settlement centered particularly on township T 158-R 68, spilling over into townships to the east and to the north.

Reverend A. B. Peters was engaged about that time by the railroad as a special immigration emissary to the Dunkards; he, thereafter, solicited more North Dakota settlers, especially from church groups who lived in Indiana. In 1896, as a result, 108 persons were present when the Cando settlement church was completed in what became known as Zion Township. In 1898 another church was erected in the town of Cando; it continues as an active congregation to this day.

Dunkards are treated here as a separate ethnic group. They were a unique, tightly knit association of people with an American-German background. Having come to America as early as 1719, they, like the Pennsylvania Mennonites, maintained their own special traditions for at least three generations before coming to Dakota. To outsiders, they were clearly "different," having distinctive beards and hair styles. The name "Dunkard" is used with a bit of hesitation, for the denomination has since 1908 been called the Church of the Brethren. The term "Dunkard" was a popular nickname for the group during settlement days. Most of the North Dakota congregations were, in fact, incorporated under the title of "German Baptist Brethren."

The Zion-Cando religious community became the parent church of at least eight similar congregations within forty miles of Cando. The favorable reports of these first Towner County settlers brought more newcomers to the region. The Bisbee newspaper said in 1897 that two hundred Dunkards got off the train at that town, and one hundred disembarked at Rolla. Two hundred horses were brought with them. The 1897 migration seems to have been a large one, for two train loads of Dunkards (with three trains of stock and farm implements) passed through Grand Forks in April of that year. This meant 1,725 new settlers, all destined for north-central North Dakota. As other Brethren arrived, little church groups sprang up accordingly. A few miles southeast of Rock Lake in Virginia Township, Towner County, the Brumbaugh, or Snyder Lake, Congregation was organized shortly before 1900; it had 125 members in 1906. In 1898 another group of Brethren moved from Waterloo, Iowa, to a location seven miles east of Rock Lake. This gathering of families was called the Rock Lake, or Ellison, Congregation; by the end of the year it had eighty-five members. Membership declined seriously within two decades of settlement, and the Ellison group merged with the Brumbaugh Church in 1938. By the late 1950's the combined church was no longer active. The township east of Rock Lake is still occupied, at least in part, by a number of families who trace their ancestry to the original Brethren homesteaders. Some attend the Cando Church, and others now belong to different religious denominations.

A Hyland church in Twin Hill Township, Towner County, began in 1902, being made up of Brethren from the southernmost portion of the Rock Lake settlement. Their church moved to Egeland in 1907 and was no longer functioning by 1937. Its maximum membership totaled 110. Of this group only an occasional family is present today.

A number of Dunkard families organized a Brethren congregation five miles west of Perth in Ellsworth Township, Rolette County, in 1901. They eventually erected a structure and called it the Turtle Mountain Church. Some sixty-six members belonged in 1908; by 1917 only five were listed as being active. Many members were said to have moved in a group "to a western state." By 1930 the church no longer functioned.

The movement to a western state was apparently not an unusual thing. The Cando Brethren community saw the departure, in the early part of the twentieth century, of a large number of members who resettled on land near Wenatchee, Washington. The migrants were said to have been motivated not just by the desire for land, but also by a sense of "mission." The same desire to spread the faith which had led some to Dakota later led others farther west.

While many Brethren were attracted by the Great Northern Railroad to the Cando area of Towner County, another early day settlement focal point seems to have been the land around Carrington. In 1896, through Northern Pacific Railroad inducements, Brethren from eastern states purchased approximately sixty quarter sections of land near that Foster County town; by the end of that year twenty families were in residence. On April 1st of the next year, 300 Brethren passed through Fargo under the leadership of Elder Noah Fisher on their way to Carrington. Other reports said that after their arrival they dispersed to farms not just in Foster, but also in Wells and Eddy counties.

The early Carrington settlement was near the city, and by November, 1896, a church had been constructed. In 1900 the Carrington Church numbered 250 members. Membership fluctuated over the years, and the congregation closed in 1960. Today only a few families remain who claim these Brethren settlers as their ancestors. One reason for the fluctuation was the dividing of the Carrington religious community in 1902, when a new church group was formed in Wells County, four miles north of Bowdon. This congregation was scattered over a relatively large area and found it difficult to maintain a stable membership. Sixty members were listed in 1903, but the 1930's saw the end of the congregation.

Northeast of Carrington, a James River Church was founded in 1902 near Brantford in Eddy County. In 1922 the congregation was divided, and the James River South Church came into being. This new group centered around a small frame structure ten miles east of Carrington in Foster County; by the 1930's, both groups seem to have ceased functioning.

The Dunkard influx into North Dakota was extensive. An 1897 report spoke of "upwards of 6,000 Dunkards" settled already in the state. By this time the Northern Pacific and the Soo Line were active in promotion projects. A contemporary newspaper said Dunkards made admirable settlers: "Not only are they sober and industrious, but they bring with them stock and implements which enable them to become profitable producers."

The previously mentioned special trains, filled with 1,725 Dunkards, which passed through Grand Forks, arrived in Devils Lake on April 4, 1897. Some embarked at that city, going perhaps a few miles north to Sweetwater. Most went farther north to Towner and Rolette counties, but many continued westward to Leeds and York in Benson County. Another party of "several hundred" Dunkard settlers was said to have come to the York area a week later. Eventually land seekers from Pennsylvania, Indiana, Ohio, Illinois, and Iowa founded the Pleasant Valley Brethren Congregation near York in 1898. A church structure was erected several years later three miles west and three miles south of that city. This country congregation is unique in that it has survived through three generations. Brethren farmers are, today, clearly visible in the townships south of York and Knox. Only two other Brethren groups, at Cando and Surrey, are active in present-day North Dakota.

Twenty-five miles south of York the Flora Brethren Congregation, established in 1913, struggled through a decade of activity before merging with the York Church. Farther west in McHenry County a White Rock Congregation began near Denbigh at the turn of the century. It had eighty-six members in 1904; by 1918 it was no longer listed on the denomination rolls.

The railroads, in their encouragement of Dunker settlements, realized their initial aim: filling the prairies with settlers. Their hope, however, that these settlers and their descendants would become loyal patrons of the railroad did not materialize. The Dunkards resembled the Anglo-Americans and Irish in that many stayed in Dakota only a short while and then moved to other states. Perhaps the harsh prairie conditions led to disillusionment.

For those who stayed, there seem to have been internal church problems, a certain disintegration. This may have been due to lack of leadership, because until 1940 the Brethren churches often had a sort of free-ministry procedure in which clergy were taken from local memberships and served without salary. Without the rallying point of a minister who would become, as in other ethnic religious groups, the teacher, perpetuator, and symbol of the national group, their loyalties may have dissipated. Perhaps, too, the German ethnic ties, which flourished in Pennsylvania and Indiana, proved less than durable in the rather extended and scattered setting of the small prairie congregations. Daily association with non-Brethren farmers may have had a diluting effect. Perhaps the Brethren, well acquainted with America, did not "have to stay" in the difficult circumstances of the primitive northern plains. Like the Anglo-Americans, they could move with ease to better climates and more fortunate opportunities.

Some Dunkard descendants remain in North Dakota, but now consider themselves to be of "Pennsylvania Dutch" or "American" background. The family names, which were Anglicized even before arrival in North Dakota, betray their German origins only through close examination.

FINNS

In Towner County the Rolla-Rock Lake Finnish settlement occupies most of Mount View and Armourdale townships and spills over into Sidney, Picton, and Monroe townships. It is, without doubt, North Dakota's largest Finnish "colony." Even the Dickey County settlement near Ludden does not compare in size.

Coming as early as 1896 from Canada, South Dakota, Minnesota, and Michigan (and later from Finland), the homesteaders centered their national life around two churches and a community center. A Finnish Apostolic congregation, which first met in 1899, built a small frame church a decade later near the center of Mount View Township. A few miles to the northwest, a Finn "Town Hall" was erected in 1905. A Finnish National Evangelical congregation began in 1901 and had services in the Finn Hall until 1926, when a church was built on the west edge of Mount View Township. The Apostolic Church brought together those Finns who sought a more fundamentalist approach to religion. The Evangelical Church was the gathering place for those with "high" church or "state" church backgrounds and more traditional theological learnings. The Finn Hall provided a rallying place for those whose religious needs were at a minimum or nonexistent.

The presence of a distinctly "religious" and "non-religious" community center was frequently — perhaps always — a part of North Dakota Finlander life. Every settlement seems to have experienced these divisions. "Finn Halls" throughout the state were the sites of entertainment such as dances and parties which were held in disdain by some local residents. The Towner County community was no exception. The Finn Hall, however, featured other things besides recreation; for example, it promoted a large Finnish-language lending library.

A strong community life was evident from the very beginning. The Finns held their traditional Midsummer Festival in June, 1897, only one year after their arrival. The Finnish spirit of mutual assistance was also present. A Finnish grain-marketing cooperative was organized in 1917.

Finns in Towner County are still very much aware of their past; a certain ethnic pride pervades the area, and a strong sense of belonging remains. But time has been hard on the ethnic institutions. The Finn Hall disappeared in a fire; the Apostolic Church has moved to Rolla and now has services only on special occasions such as funerals. The Finnish Evangelical Church (which until the 1960's had frequent Finnish-language services) has merged with the Rock Lake Missouri Synod Church, a congregation of German Lutheran background that now appropriately calls itself the All Nations Lutheran Church.

FRENCH

French frontiersmen were, without doubt, the earliest white people in the northcentral portion of the state. They antedated the farmers and ranchers by almost 150 years. La Verendrye in 1738 was the first to traverse the region; in his wake over a hundred Canadian explorers, hunters and trappers — mostly French — journeyed from outposts near Lake Winnipeg to the Mandan villages along the Missouri River in the days before Lewis and Clark.

In the middle of the nineteenth century, Joe Rolette and other traders were active in the Turtle Mountain portions of present-day Rolette and Bottineau counties. In 1875 Bernard La Riviere, one of the area's first permanent French residents, came to the east side of the mountains and soon afterwards established a store. By 1880 white settlers, both French and Anglo-Saxon, were erecting cabins along the edge of the mountains, and in 1882 the St. Claude Church (north of today's St. John) was erected to care for French newcomers and the local Métis. French-Canadian squatters were taking up land at Dunseith in 1882; others were at Bottineau in 1883 and at Willow City a little later. Within a decade, on the southern edge of the Turtle Mountains, a series of predominately French centers grew up: Laureat, Alcide and Maryville. Catholic Churches were erected and resident priests were at hand. These earliest settlers came mainly from Canada, usually by way of the American rail system and Dakota wagon trails.

A French settlement sprang up around the Tarsus Church, which was established in 1883 on Section 5 of Lordsburg Township in Bottineau County; this area still

remains French. Thorne, not far away, was another French settlement, one which, though tiny, still survives. French settlers in the area made the Thorne village the center of their life when the town was established in 1905 with the coming of the Great Northern Railroad.

The French were concerned about education. The Notre Dame Academy at Willow City, run by nuns who had immigrated from France, opened as a grade school in 1906 and added a high school in 1910; at one time it had as many as 220 pupils. Families from the surrounding towns sent their children to the school as boarders or as day-students until the 1960's.

Under the curious name of "Little Fargo," a group of French settlers located in Cecil Township in southeastern Bottineau County around the turn of the century. They came, not from Canada, but from the Wild Rice French settlement south of Fargo. Wild Rice, predating Fargo and the arrival of the Northern Pacific Railroad, was settled in 1869 and is one of the oldest North Dakota homestead communities. In the 1890's, perhaps through the impetus of local religious leaders and land agents, some Wild Rice French farmers moved to a homestead area south of Belfield in Dunn County. At the same time other French farmers established the Bottineau settlement, building there a small church which they called the "Mission of St. Genevieve." A larger church structure was constructed a few years afterwards; in 1921 the building and the parish were moved to the nearby flourishing town of Overly. The years have been hard on the settlement; few of the original French families remain. Little Fargo is now just a cemetery.

An interesting cluster of French families came to Wells County from the Gaspé area of Canada in 1889. This group, located four miles northwest of Dover, claimed a certain St. Andrews Parish in Quebec as their place of origin. Some of the original residents had worked in the lumber industry in Minnesota before coming to North Dakota. French families continued to come to the settlement during the first decade of the twentieth century, and about a dozen such families are still remembered. Only one family remains today.

FRENCH-INDIANS (Métis)

The Turtle Mountain Indian Reservation, centered in Belcourt, consists of two townships in the middle of Rolette County. This small reservation was established in 1884 as a partial settlement to the Turtle Mountain Band of Chippewa Indians, whose land had been taken from them in earlier United States government treaties. Other North Dakota reservations contain large land areas which are occupied by non-Indian farmers. The situation at the Turtle Mountain is just the opposite; Indian families occupy the entire reservation and spill over into nearby non-reservation land. The population of Belcourt and the surrounding two townships is close to 5000 people. Most of the local residents are of French-Indian (Métis) background. Chippewa and Cree ancestries are part of their more remote past.

Sometime in the early eighteenth century, the first intermarriages of French *Voyageurs* and Indian women took place in the Great Lakes region of Canada and the United States. A century later, the descendants of these unions numbered in the thousands; many of these Métis families lived along the American and Canadian Red River, in northern Minnesota, and in the Turtle Mountains. Even though their religion was Catholic, their culture was a blend of both the native and old world ways. But their life embodied more than two cultures; the century of intermingling had produced a new self-conscious people, one which was the product of the frontier, of explorations, of buffalo hunts, and of Red River commerce.

Missionaries had been with them from the beginning. In Dakota such historic figures as Fathers LaFleche, Belcourt, Genin, and Malo were living among them in the 1860's and 1870's. The St. Claude log church and the St. Ann's Church at Belcourt were erected in the first part of the 1880's, primarily for French-Indian congregations, although all the early Turtle Mountain churches — Alcide, Laureat, Maryville, St. John, and Tarsus —

numbered both French-Canadian and Métis Catholics in their membership. In 1885 Father George Belcourt set up a school for reservation people, called by the Metis *Le Couvent.* Today it has been superseded by a number of modern educational institutions.

The small-sized Turtle Mountain reservation is hardly adequate for today's population. Land to the west and north of the reservation in the wooded and hilly terrain contains many families of Indian ancestry. The Métis families live, very often, among French-Canadian neighbors; indeed, sometimes their French ancestry predominates and their Indian past is almost forgotten.

Today a tribal council is active, and the Turtle Mountain enrollment, on the reservation and elsewhere, exceeds 15,000 people. A renewed sense of heritage is developing. Celebrations, displays, educational curricula, and family activities are once again emphasizing the traditions of this unique people who combine the ways of both the French and the Indian in their colorful past.

GERMANS (Reichsdeutsch)

Germans, born in the homeland, came in great numbers to the early Dakota prairies. Some came from seaport immigration terminals; many others came from German "colonies" in Wisconsin, Iowa, and Illinois. They often formed tight little enclaves throughout the north-central part of North Dakota; but many very early Germans, after residing in America for some years and mastering the English language, confidently took up land among the first Anglo-Americans.

Some early settlements of Protestant *Reichsdeutsch* are still in existence. The Willow Creek Missouri Synod congregation (Immanuel) began in Bottineau County in early 1889. The first of these German settlers are said to have come by wagon in 1884 (or 1885) from Grafton and Pembina County. In 1886 German Lutherans who had settled in Oxford Township south of Rolla in Rolette County formed a small congregation. German farmers still reside in these localities, although the local pastors and church centers are now in nearby large towns.

At Kramer in Bottineau County, the Zion Lutheran congregation started in 1898. The first of these German settlers apparently came as part of the Willow Creek migration and spread westward in search of new and better land. Germans are still present in the Kramer area. Nearby in McHenry County, the Upham Church dates to 1898. Omemee and Bantry had German Evangelical churches in the early 1900's. They, too, served the Germans in southern Bottineau and northern McHenry counties.

German Catholic farmers comprise a large part of the population in the Bremen community of Wells County. St. Joseph's congregation of Bremen first met in 1893. Farther north in Towner County the Catholic parishes of Bisbee (begun in 1889) and Cando (1883) depend heavily on German farmers for their memberships. These parishioners are the descendants of early *Reichsdeutsch* homesteaders, some of whom had a Stearns County, Minnesota, background.

A few German farmers in the northcentral counties are the offspring of what might be called "second wave" land seekers. They tend to be scattered in the areas of mixed nationalities. Their forefathers came, often in the 1910's and 1920's, to purchase land from disillusioned homesteaders.

DOBRUDJA GERMANS

A little-known type of German from Russia can be found on the countryside in northwestern Sheridan County and in Wells County, north of Cathay. While these farmers are sometimes called "Rumanians," they are really Dobrudja Germans. Their ancestors came to North Dakota from German colonies on the west edge of the Black Sea, an area which was ruled by Turkey until 1878 and which later became part of the Austro-Hungarian empire and today is in Rumania. Indeed, some elderly Sheridan County farmers listed their birth-places as Turkey, others as Austria, and some as Rumania; all were probably correct.

The residents of the Dobrudja villages were, for the most part, Germans who migrated in the first two decades of the nineteenth century to the Russian Black Sea regions, particularly Bessarabia. In the 1840's and 1850's they moved to the Turkish Dobrudja territory. These settlers were joined by another wave of German Ukrainian families when the Russian government revoked the military exemption agreements in 1871.

The odyssey of the Wells County and Sheridan County families from the Dobrudja to Dakota was almost as varied as their origins. The Russian-Turkish War disrupted life in the villages, and some individuals left for Canada in the early 1880's, arriving in the Winnipeg area the same year they left the old country. In 1884, some first families came to Pleasant Valley south of Carrington from both Winnipeg and Regina. A few years later they moved to the Cathay area in what is still known as Germantown Township. The Germantown Baptist Church (organized in 1892) was the center of their social life for two generations. (It is now only a memory, and local Germans attend town churches.) Several years after the Germantown settlers took up their land, a second influx of Dobrudja families arrived; they took up land thirty miles to the west in Sheridan County. This later group located in an area they chose to call New German-town Township; the Rosenfeld Baptist Church, which is still an active congregation, became the focal point of their activities.

After the initial Dakota farmsteads were established, as with many other ethnic groups, the settler's communication continued with old country friends and relatives. Other families arrived, usually by railway; and the settlement areas increased in size. The land owned by the early Dobrudja settlers is in the hands of their descendants today.

No other Dobrudja colonies exist in North Dakota, but they are quite numerous in Canada, and one is said to have developed near Parkston, South Dakota.

HUNGARIAN GERMANS

Arriving some five or ten years after homesteading took place, as early as 1895, a group of Germans from the Burgenland region of Hungary purchased land immediately south and east of Sykeston in Wells County. They called themselves "Hungarians" — and so they were, for their ancestors had settled, at the invitation of government authorities, in a small and picturesque portion of the Austro-Hungarian empire which is some seventy miles south of Vienna on the Hungary-Austria border. The villages of St. Andra, Fraudenkirchen, and Tadten are often mentioned as the ancestral homes of the Sykeston Burgenland people. Some two dozen families, all Catholic in background, came to the Wells County area; less than ten remain there today.

These early "Hungarians" went initially to Parkston, South Dakota, and, after acquiring a bit of ready capital, moved north to Sykeston. Parkston is significant in the history of a number of North Dakota groups; not only Hungarian Germans but Dobrudja, Mennonite, and Black Sea immigrants passed through its environs.

The only other sizable Burgenland settlement in North Dakota is at Fingal in Barnes County. A few Hungarian-Germans, however, settled near St. Anthony in Morton County. Some contact existed between the early Fingal and Sykeston groups.

GERMAN MENNONITES

A community of Mennonite immigrants from the Ukraine settled in Delger Township in Wells County in 1897. Nearby Rusland Township's name reflects their presence. They came along the same trail used by the Protestant and Catholic German-Russians, from Freeman and Scotland, South Dakota, up through the Eureka area and northward by way of McIntosh and Logan counties. These are now known as the Mennonite Brethren.

Another Mennonite Brethren community existed near John's Lake in southcentral Sheridan County. This scattering of farmers came north from South Dakota, as did so many other people. They had close bonds with Mennonites in Burleigh County immediately to the south.

German-Russian Mennonite churches were special focal points of community activity, for the early settlers and their descendants lived on separate farmsteads with no colony-type arrangements. Their earliest homes reflected a Ukrainian German culture much like their neighbors of other eastern European traditions: clay houses, white-washed walls, and Eastern European barns.

A few of their present-day Wells County and Sheridan County descendants have affiliated with religious groups of American origin, and non-Mennonite Germans occupy some of the original farmsteads.

GERMAN-RUSSIANS

Germans from Russia are the largest national group in both Sheridan and Pierce counties; their farms and villages stretch beyond those two areas into McLean, Burleigh, McHenry, Steele, and Stutsman counties. This German region is part of an almost continuous pattern of settlements which extends southward to the most northern counties of South Dakota. This arrangement is not accidental; the Chicago, Milwaukee and St. Paul Railroad, which cuts across the upper portion of South Dakota, was a favorite avenue of entry to the Dakota Territory from German immigrants from Russia. Successive railheads — Aberdeen, Ipswich, and Eureka — became departure points for incoming Germans as they sought the prairie land which was so much like their homeland in the steppe of Russia.

A long trail stretched from Eureka in South Dakota into North Dakota near Zeeland, and then northward past what are now the cities of Kintyre, Steele, Tuttle, and Hurdsfield, and farther almost to Rugby; it followed in a rough fashion the route of modern Highway Number 3. German settlers took land along the way, branching especially to the north (Pierce and parts of Benson and McHenry counties) and to the west (Sheridan and McLean counties). Eureka was the first stop and the familiar landmark for most of central North Dakota's German-Russians. In fact, one of the first stores in Turtle Lake, 200 miles from the South Dakota border, was called the "Eureka Bazaar."

The movement northward followed the familiar pattern: scouts were sent out, reports came back, first departures occurred, and finally there began a general rush to the new area. A German-Russian poem expressed it this way: "Our people are like birds on a branch, ready to fly to another tree." The movement into central North Dakota was motivated by the usual land fever, but also by the decrease of free land in the southern counties. In some places, too, old timers were heard to say, "There were too many rocks down south."

Catholic German-Russians

The German-Russian area which centers in Pierce County is of Catholic religious background, and the people came (ninety percent at least) from six villages along the Kutschurgan River, forty kilometers northwest of Odessa in the Black Sea portion of the Ukraine. The earliest Pierce County settlement (near present-day Selz) was, indeed, called Odessa and was established by prospective farmers from Zeeland in 1894. Soon afterward a flood of German Catholics came to that locale, traveling north on the trail through Logan and Kidder counties. Within the next ten years, rural settlements were established through the Pierce, McHenry, and Benson county area: Selz, Strasburg, Kandel, Blumenfeld, Karlsruhe, Johannestal, and Fulda. Selz, Strasburg, and Kandel are the names of three of the six Kutschurgan Russian villages. The Pierce and McHenry colonies display a certain vitality even today. They have, through the ensuing generations, maintained strong links with each other, and their sense of unity is intact. Contacts with the earlier southern home colonies in the Zeeland and Eureka area exist only as memories.

Later arrivals in the area came directly from Russia, through eastern American seaports, and to Dakota by way of the Great Northern Railroad. Berwick station was the end of the line and the beginning of American life for many early families.

According to some accounts, a number of Germans in the Catholic Pierce County region made a serious mistake when they chose the sand hills which traverse Pierce and McHenry counties as the sites of their homesteads. Sandy soil in Russia was apparently good for crops, but in semi-arid North Dakota it proved to be a disaster. After the top soil was disturbed, the land began to blow away; traditional methods of farming proved impossible. Disillusionment set in, and again the Germans began to move; this time many left Dakota and sought the newly opened Canadian homestead lands. In May 1906 a local newspaper reported the departure by rail of seventeen carloads of settlers, leaving the sand hills for new homes in Canada. At the same time others went by wagon to land near Regina; many went as far away as Saskatoon and Battleford in western Saskatchewan. Whole villages in Canada have their roots in Pierce County and ultimately in Eureka, South Dakota.

The Germans flourished in spite of their occasional poor land choice. One study has it that nineteen percent of the land in Pierce County was owned by German-Russians in 1915; forty-eight percent of the land was owned by this same national group in 1965. A rural Syrian community disappeared as its farms were purchased by German neighbors. Anglo-American settlers departed, and even Norwegian farmers were displaced as the Germans sought land for their sons and other family members. In his history of Pierce County, O.T. Tofsrud writes that fifty-eight percent of the first pioneers in Pierce County were Norwegian. Today, slightly over one-fourth of Pierce County's rural people trace their origins to Norway.

Protestant German-Russians

South of the Catholic region, an extensive Protestant German-Russian settlement runs from Manfred and Bowdon in Wells County, westward to Turtle Lake in McLean County. The area's first arrivals, in their turn, followed the trail northward from Eureka. Some came even from Freeman, Menno, and Scotland in southern South Dakota near Yankton. Early Germans arrived in Lincoln Valley in 1898; major settlements were formed in that region between 1902 and 1905. Later families came directly from the eastern states by rail, following the main line and sometime the branch lines through Carrington, Sykeston, Bowdon, and Denhoff. German settlers came to the Turtle Lake vicinity in 1900 and 1902, and to the McClusky, Denhoff, and Goodrich regions also at the turn of the century.

The Germans chose land which was by no means the best that North Dakota could offer, but in many ways it resembled the topography of south Russia. Mountains and valleys were, to them, unfamiliar landscapes, and prairies seemed to be places of opportunity and even comfort. Grain fields and isolated villages were part of their past, and self-reliance was a time-honored virtue. In fact, unlike many other groups, the German-Russians during their early days on the Northern Plains seem to have displayed a great amount of confidence. They knew how to build a worthy and durable adobe home, how to lay out their farmsteads, build a root cellar, and dig a well. In short, they knew how to survive without the niceties of urban life. They set up their own systems of mutual support, their special recreation patterns, and their own information network. (One of the first newspapers in Sheridan County was Denhoff's *Dakota Staatszeitung*.)

The great majority, perhaps even 90 percent, of the Protestant Germans from Russia came from Bessarabia. Their Evangelical religious background in south Russia was for the most part Lutheran. In North Dakota, while many stayed within that tradition, great numbers joined local German-speaking non-Lutheran denominations. The Manfred Seventh-Day Adventist Church, located in Wells County's Rusland Township, is an example. This church, built of earthen blocks in the mid-1890's, was one of the first churches of that religious group in the state. In spite of its American denominational origin, the Manfred Church was a German community center for many years.

Whether in the country or in town, the church, more than any other institution, was the focus of German social life. German-Russians in Sheridan County were found in the Reformed, the Baptist, the Seventh-Day Adventist, the Evangelical United Brethren, the Iowa Synod Lutheran, the Missouri Synod Lutheran, and the Evangelical churches.

The Sheridan-McLean settlement initially had close ties with the German Protestant families of the more southern Logan and McIntosh counties. As the years proceeded, their memories dimmed and they became a settlement sufficient unto themselves. In earliest days, however, the trail back to Eureka was used to take grain to market, to visit relatives, and even to return to the mother colony for retirement.

In retrospect, one thing is clear: the German-Russians came to stay. Whether in Sheridan or McLean counties or elsewhere, if they homesteaded an area, they are almost inevitably present today. Local township names, such as Rusland, Balta, Denhoff, Berlin, Strasburg, and Rosenfeld, are not empty symbols. German farmers still live in these areas.

A small separate group of German-Russians took up land in the southcentral portion of Bottineau County, coming to the region in the late 1890's. This cluster of families, near Gardena and Kramer, is one of the most northerly of all the North Dakota Black Sea settlements. Like other German-Russians they, too, came by way of the Eureka, South Dakota, railroad terminal. Some few came north after living several years in McIntosh County. The Peace Reformed Church at Upham, organized in 1907, has been a community center for several generations. While settlers of other backgrounds left the neigh-

boring farms, this group's original land is still in the hands of the descendants of the first German-Russian Bottineau County families.

ICELANDERS

In 1886 a group of Icelandic farmers came from Pembina County to the Upham area in northern McHenry County and portions of southcentral Bottineau County. "Scouts" had been sent ahead, and the Souris River region looked favorable to them; the first families arrived thereafter. In the next years fellow countrymen took up land, and soon a clearly defined Icelandic community came into existence. Eventually at least thirty families were in residence on farms located on both sides of the Souris River. This is, perhaps, the only Icelandic community in North Dakota other than the Mountain-Gardar settlement in Pembina County.

The group must have flourished in the initial decades, for by 1904 an Icelandic Hall had been built northeast of Upham, The Melankton Church was organized in 1897 when a constitution was adopted which gave the group an Icelandic Evangelical Lutheran orientation. The congregation met in local homes and in the Icelandic Hall for a few years and by 1920 had acquired its own church structure.

The Icelandic farmers' choice of land was sometimes unfortunate, for Souris River woods, hills, and marshland ran through the heart of the Icelandic territory. In addition, government acquisition of Souris acreage for conservation programs made inroads into the settlement. As a result, while still an Icelandic area, the community has today lost some of its ethnic vigor. In 1967 the Melankton congregation merged with the Deep River Lutheran Church, which was originally of Norwegian origin.

INDIANS (American)

The Fort Totten Indian Reservation, which was established in 1870, extends from Minnewaukan southward to the Sheyenne River, eastward along the river to the Nelson County line, and north to the south edge of Devils Lake. Almost all the resident Indian families, most of Sioux background, live in the vicinity of Fort Totten, St. Michael, and Tokio. A large part of the agricultural land is now being used by Anglo-American or Scandinavian ranchers and farmers. Some farmers of Indian ancestry, however, are present.

Many non-farm Indian families live in the rural sections of the northern part of the reservation. Houses are situated on small, dispersed parcels of land. The resident families work on tribal projects or in area businesses or industries. In recent years new housing programs have been completed and educational facilities have been improved. Today, Indian families are less inclined to leave the area; in fact, reservation population totals have increased.

IRISH

Irish settlers were found among the first homesteaders throughout the entire area. They, like their Anglo-American counterparts, were at home in the American scene and seldom required the support of great numbers of their fellow countrymen. Many of them had lived in the West, having served with the United States Army or worked on railroad construction crews; coming to Dakota, they scattered hither and yon across the homestead lands. Many, too, were familiar with the frontiers of Wisconsin and Illinois and other earlier settlement regions. The Irish tended to look at homesteading in a speculative and temporary fashion. The few years required to "prove up" a parcel of land often represented only a passing phase of their lives. The cash payments received at the sales of their farms made possible their resettlement in towns and larger cities. An Irishman often became the Dakota village's first saloon keeper, hotel owner, drayman, police chief or fire department organizer.

Nevertheless, recognizable Irish settlements did develop. Some very early American Irish, many of whom came from New York, were prominent in the establishment in 1882 of Tiffany east of New Rockford (Section 29, T 149-R 64). This cluster of frame buildings marked the earliest townsite in the area. It was a speculative venture; when the railroad did not arrive, the settlement, after flourishing during homesteading times, eventually disappeared. The town did have the honor of setting up the first store in what is now known as Eddy County. Some Irish farmers are still in the region.

Notable also was the heavily Irish Sweetwater community, a few miles north of Devils Lake, which held its first Catholic service in 1886 and built a church in 1892. A similar rural Irish settlement grew up east of Carrington in Wells County. A few Irish farm families remain in both areas today.

JEWS

A group of five Jewish families settled in 1888 along the Souris River in Starbuck Township of Bottineau County. Twenty more families, although expected, didn't arrive; the settlers apparently left the area almost as quickly as they had come.

LUXEMBURGERS

Luxemburgers were present in a scattered fashion in eastern Wells County and western Eddy County. They never established a concentrated community; rather, they mixed with the German-speaking settlers of the area. Some of their descendants remain today.

NORWEGIANS

Large settlements of Norwegian farmers can be found throughout the northcentral part of North Dakota. Norwegians are not the most numerous — Germans take that honor — but they are the most widespread. They came in the earliest days, and their eagerness to embrace the American way of life has probably made them the most influential of all the national groups.

The presence of rivers and creeks seems to have affected both their arrival and their dispersal patterns. Some Norwegians lived along the Sheyenne River near Hamar and Warwick in 1882. This northeastern part of

Eddy County represents the northern extremity of the Sheyenne Valley, which is filled with Norwegian farms as it passes through Barnes, Griggs, and Nelson counties. Hamar is also the Norwegian community that marks the western edge of yet another solid Norwegian belt that extends over one hundred miles from the Red River westward along the Goose River through Griggs and Nelson counties.

The railroad was a second factor influencing Norwegian settlements. The Great Northern reached Devils Lake in 1883 and paused there for several years. Homesteaders rushed ahead of the line and chose their land, later filing at the Devils Lake land office. Among them were early Norwegians, usually single men who had lived in Minnesota or Wisconsin for a few years and were familiar with the American frontier. Norwegians and others took land as much as fifty miles west of the railhead in the mid-1880's.

The two largest concentrations of Norwegians in northcentral North Dakota occur in Benson and Bottineau counties. Today, Norwegians make up about fifty percent of the population of these two counties; they probably constituted the same proportion at the turn of the century. In Benson County, Norwegians were taking land in 1883 near Leeds and Churchs Ferry. Settlers from St. Croix County, Wisconsin, were present in the Maza vicinity in 1884. A small Norwegian Lutheran congregation first gathered near Minnewaukan in 1884. The Antioch congregation at Brinsmade organized in 1885.

In southern Benson County, township names give a clue to the Norwegian presence: North Viking, South Viking and Arne. In 1886, the first settlers in South Viking Township, six men all from Norway, filed for land on the south side of the Sheyenne River. They walked to the land office in Devils Lake to record their claims. Also in 1886, a settlement was made ten miles west of Minnewaukan in Albert and Eldon townships. There the St. Olaf Lutheran congregation came into existence, meeting first in 1887. In 1885 very early Norwegians came with American settlers to Walsh Township (T 157-R 73), Pierce County, near present-day Rugby. In 1887, numbers of Norwegians were arriving in Irvine Township west of Churchs Ferry. Some had arrived in nearby Lake Ibsen Township the previous year. In the late 1890's, Norwegians were moving into the Esmond area of western Benson County. The Immanuel Lutheran congregation had already begun six miles north of Maddock in 1887; an Esmond church started in 1901.

The present Benson County Norwegian complex extends southward into Wells County on the south side of the Sheyenne. Manfred had the Vang Lutheran Church (organized in 1894), but Norwegians were also taking land in Valhalla Township (Eden Church was its center), in Norway Lake Township (East Vang Church), in Heimdal Township (Bethel Church), and in Fram Township. Crystal Lake Township had the Evanger Church and Pony Gulch had St. Petri's Church. The last three settlements are now mixed-nationality regions. A Norwegian settlement developed on the eastern edge of Wells County between Barlow and Cathay; Stavanger

Church (organized in 1892) in Fairville Township was its center.

South of Benson County, Norwegians were checking out land along the Sheyenne River in Bush Township in northwestern Eddy County in 1882, and the next year families arrived to take up permanent residence. Swedes and Norwegians still occupy most of Eddy County's Grandfield and Gates townships. The Sheyenne Church in Grandfield Township began in 1886.

The eastern edge of Foster County represents the western portion of the Norwegian rural community which stretches all the way from Cooperstown to Hillsboro on the Red River. In Foster County a settlement centers near Grace City in Larrabee and Nordmore townships. The local Kvernes congregation was organized in 1884. Farther to the west, Norwegians are said to have first come to the Carrington vicinity in 1883.

Northcentral North Dakota's largest concentration of Norwegian farms is centered in Bottineau County. Norwegians make up almost all of the population of many of the townships along the Canadian border, especially in the central and northeastern part of the county; their settlements continue eastward into a large part of Rolette County.

As early as 1882 or 1883 a group of Scandinavians, with Norwegians among them, squatted on Rolette County land and established what came to be known as the Willow Creek Settlement on the lower edge of the Turtle Mountains, where water and wood were in abundance. An 1886 visitor reported that Norwegian houses began four miles south of Dunseith and followed the stream for eight miles on both sides.

Apparently, in 1883, other Norwegians walked from the railhead at Devils Lake and took up land in the southeastern corner of Dalen Township near what is now the village of Carbury. This was the very first of all the Bottineau County Norwegian settlements. The original group (and many other early arrivals) came from Polk County, Minnesota. In 1886, Norwegians moved into Bottineau County's Pickering Township, also at the edge of the mountains. By 1888 or 1889 a group was present in Cordelia Township, not far from Butte St. Paul. They had moved west from the mountains and were in Haram Township (named for Haram, Norway) in 1887. Farther west, a township with the appropriate name of Scandia was settled in the late 1890's.

These early Norwegians had been preceded by a great number of Anglo-Ontarians, French, and Americans. Initially, the Norwegians seem to have had little influence on local Bottineau County affairs; for example, an 1883 petition which sought to set up a county government contained over eighty names and none were of Scandinavian origin. Apparently the earliest Norwegians were country people and had little to do with village life. The 1886 visitor to Dunseith (mentioned earlier) said that there were 100 people in Dunseith, and only one was Norwegian; he ran a saloon.

The region was apparently attractive, for immigrants from Norway literally flooded into northern Bottineau County after 1885. The Starbuck settlement (from Starbuck, Minnesota) began in 1889. In 1888, Norwegians were present in Roland and Homen townships in the Turtle Mountains proper. Vinge Lutheran Church in Homen

Township was organized in 1889. Settlements were established along the Souris in Eidsvold Township in 1888. In the years that followed, the flat and treeless land began to fill up. For example, south of Antler several prairie townships are today heavily Norwegian; so also are Chatfield and Elms in the southwestern part of the county.

In northcentral North Dakota, as elsewhere in the state, community churches were early social centers: Salem Church in Homen Township, the Mouse River Church in Eidsvold Township, and the Lesje Church in Scandia Township — all in Bottineau County. By 1918 two dozen Norwegian Lutheran congregations had been organized on the prairies of Bottineau County. Many met in local homes for just a few months, or perhaps a few years, but some built frame churches which exist today.

Farther east in Rolette County, some early Norwegians came to Kohlmeier Township along Wolf and Willow creeks, and to Rice and Leonard townships on Ox Creek. An Ox Creek congregation was organized in 1884; a Willow Creek church first met in 1885 and a Vestland congregation began in 1893. Island Lake and South Valley townships also received Norwegians in the late 1880's.

Synodal differences were often of minor significance to rural Norwegian congregations. Accessibility was the major concern. In towns it was different; there, congregations arose, merged, disappeared, or flourished according to doctrinal or ceremonial preferences.

Parochial schools were conducted by several, perhaps many, of the Bottineau County Lutheran congregations. This meant a series of informal summer or weekend classes which instructed young people not only in religious matters, but also in the Norwegian language and culture.

Southeast of Bottineau County, two almost solidly Norwegian townships — Barton and Dewey — exist today in northwestern Pierce County. Here, the first arrivals came before railroad construction in 1885. The next year the Denny Norwegian Lutheran Congregation began at Barton. In central Pierce County a group of Norwegians live on the land adjacent to the village of Silva. These families are remarkable, for they continue to be an island of Norwegian permanence, though surrounded by German-Russian farmers for several generations.

The Souris River attracted Norwegians at a very early date. The first arrivals came in 1882 to McHenry County, and the Norway Lutheran Congregation was established in 1884 at Villard. The Oak Valley Congregation had its initial meeting at Velva in 1886. Farther north along the river a Towner congregation met in 1889; the Sand Hill Congregation met northeast of Bantry in the same year. Descendants of these first settlers remain today.

Away from the river, a Norwegian settlement exists south of Granville in McHenry County's Riga Township. Settlers arrived there during homesteading days at the turn of the century. Farther to the south, the land west of Bergen is still filled with Norwegian farmers. (Bergen has the distinction of being one of the rare present-day North Dakota towns with a Norwegian name.)

Itinerant Lutheran pastors served the very early gatherings of Norwegians in McHenry County. This was typical of most of North Dakota. These "circuit rider" clergymen were a devout and hardy breed whose names are still remembered with special honor.

In Sheridan County the early Norwegian homesteaders, contrary to their usual experiences, gave way to the overwhelming numbers of Germans from Russia. Near Skogmo, in the northcentral part of the county, there sprang up the West Scandia and East Scandia churches, both of which began in 1903. One has ceased to exist, and the other has moved to a new location. Comparatively few Norwegians remain in that county, and these are in areas which have a mixed national background.

SWEDES

Small Swedish communities can be found throughout North Dakota. The northcentral part of the state has a half dozen settlements which are often adjacent to larger Norwegian farm areas. The early Swedes came, for the most part, during the "land boom" period, but some individuals came in the very earliest frontier times. Where possible, the Swedish homesteaders clustered around little Lutheran country churches. The Klara settlement in southwestern Benson County's Arne Township is an example. The earliest settlers in that vicinity are said to have come in 1888; a Klara Swedish Lutheran congregation first met in 1897, and a church building was constructed in 1907. The area now is a mixture of Norwegian and Swedish families.

Immediately north of the Klara settlement, east of Esmond, another group of Swedes established the Vasa Lutheran Church in Isabel Township. Some descendants of the original settlers are still present in the locality. The Benson County village of Hesper has been associated with the Swedish settlers who live in Isabel, Arne and Hesper townships. Many of the area's first homesteaders came directly from Hesper, Iowa; they had originally emigrated from Finnskoga and Vamhus in Sweden.

Swedish settlers, many of whom came by way of Illinois, Michigan, and Minnesota, were taking up farms along the river east of the village of Sheyenne in Eddy County as early as 1883. Within the next few years others came to the land south and west of Sheyenne. Two Augustana Synod Lutheran churches were organized in that region: one in Grandfield Township, established in 1896, and the other, the Grace Lutheran Church of Sheyenne village (1933). At least some of the earliest residents claimed Skane and Smaland in Sweden as their home territory.

A Swedish Lutheran Church was established in Oberon in Benson County in 1917. Today some of the first settlers' grandchildren are still to be found in that area, living among neighbors of Norwegian origins.

In McHenry County the Elim Swedish Lutheran church of Bergen was a community center. Established in 1905, it continued at least until the 1950's. German-Russians who have moved into the area have taken up much of the surrounding territory. A few Swedish families remain, again mixed with Norwegians.

In Bottineau County, a Scandia Township Swedish settlement began with the arrival of homesteaders at the turn of the century. A Swedish Augustana Church was organized in 1910; the congregation dissolved in 1938. In this area, a major portion of the population, from the first settlement times until today, has always been Norwegian. Also in Bottineau County a small Swedish Lutheran congregation was organized in Antler in 1908; this congregation, it seems, is no longer active.

The southwestern townships in Towner County also had a collection of Swedish farmers. There may have been a local Swedish church in earlier times, but none seems to have been recorded. Some Swedish families still reside in that part of the county.

The presence of the early Swedish families in the northcentral counties was marked by at least a dozen small Swedish churches. The subsequent demise of many of these churches, however, points to a certain Swedish-American tendency to leave the farm. Quite clearly, many second and third generation Swedes were inclined to leave the rural setting and migrate to more urban environments.

The ease with which Norwegians and Swedes intermarried is also apparent. In spite of humorous references to their historically different cultures, when the two groups found themselves far from their homelands and under harsh frontier conditions, they must have discovered a certain kinship. Indeed, comments are made in pioneer accounts concerning a respected neighbor who "spoke Norwegian with a Swedish accent." An early settler, Olav Redal, made a similar observation in 1917. He wrote in his *Norwegians in Bottineau County:*

> From the beginning of the pioneers settling here, the Norwegian and Swedish men and women have struggled with the same soil, lived under the same sky, attended the same church, and treated each other as brothers of the same people. I do the same, as I refer to the poet's beautiful song about the Scandinavian people: "The north is like a sisterland, derived of the good and old mold."

SYRIANS (LEBANESE)

From 1897 to 1902, a number of homesteaders came from Lebanon (then Syria) and took up land in Pierce County's Meyer, Reno Valley, and Elverum townships. They set up a Syrian Catholic Church (attended also by local Latin Catholics) on Section 24 of Meyer Township in 1902. The church was moved to Rugby in 1906 and later was destroyed by a fire. A Syrian Catholic priest, who traveled to various missions throughout the state, came to the church once a month.

At least fifty Syrian men and women filed on Pierce County land during the land rush days. Several dozen families seem to have stayed as permanent farmers during the first decades of settlement, but by 1960 only one Syrian family still owned land in the area.

The early Lebanese homesteaders frequently moved to small North Dakota towns and became part of the business communities. There were, for example, Lebanese merchants in towns such as Fillmore and Rugby and Drake. Itinerant peddlers of the same background were regular visitors to farms throughout the entire northcentral portion of the state in the earliest decades. Some of these traveling men had previously lived on homesteads, and some later became permanent businessmen in area villages.

Riverside cemetery southwest of Dunseith has a Moslem section which contains at least twenty graves. This is indicative of the presence of a good number of Syrian homesteaders who settled near Dunseith, Belcourt, and Rolla in Rolette County. The Syrian people in this area seem to have been of both Christian and Islamic background. An occasional Syrian family settled near Perth and Bisbee in Towner County, and they seem to have been related to the Rolette County group. Apparently, no solid clusters of Syrian families developed; rather, their farms were widely scattered, and their neighbors were settlers of other national groups. One account has it that some fifty families would gather at a central point for regular fellowship in the early decades of North Dakota life. They would be joined by friends from the Rugby Syrian community. Most of the Syrian families left the farm, though several descendants remain and are prominent community leaders.

A small Syrian settlement area exists north of Glenfield in Foster County. Families of this group are said to have come from the Ross community in Mountrail County and were, at least until recently, of Moslem background.

Around 1910 a group of Syrian homesteaders moved into the central portion of Sheridan County. They tended to be in the townships immediately to the south and east of Lincoln Valley. Some were in Lincoln and Mertz (T 148-R 76) (T 147-R 75) townships; most were in Hellman (T 147-R 76) and Schiller (T 148-R 75) townships. No particular rural concentration developed; like other Syrian groups, they were individuals surrounded by non-Syrian people, in this case, German farmers of Russian background. Most of the settlers were of the Orthodox Christian tradition, having come from the Christian parts of Lebanon. Within two decades many had left the farm, although some remained until World War II and at least one was present in the mid-1960's.

UKRAINIANS

South McHenry County contains an area which is at least half Ukrainian, particularly Cottonwood and Land townships. Kief is the trade center, and the name indicates the general district in Russia from which most of the local residents originated. This group of farm families is part of a Ukrainian settlement which first developed in 1899 and now extends into McLean and Ward counties including the communities of Butte, Ruso, and Max. Their religion tended to follow a kind of Baptist Russian tradition. Apparently Russian churches were not in existence, and American denominations claimed the allegiances of the early and present-day residents. Part of this settlement is found in Highland Township (T 149-R 77) in Sheridan County.

FATHER WILLIAM C. SHERMAN is a well-known and celebrated North Dakota scholar and educator. He taught Sociology of the Great Plains and Religion at NDSU from 1971 to 2001. He served at St. Michael's Catholic Church in Grand Forks from 1976 to 2003. Father Sherman has been awarded two honorary doctorates, one from the University of Mary, Bismarck, and one from the University of North Dakota, Grand Forks. His work highlights the unique and complex history of North Dakota inhabitants, especially that of the Germans from Russia.

THE COMPLETE COLLECTION encompasses over 13,000 black and white photographs, negatives, color slides, floorplans, and site survey documents. The subjects of interest include houses, barns, sheds, and various agricultural structures. Today, many of these structures no longer exist.

More information is available about each photo by entering the Digital ID number (ex: 110.307.n11) in the search box on DigitalHorizonsOnline.org.

VIEW THE ENTIRE COLLECTION ONLINE AT:

digitalhorizonsonline.org ➜William C. Sherman Photograph Collection

Hungarian German • Stark County, ND (110.307.n11)

German Russian • McIntosh County, ND (110.400.n09)

German Russian • Grant County, ND (110.77.n10)

German Russian • Emmons County, ND (110.227.n01)

German Russian • Grant County, ND (110.331.n09)

Hungarian German • Stark County, ND (110.161.n07)

German Russian • Stutsman County, ND (110.261.n04)

German Russian • Grant County, ND (110.387.s09)

German Russian • Grant County, ND (110.83.n03)

German Russian • Grant County, ND (384.n09)

German Russian • LaMoure County, ND (110.110.s04)

German • Williams County, ND (110.147.n01)

German Russian • Grant County, ND (110.30.s04)

German Russian • Dunn County, ND (110.329.s02)

German Russian • Morton County, ND (110.202.s01)

German Russian • Stark County, ND (110.20.n08)

German Russian • Stark County, ND (110.20.n10)

Hungarian German • Morton County, ND (110.93.n14)

Hungarian German • Morton County, ND (110.93.s07)

German Russian • Hettinger County, ND (110.363.n20)

Bohemian from Crimea • Stark County, ND (110.181.s01)

Ukranian • Burleigh and McLean County, ND (110.395.02)

Jewish • McIntosh, ND (110.104.s08)

Hungarian German • Stark County, ND (110.198.n34)

German Russian • Stark County, ND (110.189.n01)

Mennonite • Wells County, ND (110.327.n08)

Mennonite • Wells County, ND (110.327.n23)

Belgian • Morton County, ND (110.310.n18)

Ukranian • Stark County, ND (110.39.s01)

Ukranian • Stark County, ND (110.39.n01)   **German Russian** • Stark County, ND (110.180.s03)

German Russian • Morton County, ND (110.402.n06)

German Russian • Morton County, ND (110.402.n57)

German Russian • Wells County, ND (110.102.s03)

German Russian • Wells County, ND (110.102.s01)

German Russian • Mercer County, ND (110.14.n02)

German Russian • McLean County, ND (110.80.n02)

German Russian • Grant County, ND (110.369.n16)

German Russian • Dunn County, ND (110.135.s04)

Hungarian German • Stark County, ND (110.125.s05)

Norwegian • Billings County, ND (110.90.n01)

Ukranian • Burleigh and McLean County, ND (110.395.01)

German Russian • Grant County, ND (110.338.s07)

German Russian • Emmons County, ND (110.11.n02)

German Russian • Stark County, ND (110.383.s02)

German Russian • Stark County, ND (110.192.n03)

German • Emmons County, ND (110.04.n36)

Ukranian • McHenry County, ND (110.325.n01)

German • Emmons County, ND (110.04.n16)

Estonian • Stark County, ND (110.150.n16)

English American • McLean County, ND (110.142.n03)

English American • McLean County, ND (110.142.n01)

English American • McLean County, ND (110.142.n04)

Ukranian • McKenzie County, ND (110.96.n25)

German Russian • Morton County, ND (110.143.n17)

Ethnic Population Distribution
Southeast Section of North Dakota

1. Swiss 50%; Anglo-American and Anglo-Ontarian 50%
2. Anglo-American and Anglo-Ontarian 50%; German 45%; Norwegian and Swede 5%
3. Norwegian and occasional Swede
4. Norwegian 50%; German 30%; other 20%
5. Anglo-American and Anglo-Ontarian 40%; German 40%; Norwegian 20%
6. Anglo-Ontarian and Anglo-American 90%; others 10%
7. Norwegian 40%; Anglo-Ontarian and Anglo-American 35%; German 15%
8. German 50%; Anglo-American and Anglo-Ontarian 50%
9. Anglo-Ontarian and Anglo-American 50%; German and Norwegian 45%; others 5%
10. Mixed: Norwegian, Dane and Swede
11. Norwegian 90%; Swede and Dane 10%
12. Swede 75%; Norwegian 25%
13. Luxemburger 35%; German 35%; Polish 30%
14. Norwegian 75%; Anglo-American 25%
15. German (Moravian) 90%; others 10%
16. German (Moravian) 50%; Norwegian 50%
17. Mixed: German, German (Moravian), Bohemian-German, Anglo-American, Norwegian, others
18. Bohemian-German 75%; others 25%
19. Anglo-American 75%; others 25%
20. Dane 75%; others 25%
21. Hungarian-German
22. Mixed: Hollander, Dane and Anglo-American
23. Anglo-American 40%; Norwegian 40%; Dane 20%
24. Hollander 35%; Norwegian 30%; other 35%
25. German 60%; Norwegian 40%
26. German 50%; others 50%
27. German 50%; Anglo-American 40%; others 10%
28. German 40%; Anglo-American 40%; Norwegian 20%
29. German-Russian (Catholic)
30. German-Russian (Protestant)
31. Mixed: German, German-Russian (Catholic), Polish
32. German 40%; German-Russian 40%; Anglo-American 20%
33. German 60%; Anglo-American 40%
34. Swede 60%; Norwegian 40%
35. Anglo-American 50%; German 50%
36. Mixed: Anglo-American, German, Norwegian and Swede
37. Mixed: German, Anglo-American, Norwegian and a few others
38. Swede 50%; Anglo-American 30%; Norwegian 20%
39. Norwegian 60%; Anglo-American 40%
40. Mixed: German, Norwegian, Anglo-American, Bohemian, a few others
41. Dane
42. Mixed: German and Bohemian
43. German 50%; Anglo-Americans 40%; others 10%
44. Norwegian 60%; Swede 40%
45. Norwegian 80%; Dane 20%
46. Anglo-American 50%; Norwegian 30%; Swede 15%; others
47. Anglo-American with some Bohemians
48. Luxemburger and German
49. German-Russian (Volga)
50. Bohemian 40%; others
51. Mixed: Finlander, Anglo-American and Norwegian
52. Anglo-American 50%; German-Russian and German 50%
53. Bohemian and other
54. German and Bohemian-German

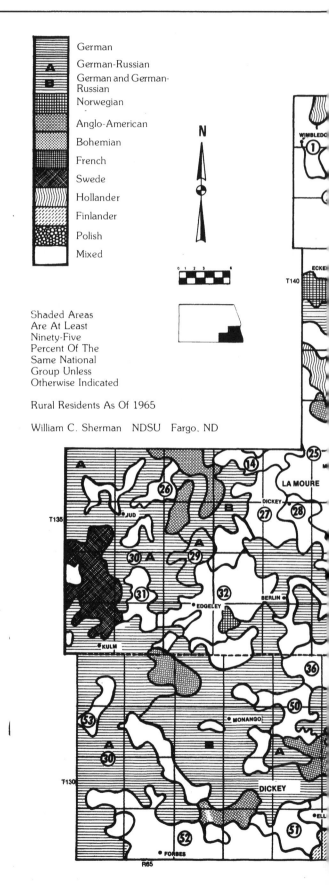

Legend:
German
German-Russian
German and German-Russian
Norwegian
Anglo-American
Bohemian
French
Swede
Hollander
Finlander
Polish
Mixed

Shaded Areas Are At Least Ninety-Five Percent Of The Same National Group Unless Otherwise Indicated

Rural Residents As Of 1965

William C. Sherman   NDSU   Fargo, ND

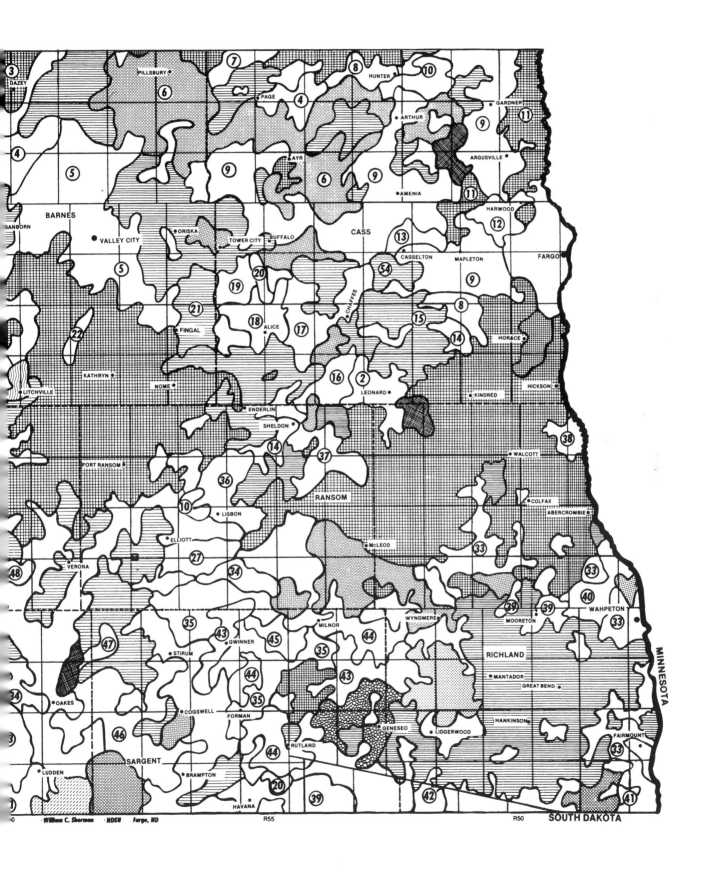

Township Names
Southeast Section of North Dakota

BARNES CO.

PIERCE	LAKE TOWN	DAZEY	SIBLEY TRAIL	Sibley BALDWIN	ELLS-BURY	Pillsbury	CASS CO. ROCHESTER	PAGE	DOWS	Hunter	BELL	Grandin KINYON	NOBLE
Wimbledon		Dazey					Page			HUNTER			
UXBRIDGE	Leal EDNA	ROGERS	ASHTA-BULA	GRAND PRAIRIE	MINNIE LAKE	LAKE	RICH	ERIE	Arthur ARTHUR	GUNKEL	Gardner GARDNER	WISER
		Rogers										
BRIMER	ANDER-SON	STEW-ART	GETCHELL	NOLTI-MIER	WEIMER	COR-NELL	Ayr AYR	EMPIRE	AMENIA Amenia	RUSH RIVER	Arguaville BERLIN	HAR-WOOD
ECKEL-SON	Sanborn POTTER	HOBART	140-58 Valley City	ALTA	ORISKA Oriska	Tower City TOWER	BUFFALO Buffalo	WHEAT-LAND	CASSEL-TON Casselton	HARMONY	RAYMOND Mapleton W Fargo	REED FARGO
MANS-FIELD	HEMEN	GREEN	MARSH	CUBA	SPRING-VALE	HILL	HOWES	GILL	EVEREST	DURBIN	S W Fargo MAPLE-TON	Fargo BARNES
MEADOW LAKE	SVEA	SKANDIA	NELSON	NORMA	BING-HAMPTON Fingal	CLIFTON	ELDRED Alice	WAL-BURG	MAPLE RIVER	ADDI-SON	WARREN	Horace STANLEY
GREEN-LAND Litchville	ROSEBUD	SPRING CREEK	Kathryn OAKHILL	THORDEN SKJOLD	Nome RARITAN	PONTIAC	HIGHLAND	WATSON	Davenport LEONARD Leonard	DAVEN-PORT	NOR-MANNA Kindred	PLEASANT

LA MOURE CO.

GLEN	MIKKEL-SON	KENNI-SON	ADRIAN	SARA-TOGA	Marion SHERI-DAN	PRAIRIE	LITCH-VILLE	RANSOM CO. NORTH-LAND	PRESTON	MOORE	LIBERTY	Enderlin Sheldon GREENE	COBURN	RICHLAND CO. HELEN-DALE	BARRIE	WALCOTT
RANEY	Jud BLUE-BIRD	GLEN-MORE	RUSSELL	Dickey ROSCOE	GRAND-VIEW	GLAD-STONE	BLACK LOAM	FORT RANSOM	SPRINGER	TULLER	CASEY	SHEN-FORD	OWEGO	SHEYENNE	VIKING	COLFAX Colfax
SWEDE	RAY	NORA	WANO	HENRIETTA Berlin	GRAND RAPIDS	PEARL LAKE	GREEN-VILLE	HANSON	ELLIOTT Elliott	Lisbon ISLAND PARK	BIG BEND	SCOVILLE	SANDOUN	FREEMAN	GARBORG	NANSEN	Abercrombie ABERCROMBIE
NORDEN Kulm	POMONA VIEW	Edgeley GOLDEN GLEN	WILLOW-BANK	BADGER	La Moure DEAN	RYAN	Verona OVID	ISLEY	ALLE-GHANY	BALE	ALICE-TON	SYDNA	ROSE-MEADE	WEST END	HOME-STEAD	ANTE-LOPE	IBSEN	DWIGHT Dwight

DICKEY CO.

NORTH-WEST Merricourt	YOUNG	POTSDAM	VALLEY	PORTER	WRIGHT	JAMES RIVER VALLEY	DIVIDE	SARGENT CO. DENVER	VIVIAN	WHITE-STONE HILL Gwinner	WILLEY	Milnor MILNOR	HALL	WYND-MERE	Wyndmere DANTON	Barney BARNEY	Mooreton MOORE-TON	Wahpeton CENTER
GERMAN	WHITE-STONE	HAMBURG	Monango KEY-STONE	Fullerton MAPLE	YORK-TOWN	CLEMENT	BEAR CREEK Oakes	IVERNER	HARLEM Cogswell	BOWEN	DUNBAR Forman	SHUMAN	HERMAN	DEXTER	LIBERTY GROVE	Mantador BELFORD	Great Bend BRANDEN-BURG	SUMMIT
SPRING VALLEY	GRAND VALLEY	ALBION	ELDEN	KENTNER	KENT	HUDSON	RIVER-DALE	JACK-SON	SAR-GENT	FORMAN	RUT-LAND Rutland	RANSOM KINGS-TON	Cayuga GRANT	Lidgerwood MORAN	Hankinson BRIGHT-WOOD	WALDO	Fairmount DE VILLO
AL-BERTHA Forbes	LORRAINE	Ellendale ELLEN-DALE	VAN METER	ADA	PORT EMMA	Ludden LOVELL	SOUTH-WEST	BRAMP-TON	TAYLOR	WEBER Havana	TEWAUKON	MARBOE	DUERR	ELMA	GREEN-DALE	LA MARS

EAGLE

FAIRMOUNT

Commentary

ANGLO-AMERICANS

The term *Anglo-American* is used to refer to Americans whose ancestries date back to colonial times; and in most cases the label means "Old Americans" of British Isles backgrounds. It also embraces an occasional German or Irishman with three or four generations of American family heritage. These "Yankees," as others called them, were the classic frontiersmen — their forebears were the people who had organized farm and town life along the edge of America's earlier primitive West in Pennsylvania and later in Illinois, Iowa and Wisconsin. They had the honor of being, in most cases, the very first Dakota arrivals. During the original settlement decade, they frequently made up the largest number of residents in the dozens of townships and villages that sprang out of the prairies.

Often they came as individuals. The first trickle of settlers into the Fargo area was almost all of Anglo-American background (with a few of their Ontario "cousins"). They were the first along the Sheyenne River; Colonel Marsh took land south of Valley City in 1874; Joseph Colton was the original settler at Lisbon. Earlier, along the Red River, Morgan Rich of New York had acquired the first parcel of Richland County land in 1869.

They also came in organized groups — sometimes as an informal collection of family friends, sometimes under church or land company leadership. Regularly, in the earliest years, a cluster of wagons or a line of railroad cars would halt at a pre-selected site and discharge its hopeful families. What was soon to be called a "Wisconsin Settlement" or an "Illinois Settlement" would come into being. Helping each other during the first difficult years, the pioneers managed to struggle through the harsh winters; soon "civilization" had taken root.

The Anglo-American migration followed predictable routes: the rivers and valleys, the trails, and later the railroads. In the beginning it seems that rivers were favored avenues of entry into Dakota Territory. Military and commercial trails frequently followed a river course, and the available water and wood made early settlement more feasible. At a remarkably early date (1870) the Sheyenne River Owego settlement sprang up on Section 16 of Owego Township in Ransom County. By the end of that year, twelve families (sixty-four people) were already in residence. Captain Hadley, the organizer, named the village after his New York home. The captain hoped that this special location would be the spot where a proposed railroad would cross the Sheyenne and that a bustling trade center would eventuate. Nearby Pigeon Point and Bonnersville were examples of contemporary clusters of cabins along trails which skirted wood and water supplies. On the Wild Rice River the Hamlin Anglo-American settlement developed in Herman Township in Sargent County in 1879. In 1878, the Michigan Settlement began near Fairmount on the Red River in Richland County as forty families came from Hartford, Michigan. Soon afterwards, a Wisconsin Settlement grew up south of Fairmount.

The James River was an artery which brought a number of American groups into Dickey County. Going

north, a number of very early settlers began to fill the prairie with communities. Port Emma was founded by north, a number of very early settlers began to dot the prairie with communities. Port Emma was founded by Americans and Ontarians in the early 1880's, and at the same time, Eaton was founded and named by "a scholarly gentleman" of New England background. Nearby a Hudson Townsite became home for a colony from New York State which arrived in 1883. Kentner Township had another New York colony; its early residents were from the Livonia, New York, area. A Michigan Settlement began not far away in the Merricourt area (Young and Potsdam townships). Another New York Settlement was established in Yorktown Township in 1883. In the same general region, an Illinois group was present in the earliest of days.

Elsewhere, Franklin, in LaMoure County, was named by settlers from Franklin, Michigan. Erie, in Cass County, began with the arrival of settlers from Erie, Pennsylvania. Many of these later groups came not by river, but through the services of the newly established railroads.

The railroads, with their speed and efficiency, were destined to bring the great majority of immigrants to North Dakota. Riverboats and wagon trains would be utilized until the turn of the century, but increasingly the railway coach brought newcomers to their promised lands. Indeed, in the southeastern part of North Dakota, the Northern Pacific asserted its dominance at a very early date, for it arrived at Moorhead in 1871 and was completed to Bismarck in 1873. All along its path, it distributed the earliest land seekers, particularly those of American descent. Thus, a great number of Anglo-American families settled (and their descendants still remain) in the northern portions of Cass and Barnes counties. In this region, Tower City, Oriska, and Buffalo were American centers. Town names like Urbana and Ashtabula reflect the origins of town organizers from Illinois and Ohio.

From the beginning, even before small family-type farmers arrived, the huge areas of railroad land, acquired through land-grant legislation, had established Anglo-American influence throughout Cass and Barnes counties. The land grants brought about the development of bonanza farms and made possible the activities of a speculator type of real estate agent. These opportunists organized and promoted many of the first large-scale immigration movements to the region.

Northern Cass County and northeastern Barnes County is a unique area, for it reflects the special fact that large commercial agricultural concerns broke the sod and settled the region initially; only afterwards did serious immigrant settlement take place. This was land-grant country where the odd-numbered sections in most townships were railroad property. These parcels of land were subsequently transferred either to a bonanza farm concern or, very often, to an individual "absentee owner." In 1893, for example, a Mr. Charles Wright owned sixteen of the eighteen odd-numbered sections in Rich Township, Cass County; forty-six individuals owned the land in the remaining even-numbered sections throughout the township. Many parts of northern Cass and Barnes counties saw substantial early day small-farm ownership only on even-numbered sections.

After several decades, however, as bonanza farms and "absentee" owned properties proved unprofitable, an influx of Anglo-American and second generation German and Scandinavian farmers from Minnesota, Iowa, Illinois, and from elsewhere in North Dakota arrived to become small resident farmers. This second wave of settlement occurred especially between 1910 and 1930. The present inhabitants of the above mentioned areas represent the following: (1) survivors of the first "even-numbered" original small farmers from the 1880's; (2) the second wave out-of-state arrivals dating from 1910 to 1930; (3) a random influx of North Dakotans spilling over from ethnic communities in neighboring counties between 1910 and 1950.

The first Anglo-American residents of these northern Barnes and Cass townships and, in fact, the whole southeast area tended to belong to churches of old American background. The abundance of Presbyterian congregations testifies to this fact; at least eight small-town churches of that affiliation dotted Cass and Barnes counties at the turn of the century. By 1873 the initial Presbyterian activity had begun along the Northern Pacific line with informal services at many of the newly established railroad sidings. For example, the first service in Casselton took place in a farm house in 1879; a church was built in 1881. Tower City Presbyterians organized at the same time and built their church in 1881. The Buffalo Church, built in 1886, is still active. Mapleton, Wheatland, Ayr, and Galesburg had similar churches. Presbyterians often represented people of Ontario background, but Yankees predominated in the southeastern part of the state.

The presence of old American families in Cass and Barnes counties is indicated by the existence of some twelve early Methodist churches along with a smaller number of Congregational, Baptist, and Episcopal churches. The Methodist church in Casselton was erected at the very early date of 1874 and was the third structure built by that denomination in the state.

An Episcopal church was built in Buffalo in 1887. Fellow churchmen in Valley City had held their first service in a home in 1878; by 1881 they had erected a beautiful stone church in that town. A Tower City Episcopal church was constructed in the 1880's; it flourished for several decades. The Episcopal church in Casselton, which was erected with the special assistance of General George Cass, continues to be a building of architectural merit; it now belongs to the Mennonites.

Baptists were active, too. They built a church in Tower City in the first years of the 1880's. In their enthusiasm they also erected an adjoining Baptist University which opened in 1886; the institution closed within three years.

The prestige and the power of the early Anglo-Americans are evidenced by the overwhelming number of southeastern North Dakota villages with English-type names. This was often due to the influence of railroad

officials of Yankee origins. Names of railroad executives are frequent: Cass, Durbin, Fargo, Canfield, Nortonville, Lynchburg, Tower City, Hobart, Milnor, Sanborn. Sometimes these same men named the newly established railroad sidings after their daughters: Marion, Elizabeth, Alice, Kathryn. Real-estate men of British Isles background also left their mark: Alfred was a titled Englishman in the land business; Hunter was a large land holder in Cass County. The Bonanza farms' Yankee managers and owners were also in the naming game: towns such as Chaffee, Amenia, Sharon, Grandin, Dwight, Adams, Glover and others. Township names almost inevitably show an Anglo-American background. Allegheny, Saratoga, Binghampton, Rochester, and Buffalo reflect either the aspirations or homesickness of displaced New Yorkers. Cornell, Cayuga, and Kenyon — each harkens back to someone's early college days. Over them all, Albion in Dickey County shines triumphant and with special brilliance.

Today the "Michigan," "Wisconsin," "New York," and "Illinois" settlement lands are, as a general rule, owned by Norwegian and German farmers. The prospect of a prosperous life elsewhere in the developing American West, or in the nation's cities, was too inviting and too accessible for most of the Yankee families to stay long on the harsh northern prairies. Institutions founded by the Anglo-Americans — the schools, business establishments, courthouses — are now usually in the hands of capable descendants of European immigrant settlers. Institutions such as churches and clubs built specifically on Yankee membership have suffered a serious decline in numbers. Numerous small church structures, often done with exquisite architectural taste, have been abandoned or sold to later-day religious groups.

This Yankee exodus, however, did not affect some of the more prosperous land areas of northern Cass and Barnes counties, where there remain many townships in which "Americans" are still in abundance. Cass County's Lake, Rich, and Empire townships (all near Ayr) have areas in which ninety percent of the present residents are of American or Ontarian backgrounds. Half of the farm families around Amenia, and in the area north and south of Gardner in Kenyon and Gardner townships, are Anglo-American or Canadian in origin. South of the Burlington Northern Railroad, Durbin and Mapleton townships are much the same.

In Barnes County near Pillsbury, the Baldwin, Ellsbury, Grand Prairie and Minnie Lake townships are to a great extent of Anglo-American and Anglo-Ontarian origins.* Townships such as Stewart (partially settled by a colony from Michigan), and Uxbridge (settled from Ontario, Illinois, Wisconsin, and Iowa), and Hemen (settled from Ontario) are still strongly Anglo-Ontarian or Anglo-American in background. Oriska township (settled from Wisconsin, Illinois, Ohio, and elsewhere) has a strong American flavor.

In other southeastern counties today, Anglo-Americans occupy only occasional areas. LaMoure County's

---

*In northern and eastern North Dakota, Anglo-American and Anglo-Ontarian communities were often adjacent to each other; in fact, farms of the two groups were frequently intermingled. Both situations existed in parts of Barnes and Cass counties.

Kennison Township has some solidly Anglo-American concentrations. Isolated areas in Dickey County still reflect some of the early American influence, but such places are rare; one exists about eight miles north of Ellendale, and another is the same distance west of that town.

In the late 1870's an Illinois settlement sprang up in Barrie Township, Richland County, on the Sheyenne River. A small Congregational Church is still present, but many descendants of the original settlers have disappeared. Also in Richland County, the Antelope Township settlement was predominantly of Scotch background. Its first people (some came in the 1870's) were mostly Presbyterian from both the United States and Ontario. They eventually became Congregationalist; but, because of the difficulty in obtaining ministers, in the 1930's they affiliated with the Methodists. Their first Sunday School was organized in 1882. The Antelope Church building was erected in 1901 next to the community school house. The settlement still exists and takes pride in the fact that its consolidated grade and high school (in the center of the township) was one of the first in the State of North Dakota.

As in other parts of the state, land of a more "rough" character, suitable for ranching, still contains large numbers of people of British Isles background. There seems to be a natural affinity between cattle raising and a British background. Accordingly, Southwest Township in Sargent County is almost solidly Anglo-American, and the area east and west of Forbes along the southern boundary of Dickey County is at least half Anglo-American. The sandhills region of southeastern Ransom County, particularly Rose Meade and Sandoun townships, has a goodly number of Anglo-American ranchers. This collection of families extends into Richland County's West End Township, north of Wyndmere. In southern Richland County, LeMars Township has many of the same type of Anglo-American settlers.

ANGLO-ONTARIANS

Coming with the earliest Old American land seekers were immigrants from Canada who were fluent in English, and to some extent, familiar with American traditions. In many, if not most, localities along the southern portion of the Red River and along the Northern Pacific Railroad, one out of every five English-speaking newcomers was of Anglo-Ontarian background. An 1891 magazine said of the Buffalo vicinity in Cass County, "The country is settled mainly by Americans though there are settlements of Germans and Scandinavians here and there, and a sprinkling of Canadians." The phrase "sprinkling of Canadians" was accurate, for many Canadian land seekers who journeyed on the Red River toward Manitoba* were deflected by attractive American settlement prospects. They never reached the Canadian border; instead, they took land in the United States. Many other Ontarians, having heard of Dakota oppor-

*Movement to western Canada, with any degree of comfort, required a journey through the United States until the Canadian transcontinental railway route was completed in the early 1880's.

tunities by word of mouth or advertisement, came directly to the newly developing territory.

Ontario people were, therefore, among the very earliest settlers. Being of Scotch, British, Scotch-Irish, and Catholic-Irish backgrounds, they rapidly adjusted to the local social and economic landscape. They entered politics, engaged in business, and were welcomed into the various lodges and churches of Anglo-American origin. In general, wherever Anglo-Americans settled, some Ontarians were also present. This was particularly true in the central and northern portions of Barnes and Cass counties. Thus, we see Hemen Township south of Sanborn filled, at an early date, with great numbers of Ontario settlers. Also near Sanborn, a cluster of "Germans from Canada" are said to have settled in the same time period (the early 1880's). Noltimier Township northeast of Valley City had many Irish Catholics from Ontario. Uxbridge Township in Barnes County also listed a considerable number of Ontarians among its first settlers. In Cass County the Amenia, Arthur, Gardner, Page, and Ayr regions had many Anglo-Ontarian homesteaders.

Like their Anglo-American "cousins," the Ontarians tended to move readily to other regions of America. In general, only a small proportion of their descendants are still on North Dakota farms. The Cass County and Barnes County regions mentioned above are exceptions; here some farm families still look back to Ontario as their place of origin.

Ontario people were present in many places, often as isolated but successful individuals. Elliot, in Barnes County, was named by a Canadian bachelor who settled there in 1878 and platted that town. Fife and Barrie, in Richland County, were given their names by other Ontario immigrants. Brampton, in Sargent County, was named in honor of Brampton, Ontario, by still another Ontario homesteader.

In Richland County, Ontario-Scotch immigrants were with the Anglo-Americans in Antelope Township. Immediately west of Wahpeton in Center Township, American Irish settlers (some arriving before 1880) joined with Ontario Irish to form a small Catholic community. A local barn still has the name "Montreal Farm" emblazoned in pride across its front.

A surprising number of Ontarians were present at the early Dickey County settlements along the James River. The first settler in the Port Emma area was an Ontario land seeker who located at the head of Crystal Lake. Port Emma had an Ottawa House, which was a prominent social gathering place throughout the town's history. A few miles west of Port Emma is Guelph, named after the well-known Ontario city. Dundas, also on the river, was another town of Ontario background.

BOHEMIANS

In 1871, a group of Bohemians came very early to the Richland County portion of North Dakota, settling at Richville, along the Red River. They also squatted on land immediately north of the present city. The first settlers were born in Bohemia, but came to Dakota from

Muscoda, Wisconsin. In 1872, others came to the new settlement from the same Wisconsin area. Richville, later named Wahpeton, consisted in those days of a mere three or four houses or dugouts which had been put up a year or two previously by Anglo-Americans. The incoming Bohemians, in fact, became the town's pioneers; in 1872 one of the new arrivals became the first county sheriff and assessor. This is unique to the state's experience, for "immigrant" peoples seldom, if ever, played an important role in the initial settlement of North Dakota's major towns. Railroads brought Yankee and Ontario people who established the first enterprises and they became the pioneer families of the cities.

The Catholics in the Richville area, mostly Bohemian, had their first Mass in a dugout in 1871. A priest who served the local Métis and Fort Abercrombie soldiers presided over the event. Five years later, a small frame St. John's Catholic Church of Wahpeton was built. As other national groups, especially Germans, moved into the area, the Bohemian church members separated to build St. Adalbert's Church in 1884. The Bohemian language was part of the life of that parish until the 1950's. The congregation later merged with the larger St. John's Church in 1967. A Bohemian lodge of ZCBJ background was founded in 1897; by 1915 it had a membership of seventy-one adults. It eventually acquired its own hall and cemetery.

Also in Richland County, another group of Bohemians began arriving in 1880; they chose land between what are now the towns of Lidgerwood and Wyndmere. The first few individuals to arrive came from Spillville, Iowa, and had in their midst a prolific letter writer who extolled the beauties of the local situation in Czech-language newspapers for some thirty years. As a result, Bohemians from five or six eastern states came to take up homesteads. The region north of Lidgerwood, particularly Liberty Grove and Dexter townships, is now heavily occupied by people of Bohemian background.

Lidgerwood Catholics of German background (with some Irish) and those of Czech origin worshipped together in a church with a resoundingly Slavic name, Saints Cyril and Methodius, which was built in 1887. After this church was destroyed by fire in 1904, the two nationalities separated and established different parishes. The Germans built their church in 1906, naming it after the great German missionary, St. Boniface. The Bohemians built their church in the same year, dedicating it to the Czech martyr, St. John Nepomucene. German-language sermons continued, at least occasionally, until the mid-1930's in St. Boniface. Bohemian sermons were a regular feature at the St. John's Church until the 1960's. The two Catholic parishes merged again in 1968.

As in other Bohemian communities, a portion of the population represented a non-religious tradition; this group in Lidgerwood formed the nucleus of a Bohemian national lodge which was organized in 1897. A large hall, which became a center for social and ethnic activities, was built on the Main Street. Many members were buried in the organization's special cemetery on the south edge of town. Today, the ZCBJ Lodge building is the city's

Knights of Columbus Hall, and the descendants of the original members are often active in either Protestant or Catholic congregations.

Two small groups of Bohemians reside in Dickey County today, intermingled with other national groups. Immediately west of Fullerton a group of Bohemians can be found in Maple and Porter townships. The ancestors of these farmers came from Butler County, Nebraska, in the latter part of the first decade of the twentieth century. Farther west in the same county, a second and smaller group of Bohemians live among non-Czech farmers in German and Northwest townships.

DANES

Danes came to the northern part of Cass County at an early date, the mid-1870's. They took land in Bell Township along the Elm River. The group was small in size and only a few of their descendants are present today, living among Swedish and Norwegian neighbors.

In 1877 Richland County received its earliest Danish settlers. In that year three families — one of Danish, one of Polish and one of German origin — became the first permanent residents of Fairmount Township. Their land was in the extreme southeastern part of the county, close to the Red River. This first Danish family was eventually joined by others of that nationality who occupied the area south of the town of Fairmount. Many Americans were also coming to the region at that time; a Michigan settlement and a nearby Wisconsin settlement both began north of Fairmount in 1879. The arrival of the early Dane family must have been an isolated event, for the many Danes who eventually came to the Fairmount area seem to have done so around the turn of the century. At that time, a small but compact Danish settlement came about as later Danes purchased land from the above mentioned Americans who were then moving out of the region. These late arrivals came, in part, from the old country; but a large number came from nearby American states. At least part of the group had lived previously in Farmington, Minnesota, where they had acquired some financial resources by working for the railroad.

Eventually, enough families were present to enable the group to found a Danish Lutheran Church in the town of Fairmount. This little congregation continued until perhaps the 1930's; the building remained in the 1940's. A few Danish families still live in this Richland County area. The descendants of most of the original residents have left; some have intermarried with other national groups.

In the spring of 1878 two Danish brothers from Minnesota arrived in Hill Township on the western edge of Cass County. A few weeks later, after other members of their family arrived, they preempted land along the Maple River and erected a dugout type of home. This first contingent of Danes had originally come to America from the Jutland region of Denmark and had worked for awhile in Illinois and Minnesota. In the next several years, they were joined by fellow countrymen from Danish Schleswig. The settlers established farms and eventually erected houses in a Danish tradition with walls of sun-baked brick. They even constructed a Jutland type of pleasure boat which was used for outings on the Maple River. Four small windmills were also built by the first Danes as they sought to process their grain. Some 20 miles farther south at Lucca in Ransom County, a Danish millwright erected a large windmill complete with canvas sails and steel grinding mechanisms.

The Danish Lutheran church seems never to have taken permanent root in Hill Township. Apparently, many of the Cass County settlers resented the traditional Danish church organization, and they affiliated with various American Protestant churches. Danish foods and dances persisted through the early years, but the people's affiliation with local English language churches and schools made cultural survival difficult.

There was an additional problem: the initial choice of land was not a fortunate one; marshes and rough terrain caused many to become disillusioned. An area history says ominously: "Hill Township was blessed with an abundance of gravel." By 1910, many of the original settlers had moved away; nevertheless, the group's cohesiveness continued. A private phone line served the Dane portion of the township from the 1890's until the 1920's. Today, however, relatively few Danish descendants are present in the township.

At times a Danish family name is found today on the lists of residents in predominately Norwegian and Swedish parts of southeastern North Dakota. These citizens are often the grandchildren of an occasional Danish farmer who came to the region and settled alone or in tiny groups among other land seekers. Some are individuals who trace their ancestry to a few Danish-Americans who took up land in the re-shuffling period of the early decades of this century as the initial homesteaders moved away. A few such families, mixed with Norwegians and Anglo-Americans, reside in southern Barnes County west of Litchville. Others are found among Norwegians in an area east of Gwinner in Sargent County.

In general, the Danes in eastern North Dakota proved to be among the less-persistent homesteaders. Their prior experience often had been in the more "gentle" dairy and garden regions of Europe. They left their Dakota farms rapidly, and their land was taken up by others.

DUNKARDS (Brethren)

A small group of German Dunkards settled south of Englevale in Ransom County at the turn of the century. Their original group, probably only a scattering of families, was spread through much of Alleghany Township. Coming after the homestead days, they purchased their farms and homes. A Brethren congregation was organized in 1910; in 1911 it was said to have twenty-four members, and a church was eventually constructed. The little religious community dissolved in 1934; the church building was moved to town where it became a shed; even the cemetery graves have since disappeared. The Englevale farm neighborhood contains many German families today; some of these are the descendants of the original Dunkard farmers.

FINNS

In 1882 a "scout" of Finnish background described as favorable the land along the James River north of Aberdeen in present-day South Dakota. There followed, over a period of years, a westward movement of his fellow countrymen from northern Michigan, Ohio, Pennsylvania, and Massachusetts. These people took the Chicago, Milwaukee and St. Paul Railroad to Aberdeen, and from there went northward to Frederick, where they founded a large rural Finnish community. (Hecla and Frederick are still Finnish farm settlements.) The northern portion of this group of homestead families found themselves in North Dakota when the territory was divided at the time of statehood. They make up most of the residents of Lovell and Ada townships in southeastern Dickey County and also are present in nearby Port Emma and Van Meter townships. (Their neighbors commonly refer to them as "Finlanders.")

A Finnish Apostolic Lutheran Church, first in South Dakota and later in North Dakota, served their religious needs. As was common in Finnish communities, a Finn community hall was built. Ludden, in Dickey County, became a favorite shopping center. Also, following the traditions of Finns elsewhere, local cooperatives grew up on both sides of the border: a creamery, a telephone system, an oil company, and a livestock association.

Close ties developed and continued for several generations with fellow countrymen who resided in settlements throughout northern Minnesota. An active communications network seems to have been in effect, for several Finnish colonies in other parts of North Dakota received some of their first settlers from this early Ludden community.

FRENCH

Beginning in 1869, French settlers from Trois Rivieres in Quebec settled near the junction of the Red River and the Wild Rice River in what is now Cass County. This early date represents a time well before the coming of the railroads and the establishment of any of the major present-day North Dakota towns. In fact, only a handful of river-oriented immigrants were in all of the Red River Valley. The early French settlers came, not by the cross-Canada route (for such railroads were non-existent), but through the United States via railroad and ultimately by Red River cart caravan from St. Paul.

The religious needs of the first arrivals were fulfilled in a log structure called the Holy Cross Mission, located on Section 13 of Stanley Township. This church was built to care for the Métis settlers and the arriving French Canadians. (Missionary Father J. B. Genin said that in 1867 there were 100 Métis families present between Fort Abercrombie and the Buffalo River.) The religious structure was standing in 1870 and was, thus, the earliest in this part of the state. This first Holy Cross Church burned; a second was constructed beginning in 1872 and completed in 1875. In 1883, the French-speaking settlers built a church at a more central location in the southern portion of Stanley Township. This became known as the St. Benedict Parish and is an active congregation today.

The modern-day French descendants still own approximately the same area and the same amount of land as their ancestors did in pioneer days.

In 1903, a school building was erected at St. Benedict's by the parish and newly arrived French Presentation Sisters. A grade school and eventually a high school (1935) were established. The French language was initially the basis of all education, with English in a secondary position. The process reversed itself slowly, and by the 1930's English was the primary and French the secondary language. The high school closed in 1964; grade-school classes ended in 1966.

This French community is probably the earliest agricultural settlement in the southeastern part of the state. French and Metis communities in Pembina County date their farming activities from the 1850's or, at the latest, the 1860's. (It is difficult to distinguish between gardening and small farming.) But on the southern part of the Red River, the Wild Rice or St. Benedict's settlement seems to have been the first collection of permanent farmsteads.

GERMANS (Reichsdeutsch)

The southeastern part of North Dakota has proportionately more people of un-hyphenated German background than any other part of the state. Some individual Germans were with the Anglo-Americans who took up land to form the first tiny log and dugout villages along the Red River in the early 1870's. These tended to be Germans who had lived previously in such states as Wisconsin, Illinois, and Minnesota. This same kind of German, already somewhat versed in English and American ways, seems to have made up the majority of first settlers in the earliest German homesteaded areas in the Red River region of North Dakota.

Since the number of *Reichsdeutsch* communities in the southeastern counties is considerable, it might be helpful to divide and discuss them in terms of religious affiliations, Catholic and Protestant (especially Lutheran). There is some basis for this categorization, for often the groups lived side by side, sharing a common language and customs and yet refraining from inter-marriage for several generations. Indeed, as the years passed, German Protestants would marry non-German Protestants, and Catholic Germans would marry non-German Catholics, but the two German religious groups seldom intermingled.

German Protestants

As early as 1872 German Lutherans came to what is now Brandenburg Township in Richland County, locating immediately west of the present Great Bend village. In 1874 they organized a congregation; their first services were held in tiny frontier homes before a small church was built in 1875. By 1881 a permanent pastor was at hand. Thus, the area's well-known Missouri Synod Lutheran community came into being; for four generations it has been a flourishing church group. Brandenburg Township is still almost entirely German Lutheran, and that national group extends beyond its borders in almost every direction.

Southwest of Great Bend, another German Lutheran settlement began in 1875 with Germans taking up land in what is now Belford Township. In 1886 a religious congregation was organized; St. John's Church, situated a few miles south of Mantador, was built a little later. Descendants of the early settlers live in the area today.

The prairie south of Lidgerwood began to receive Germans at settlement time, in this case about 1880. Duerr Township was and still is the location of many of the first arrivals and their descendants. The Immanuel Lutheran Congregation, Missouri Synod, began here with the occasional visits of a Great Bend pastor. The first members worshipped in the local school building; eventually, the Immanuel Church was built some six miles southeast of Lidgerwood.

Also in Richland County, another Missouri Synod German congregation was formed by the people who resided east of Great Bend in Summit Township. As early as 1880, church services were held in homes and schools in the Tyler area. Planning for a church began in 1887, and the St. John's Church was finally built in 1903. The northern portion of the Richland County German Lutheran group founded a congregation and built a church at Barney in 1899.

Lutheran Germans occupy much of the southern half of Richland County. Catholic Germans live in the neighboring townships. Together, they constitute the largest *Reichsdeutsch* settlement in the state.

The educational element of their tradition was vitally important to Richland County German settlers. Lutherans built parochial schools in Great Bend, Barney and eventually in Hankinson. Their fellow countrymen, the Catholic Germans, built parochial schools in Mooreton, Mantador, Lidgerwood, Hankinson, and Wahpeton.

West of Richland County, Germans moved into LaMoure County's Marion, Edgeley, and LaMoure areas in the 1880's. A Missouri Synod congregation was established in Jud in western LaMoure County in 1909. The St. John's Missouri Synod Church of Marion was organized in 1897; services had been informally held in homes and schools as early as 1884. In 1890 a German congregation was founded at Stirum in Sargent County; later, one began at Gwinner.

Of particular significance, however, was the establishment of the Missouri Synod Christ Church, which was organized in Albion Township, in Dickey County, in 1883. From this center early pastors ministered to newly arrived Germans as far away as Kulm, Leola, and Oakes. Also in Dickey County, a German Lutheran church was organized in 1892 in a local home in Monango. A church was built in 1903. This congregation was unusual in that it was made up of *Reichsdeutsch* and Germans from Russia (the townships to the west of Monango form the east edge of southcentral North Dakota's great German-Russian settlement). The combination of Germans and German-Russians in a church community was infrequent in North Dakota; usually the two groups insisted on forming separate churches. Eventually, other Dickey County German Lutherans of Missouri Synod affiliation built churches in Edgeley (1904), Oakes (1920), and Kulm.

Early German Protestants affiliated with groups other than the Missouri Synod. In Barnes County's Getchell and Stewart townships, north of Valley City, a number of German families organized the rural Zion Lutheran congregation which met for the first time in 1895. Their church was built in Getchell Township in that same year; it remained active until 1959. Settlers in townships northwest of Valley City organized a German Methodist mission (the Salem Church) in 1881; it continues today. A Zion Lutheran Church at Oriska, organized in 1891 and built in 1904, served Germans who settled around that town. The religious needs of the numerous Protestant Germans in the eastcentral part of Barnes County were served by both the Oriska Zion Church and the St. Paul's Lutheran Church in Tower City, which was built in 1904. Many of these Germans came as "second wave" settlers from Iowa and eastern states; they purchased land from departing Anglo-Americans.

Families of German Protestant background are found today sprinkled throughout central Cass County. A rather solid group exists a few miles west of Arthur, and many are on the land between that city and Casselton. Some Germans reside among other national groups between Casselton and Mapleton. A number of these individuals are descendants of settlers who, in 1886, organized the Martin's German Lutheran Church in Casselton. In 1889, German Lutherans from Arthur, Amenia, and Casselton formed a joint parish; they erected a church building in 1891. The initial congregation was decidedly ethnic in tone with services in German and a ladies aid called *Der Frauen Verein*. By 1909 the German emphasis had proved to be a hindrance, and English became the language of worship and instruction.

The congregation, thereafter, attracted a variety of national groups.

From 1881 to 1887, a great many German families moved onto Cass County land north of Enderlin, especially in Pontiac township. In 1884, they organized the Trinity Lutheran Congregation (Iowa Synod); a church building was dedicated in 1895. This German region extended southward across the line into Ransom County where other farmers built a church at Anselm in 1905. For a time another congregation of German background was at Lucca, and a St. Luke's Church was at Enderlin. By 1964, several of the groups had merged, as Trinity Lutheran in Enderlin embraced much of the same territory. German farmers still reside to the north and west of Enderlin.

A small German settlement can be found about five miles northwest of Colfax in northern Richland County. That community seems to have always been an island of German farmers centered around what for many years was an Evangelical United Brethren Church. This group of Germans had their first church services in 1881. To this day, they are called the Zion community.

It can be said that each of the above rural churches was, and still is, central to some German Protestant rural neighborhood. Germans arrived in the earliest decades, took the land, and retain it today. Succeeding generations kept the land in the family, or at least passed it on to people of their own kind.

German Catholics

In the 1870's German Catholics joined the first immigrant rush into Richland County. The land north and west of Mantador and also south of Hankinson received great numbers of these land seekers. In 1881 a small church structure was erected two miles east of Mantador, and the SS. Peter and Paul parish came into being. A later church was built in the newly established Mantador village, and it is active today.

The Lidgerwood German Catholics joined with Bohemians and Irish to erect the St. Boniface Church in 1887. Some of these farm families had come as early as 1881. Later, the Germans and Bohemians separated to form two parishes. A new "German" church was constructed in 1906; the Bohemians built their church on the other side of town.

On the northern edge of Richland County's German area, the Mooreton St. Anthony's Church was erected in 1884. It served German Catholics, but other nationalities also attended.

Catholic *Reichsdeutsch* in the Hankinson area began arriving in the late 1870's. Early religious services were held in homes in the town; a church was built in 1892. Eventually, a large grade and high school was established; it was staffed by nuns from Germany. Boarding students came to the school in great numbers, particularly from German and German-Russian settlements in the southcentral part of the state. The Catholic German rural communities in Richland County are intact today. Little change in the boundaries has taken place, because the farms are most often passed on to sons or other family members.

In Barnes County, Catholic Germans took up land in 1880 near the present village of Wimbledon. Church services were held by itinerant priests in 1882; by 1886 a church with the German name St. Boniface had been built five miles south of Wimbledon. It was later moved to town, and the parish is presently very active.

Also in Barnes County, German farmers near Dazey convinced the Catholic bishop that a parish should be established for local residents. The St. Mary's Church was built in 1904. In the same county, German Catholics joined with other nationalities to erect a church in Oriska in 1908.

West of Valley City, at Sanborn in Barnes County, German Catholic settlers moved on to the land in the early part of the 1880's. This group was unusual in that many of the first Germans came from Canada. They erected the Sacred Heart Church in 1884.

The Barnes County Catholic parishes flourish today. Most have resident pastors, and the areas they serve are still heavily German in background.

BOHEMIAN-GERMANS

Sudeten Germans took up land in Cass County south of Casselton in 1880. Some acquired the "in-between" sections of the bonanza farm plots, and some purchased land from earlier agricultural settlers. Michelsdorf in Bohemia was the home village for most of these early arrivals. The Germans described themselves as being from Bohemia, and they were known locally as being just that, "Bohemians."

Several early families, including the famous Langer family, prospered almost from the start. A pattern seems to have been set up: immigrants would come to Casselton, work for a while on the large farms, and later would acquire land of their own. Many local Bohemian-Germans speak of "working for the Langers" or other such farm enterprises.

Early Casselton Sudeten Germans moved westward in the county to Clifton and Eldred townships; some homesteaded there in the mid-1880's. Alice, a village in the middle of the Bohemian settlement, became a community center; here the St. Henry's Catholic congregation began with services in farm homes as early as 1888. Ultimately, a church was erected in 1903. For a number of years before the Second World War, Alice was the site of an annual Bohemian-German festival which drew great numbers of people from Casselton and from the Jessie, North Dakota, Sudeten German community.

Little of the German culture survives. The Casselton families quickly assimilated into the American scene, attending English-language schools and the mixed-nationality Catholic church in Casselton. With the passage of time, the Alice Church came to serve a number of national groups and lacked a real "ethnic" tradition. Nevertheless, today seventy-five percent of the farm families who live north and west of Alice are of Sudeten background.

HUNGARIAN-GERMANS

A distinctive group of Germans is found around Fingal in Barnes County and nearby in an area that extends into Cass County. These are Germans from Hungary — in fact, from the far western edge of Hungary near the border of Austria. They came from small *dorfs* in the region of Burgenland, which is about eighty kilometers south of Vienna. Their home villages include the towns of Pilgersdorf and Geresdorf. Apparently, the original inhabitants of that region were displaced by the Austro-Hungarian rulers, and Germans were invited into the area for settlement. "Maria Theresa" is a name which for many years was popular among the Germans of the Fingal area. These Hungarian-Germans are not of Hungarian national origin, but are completely German in their family backgrounds. Curiously, their North Dakota neighbors always called them "Hungarians," not "Germans."

The first settlers arrived in the Fingal area in 1879. The newcomers were Catholic and the church was important in their lives. The first Mass took place there in 1881. A stone country church was eventually built on Section 34, Springvale Township. An adjoining St. Gerhard's Parochial School was established in 1909; it closed during World War I. At that same time, 1918, a church was built in Fingal; it serves an active congregation today. Only a cemetery marks the prior rural parish site. Today, the German-Hungarian community occupies most of Binghampton and Springvale townships.

The Fingal community is the larger of two Burgenland settlements in North Dakota. The other is at Sykeston. A scattering of Burgenland people also settled near St. Anthony in Morton County and near Foxholm in Ward County. The Sykeston and Foxholm "Hungarians" seem to have had occasional early day ties with the Fingal community.

GERMAN MORAVIANS

Early in 1878 a group of Germans of Moravian religious background arrived at the Casselton railroad station in Cass County to occupy land a few miles south of that city in Maple River and Addison townships, which they had purchased from the Northern Pacific Railroad. While their earliest American origins were in Pennsylvania, the original Dakota group came from Minnesota and Wisconsin. In May, 1878, a group of Moravian settlers met in a farm home near Casselton to organize Dakota Territory's first Moravian congregation. They called themselves the Goshen Church, and the charter members numbered almost thirty adults. For several years they had services in their homes and in a school house. They built a parsonage in 1881, and in 1885 dedicated a church on Section 5 of Maple River Township, six miles south and two miles west of Casselton. This same building, with some modifications, serves the Goshen community today.

In 1881, another Moravian congregation, the Canaan Church, was organized with thirty-two original members; a church was built in Addison Township in 1886. The Bethel Church in Leonard Township was built in 1900. Churches were later erected in Embden and Alice. Moravian church services were held in homes in Casselton in 1891, and a church was built in 1909; this congregation remains very active today. A total of five Moravian churches were, thereby, scattered through rural Cass County, allowing the German language and special Moravian customs to prevail for several generations. Their graveyards (with separate sections for men, women, and children) were unique in the eyes of their non-Moravian neighbors; so also were their flat-lying tombstones. By 1930 the German language was no longer used with regularity in the church services.

Moravian farmers were highly successful, and their young men and women eventually moved into local towns to enter business and civic affairs. By the 1960's, though almost all the land was still in the hands of the descendants of the original settlers, some of the unique traditions of the early days had disappeared. Intermarriage became frequent, and a Methodist minister, at times, served some of the Moravian churches. The Canaan, Goshen, and Bethel churches still have English-language Moravian services and have pastors of that religious background.

GERMAN-RUSSIANS (Catholic)

German-Russian homesteaders in the southeastern part of the state were almost invariably of Protestant background. Catholic German-Russian areas were located in counties farther west. Today, an occasional Catholic farm family can be found in the southeast, but these are American-born individuals who moved into the region during the thirties, or shortly after the Second World War.

One exception, however, is a group of German "Black Sea" Catholics who settled in an organized manner in LaMoure County in the mid-1930's. Some can be found, living among other nationalities, in Ray and Bluebird townships; they are particularly present in Wano and Russell townships, a few miles north of Edgeley. During the drought of the thirties, when the original settlers of Irish and Anglo-American Catholic background were leaving the area in great numbers, a local priest went on a recruiting trip to German-Russian communities in Emmons and McIntosh counties. There, whole families of Germans were loaded into trucks and assisted in acquiring the land that was being vacated in LaMoure County. These families stayed on their newly obtained farms and are prosperous residents today.

GERMAN-RUSSIANS (Protestant)

The townships on the western sides of LaMoure and Dickey counties are part of a massive series of German-Russian settlements which extends westward to the Missouri River, and even beyond to the edges of the North Dakota Badlands. This ethnic group spreads down into the northern South Dakota counties and fills central North Dakota as far north as Pierce and McHenry counties. The favorite immigration route of the Germans from Black Sea Russian colonies was the Chicago, Milwaukee and St. Paul Railroad, which traversed northern South Dakota. From railroad centers at Aberdeen, Ipswich, and Eureka, the settlers moved northward into the vacant lands of what was to become central North Dakota. Once the availability of suitable free land became known, a continual stream of newcomers arrived by rail from immigration ports. Some of the first, however, came overland by wagon from earlier German-Russian settlements near Yankton, South Dakota.

In general, it can be said that the great majority of German-Russians who came to Dakota did so "right off the boat." In this they differed from other groups. Many, if not most of the first Bohemians, *Reichsdeutsch,* Finns, and even Norwegians had served a few years of American apprenticeship in states to the east. Ethnic home colonies in Michigan, Minnesota, Wisconsin, and Iowa gave newcomers an introduction to the language and procedures of the new country. In contrast, the Germans from Russia had to undergo a certain "on the job training"; they learned about America in Dakota. This may explain something of the Germans' reluctance to enter the mainstream of American life and it may, also, partially explain the more long-lived character of their national traditions.

Germans from Russia were taking up land in the Monango and Kulm area in 1886. They were in the Merricourt vicinity by 1888. Almost without exception, the first Germans into this southeastern part of North Dakota (Dickey and LaMoure counties) were Protestants who affiliated with German-speaking American denominations; they remain Protestant today. Little country churches sprang up in the lands surrounding Kulm, bearing names that reveal their origins: Hoffnunsfeld, Postal, Friedensfeld, Eigenheim, Gnadenfeld, New Beresina. All these names, including Kulm, are from Bessarabian colonies.

Farther north in LaMoure County, the Germans were arriving in 1889 in the Jud vicinity; they were near Fullerton by 1900. At the same time, they helped found the St.

Paul's Lutheran Missouri Synod Church in Monango, Dickey County.

Early land records indicate that great numbers of non-Germans also took up land in western Dickey and LaMoure counties. In certain areas, pockets of non-Germans constituted the majority of original settlers. Swedes still remain north of Kulm, but most of the other nationalities have departed; today one may travel fifty miles westward from the Dickey County German settlements and never pass a non-German-Russian farm.

GERMAN-RUSSIANS, VOLGA

A handful of "late arriving" German settlers moved into Ransom County near Elliott. These families established one of the rare Volga settlements in the state. They came from Nebraska in 1907, but their ultimate origins were villages in Russia, particularly Neu-Norka and Neu-Hussenbach. Their descendants live today in Ransom County's Alleghany and Elliott townships. Their neighbors are usually Germans of non-Russia backgrounds.

In northcentral Dickey County, a group of "later arriving" Germans (some from the Volga and some from the Black Sea areas of Russia) took up land near Fullerton. These came from Sutton, Nebraska, around 1900. Their sons and daughters are present today.

HOLLANDERS

The southwestern corner of Barnes County has two groups of Hollanders, separated by a few miles, yet with a common heritage. One settlement spreads northward from Litchville through portions of Rosebud and Spring Creek townships. A second and larger group of Dutch farmers resides about six miles farther to the northwest in Meadow Lake Township. These farm families are the grandchildren of settlers who apparently came later than the nearby Norwegians and Anglo-Americans; they purchased their lands from departing homesteaders. The first arrivals came in 1903 from Iowa communities such as Orange City, Sheldon, and Boyden. Later farmers migrated to the area from Wisconsin and Illinois, and some came from the Netherlands.

Two Dutch Reformed churches served their special needs: the Litchville congregation (organized in 1906) and the North Marion congregation (organized in 1908). The North Marion church is a rural structure located on the southern edge of its settlement area on Section 17 of Greenland Township. Both the Litchville and North Marion churches are active today, and a local pastor serves both groups. Together, the two communities form the second largest cluster of Hollander farms in the state; only the Emmons County settlement surpasses it in size.

Dutch settlers established two other colonies in the eastern part of the state; for a time they had a lively community life and built churches of their own special background. One, in Grand Forks County, is discussed in the northeastern portion of this volume. The other group, which settled in the northwest corner of Barnes County, consisted initially of five Dutch families who came to Pierce Township in 1914 from Fulton, Illinois. Other families joined them in the following years, and a small

rural Dutch Reformed church was built. The congregation was small, and visiting ministers (often from Litchville) cared for its needs. Some families returned later to Illinois and others went elsewhere. In the 1950's the church merged with the Presbyterian Church of Courtenay and finally closed its doors in 1963. Remnants of this Hollander community live today north of Wimbledon in a small area which extends a few miles farther into Griggs County.

LUXEMBURGERS

Coming particularly from Minnesota settlements, and mixed among German immigrants from Minnesota, Iowa, and Wisconsin, a number of families of Luxemburg background settled throughout North Dakota. Their presence in the state has seldom been noted, for their numbers were generally small and they were not highly visible. Their low visibility was due partly to the fact that, while they saw themselves as distinct from the Germans, they, nevertheless, spoke the German language and would — at times, perhaps for simplicity's sake — classify themselves as Germans. Some even listed their origin as "Luxemburg, Germany." As a result, they tended to melt into the surrounding larger German communities.

Two small areas in southeastern North Dakota contain clusters of identifiable Luxemburg families. One is between LaMoure and Verona in LaMoure County. The other is immediately north and northeast of Casselton in Cass County. Being few in numbers and widely dispersed, they formed no national organizations, religious or social, to care for their needs.

MENNONITES

A Barnes County Mennonite settlement existed between Rogers and Valley City in the 1920's and early 1930's. After purchasing several farms, this Mennonite group (apparently a colony-type enterprise) found North Dakota life difficult. The hard years of the 1930's led them to sell their property and move elsewhere. The group, it seems, came originally from Iowa.

Casselton, in Cass County, has today a few Mennonite families, enough to support a small town church. The group organized officially in 1929 and is of the same tradition as the Mennonite congregations at Surrey and Wolford, North Dakota. Its basic membership comes from families who moved to the Casselton vicinity starting in 1928 and especially in the 1930's. In 1950 they purchased an Episcopal church, and by 1956 their membership numbered forty-five. These members live on farms surrounded by other nationalities; but some live in Casselton, where several are prominent in civic affairs.

NORWEGIANS

The earliest Norwegian settlers in the southeastern portion of the state seem to have arrived on the Red River as occasioned individuals in 1869. In the spring of 1870 a larger number of Norwegians came across the river near the Wild Rice River in Cass County and also near Fort Abercrombie in Richland County. There they carved primitive farms from the woods and prairie; since steamboats already traversed the river and military trails crossed the region, they were able to sell their produce and eke out a meager livelihood.

Norwegians, thereafter, were seen arriving at several other points along the Red River north of Wahpeton and south of Georgetown. Movement into the Red River Valley was facilitated by the fact that railroad construction was moving toward Breckenridge (arriving in 1871), and by favorable early reports which filtered back to Minnesota and Wisconsin Norwegian settlements by way of newspaper, letter, and word of mouth accounts.

North of the future Fargo, in present Harwood Township, Cass County, the first Norwegians seem to have arrived also in 1870. The northeastern corner of the township was soon called *Osterdahl*, in contrast to the "American settlement" a few miles to the south. The Norwegian settlement was an enduring one; today the eastern portions of the townships north of Harwood

village (the areas adjacent to the river) are still heavily Norwegian.

The pioneering settlers saw the church as both a religious and a social rallying place. Congregations were formed very quickly. In the Wild Rice area the Hemnes Congregation — which some regard as the first Lutheran church organization in North Dakota — began at a farmstead between Christine and Hickson on September 4, 1871. The Nora Church, east of Gardner in Cass County, is also said to have been established in 1871. In 1872 the St. John's Lutheran congregation in Abercrombie Township was organized, and other Richland County churches date back to that same year: the South Pleasant congregation near Christine and the Pleasant congregation northeast of Walcott.

Newcomers from Norway had moved away from the Red River and were already on the Sheyenne River by 1871; in that year the influx reached Normanna Town-

ship in Cass County near present-day Kindred. The Sheyenne (later Norman) Church, located in Section 24, Normanna Township, adopted a constitution and became active in May, 1872. Farther north on the river in Warren Township, the North Sheyenne (Horace) church group began at about the same time. Many of these first Cass County residents came from Goodhue and Rice counties in Minnesota. A log cabin from near the Norman Church acreage, dating back to 1873, was sent in 1954 to Oslo, Norway, where it is part of a national museum.

An editor of a Norwegian-language newspaper visited Fargo in 1874 and, after a short trip, reported that Norwegians owned almost all the farms along the Sheyenne River. Their small log houses and wheat stacks stood at the edge of the woods bordering the river, and their farms extended out into the prairie. In Fargo, however, the newspaperman found only a few Norwegian tradesmen.

In retrospect, it seems that Norwegian land seekers filled the Wild Rice and Sheyenne lands with amazing rapidity; they seemed almost to leapfrog one another. Walcott Township, in northeastern Richland County, received settlers along the Wild Rice in 1871. The Maple River congregation at Mapleton in Cass County was organized in 1872. From the Hickson and Kindred areas in Cass County, Norwegians in the next few years pushed southeast, filling townships on either side of the Sheyenne River, almost as far west as Lisbon. Earlier Anglo-Americans intercepted the movement south of Lisbon, but up-river the Sheyenne became the basic backbone of Norwegian settlement from Fort Ransom north to the vicinity of Valley City. A dozen miles north of that city, Norwegian townships began again and, even today, form an almost unbroken series of settlements which pass through Griggs, Steele, and Nelson Counties, and through northern Eddy County into Wells County almost as far west as Harvey. The Sheyenne, in effect, is an almost exclusively Norwegian river from southern Cass County, running west and north for almost 200 miles until it reaches Wells County.

Earlier French and Anglo-American settlements south and west of Fargo prevented Norwegian settlement in that area, but from Horace southward intensive Norwegian homesteading took place. Normanna Township, Cass County, is today almost solidly Norwegian. Nearby townships such as Davenport, the southern portion of Pleasant, and Warren west of Horace are still very much Norwegian settlements.

In Richland County, Norwegians pressed inland from the Red River and began to settle the townships to the west. Ibsen Township, west of Abercrombie, received settlers in 1879. Nansen Township, immediately to the north, was settled three years later. At the same time, Norwegians were taking land near the German colony which had been established in Colfax Township.

Norwegian settlers, moving along the Sheyenne in Barrie Township, Richland County, organized their first congregation in 1880. The nearby Standy Dovre Church in Viking Township first met in 1879. These townships, along with Freeman and Garborg, are today almost com-

pletely Norwegian. A central church which served a wide area in west central Richland and eastern Ransom County was the Silver Prairie congregation founded in 1888 some nine miles northeast of McLeod. Village and open country churches were, in almost every case, community centers for the newly established immigrants. It is impossible to list them all. Richland County in 1910 had at least twenty congregations, often of different synodal background, serving the resident Norwegian populace.

During settlement times (and today) it could be said that the northern half of Richland County was, for the most part, Norwegian territory. Some earlier groups — Germans, Anglo-Americans, and Swedes — still remain, but twelve townships are almost exclusively Norwegian in background.

In northwestern Ransom County, the Sheyenne Valley (as mentioned above) was an attraction to early Norwegian settlers. The first arrivals were often from southeastern Minnesota and Iowa; later groups came directly from Norway. In 1878, Norwegian settlers began to move into Northland Township. Preston Township on the east side of the Valley received immigrants that same year. The Preston settlement eventually had a post office and church (1882). Springer Township, east of Fort Ransom, received Norwegians in 1883. Fort Ransom Township received its first Norwegian settlers in 1878. The Sheyenne Valley Church was organized in 1879; a church building was erected in 1897. The Standing Rock congregation at Fort Ransom organized in 1882, and a church was built in 1887. Farther up the valley, the Stiklestad congregation organized in 1887 and built a church in 1897.

During the next few years large numbers of Norwegian farmers moved from the river areas westward into Litchville, Black Loam, and Gladstone townships in LaMoure County. The North LaMoure Church, which began in 1883, served the region. A scattering of Norwegians took land near Marion and Grand View. Others were near the James River town of Grand Rapids. Townships adjoining the Sheyenne River in Ransom, LaMoure, and southern Barnes counties remain today almost exclusively Norwegian in background.

Barnes County apparently received Norwegians from two directions. Some came up the Sheyenne; others came to Valley City by rail and flooded out along the river valleys and side hills. Some Norwegians are said to have settled above Valley City as early as 1877. While some went up river (to the Dazey area in 1879), by far the most went downstream. Valley City was a favorite dispersal point. The resident land agent for the Northern Pacific was a Norwegian from Minnesota, whose encouragement brought many to the region.

South of Valley City in Barnes County, Thordenskjold Township received its first Norwegian settlers in 1878. Across the river, Oakhill Township land was claimed at the same time. Kathryn eventually was founded, becoming a social and business center for a large Norwegian territory. Immediately to the north, Nelson Township saw its first Norwegian in 1878. Across the river, Norma Township received Norwegians at the same time. Fellow countrymen spread out from the valley and took land in the western portion of Raritan Township. Nome became another busy focus of Norwegian activity; the local St. Petri's church was organized in 1883. West of the valley, Spring Creek Township was settled in the early 1880's. Skandia was settled in 1880. The Ringsaker Church came into being in 1881. Farther north, Green Township received its first settlers in 1881. Perhaps the first Scandinavian Lutheran church in the entire Barnes County area was organized in the railroad town of Valley City in 1879; it continues today under the title of the First Lutheran Church. Today, Oakhill, Thordenskjold, Norma, Nelson, and much of Green, Skandia, Spring Creek, and Raritan townships are completely Norwegian.

North of Valley City a scattering of Norwegian farmers exist today along the valley, although Anglo-Americans, Anglo-Ontarians and others who settled the area at an earlier date still remain. The Rogers vicinity has a great number of Norwegians; the Bethel Lutheran Church, organized in 1886, serves the local residents. Farther north around Dazey and Lake Town townships, a solidly Norwegian area exists. This is, in fact, the lower portion of the almost completely Norwegian belt which extends along the course of the Sheyenne River through Griggs, Eddy, Benson, and Wells counties. To the east in Cass County, Page, Dows, and Hunter townships mark the beginning of the very large and well-known Steele-Traill County Norwegian area. The northern portions of these Cass County townships are heavily Norwegian; and this same nationality continues north in a concentrated fashion for at least forty miles, reaching almost to Larimore and Grand Forks.

The lower Sheyenne Norwegian communities are probably larger and more intensely Norwegian today than they were fifty years ago. Other nationalities, if we may believe early township maps, once owned farms within the Norwegian concentration. Their land was eventually purchased by second- and third-generation Norwegian farmers. The township names reflect the presence of these sturdy Norwegian pioneers: Ibsen, Viking, Skandia, Normanna, and some resoundingly ethnic names such as Thordenskjold and Svea and Sydna.

Elsewhere in the prairie regions beyond the Sheyenne vicinity, emigrants from Norway arrived in smaller numbers. Beginning about 1882 they came to Sargent County in scattered groups, settling in the east half of Wiley and the west half of Milnor townships, and also in Hall Township west of Milnor. The Immanuel congregation near DeLamere began in 1883. This area is still sixty percent Norwegian. South of Gwinner in Dunbar Township, many Norwegians were and still are present. Rutland and Ransom townships received many Norwegian settlers. The population of this area is today at least sixty percent of Norwegian origin. In Dickey County, a group of Norwegians took land west of Oakes in Clement (formerly Norway) Township in the early 1880's. In southeastern Ransom County, Sydna Township received a goodly number of Norwegians at the same time.

Some, perhaps many, of the early settlers came after "scouts" had looked over the land and sent back favorable reports. Immigration caravans, thereafter, arrived regularly throughout all the counties. Almost all the new arrivals had been born in Norway. Many, if not most, had lived in Minnesota or Iowa for a short time; but many others were "right off the boat."

In retrospect, one may say that Norwegians must have looked on the eastern Dakota lands with special delight, for they came in such massive numbers, they endured with such determination, and they continue to farm with such success. Some unique qualities must have been present in the Norwegian character; they seem to have been almost predisposed to prairie life. It was not just a matter of timing; others had come earlier. It was not just numbers; other immigrants were coming to the United States by the millions. They were a special people for a special region.

POLES

Coming very early, almost at the same time as their Bohemian neighbors in western Richland County, a large group of Poles arrived west of Lidgerwood and centered eventually around the Sargent County town of Geneseo. Some Polish settlers came from Pennsylvania (1882); others came from Independence and Arcadia, Wisconsin. Apparently, one Catholic church, St. Martin's of Geneseo, served not only the developing Polish community, but also some nearby Irish settlers. Later, the nationality difference brought about a split; and a second Catholic parish, one with an Irish and American flavor, was organized in 1910 at Cayuga. This latter church, SS. Peter and Paul, was built without the consent of the Catholic bishop and had to wait four years before a pastor was appointed. The Polish community today extends from Geneseo to about ten miles west and six miles north and south of that town. It includes Kingston, Herman, and Ransom townships. The Geneseo and Cayuga churches, now both predominately Polish, are brick structures and remarkably substantial, considering the early date of construction and the rather meager finances of the congregations at that period.

An occasional Polish farmer is found mixed with other groups in almost every county in the southeastern portion of the state. A small group can be found west of Edgeley, and another is located north of Casselton. The forebears of these rural families came, in some instances, with the first homesteaders; but many came as individual farmers between 1910 and 1930 from such states as Iowa and Illinois.

SWEDES

Swedish immigrants came into the southeastern part of the state in considerable numbers at a very early date. Their eventual totals never matched that of their Scandinavian neighbors of Norwegian background, but they came as early and were spread liberally throughout almost every county. Their immigration was an interesting one. Almost inevitably an occasional Swede was with the masses of Norwegians who moved into their particular homestead regions. Some, however, settled in clusters, usually a handful, but at times, as a large group.

Solitary Swedes came on their own and were remarkably self-sufficient. In this they resembled the Anglo-American frontiersman who was capable of running ahead of the migration wave and squatting, almost in isolation, along river courses and in wooded regions. We read, for example, of a Swedish immigrant erecting in 1869 log cabins in Eagle Township, Richland County, along the Red River north of Fort Abercrombie. The arrival of a foreign-born settler at such an early date is remarkable; nevertheless, we find lone Swedes present among the first Anglo-American settlers elsewhere: for example, on the Sheyenne River south of Valley City and along the James River north of Ludden in Dickey County. In fact, Swedes of the first decade out-numbered other groups in some townships which are now solidly Norwegian or German.

This early-arrival characteristic of the Swedes can be seen not only in the southeastern part of the state, but also along the Missouri and the Souris rivers. Perhaps it was due to the fact that the Swedish immigration wave antedated that of other Scandinavians by a few years. Familiar with the American scene, they might have moved westward in a more easy fashion.

Swedish settlements grew up in most of the southeastern counties. As with many other groups, their churches marked their presence. The Richland County settlement in Eagle Township, mentioned above, built a Swedish Evangelical Church (the Mission Church) in the early 1880's. In Cass County, very early Swedish settlers moved into Reed and Raymond townships, and also into Gardner and Berlin townships. Accordingly, the Maple-Sheyenne Lutheran Church was organized in 1878 at Section 13, Raymond Township. Some of its members had come to Cass County in 1871. A few miles to the north, Herby Church in Berlin Township (Section 18) came into existence in 1891. Its first settlers had arrived in the region in 1877. Both of these churches are active today.

In Barnes County the Hobart Lutheran Church near Valley City was organized by Swedes in 1890. Some of its members had come to Dakota in 1879. The Vasa (Wasa) Church in southern Barnes County at Litchville was founded by settlers who came as early as 1881; this group held its first service in 1884.

In 1882 a handful of Swedish families journeyed by wagon from Fargo to Ransom County's Aliceton Township. They founded a Swedish enclave which, though diminished in size, is still present. Farther south in Sargent County, Gwinner was often called "Little Sweden" by seasonal farm workers. Present were Swedish families who came not only from Aliceton Township, but also from the nearby Sargent County townships of Dunbar, Wiley, and Rutland, which were heavily Swedish in background. Many local families today have Swedish ancestry. The rural Forsby Swedish Lutheran Church near Gwinner was organized in 1897, and a church was completed in 1899. Farther south, the First Swedish Baptist Church was incorporated in

Rutland in 1890 and continued to be a Swedish social center for several decades.

In Dickey County, a group of Swedish settlers came to an area northeast of Oakes in Bear Creek Township; a few were west of town in Clement Township. The original Swedish land seekers are said to have come in the early 1880's, "either on foot or by ox cart." Some of their descendants still remain. A Salem Lutheran Church of Augustana background served their needs during the first few decades of settlement.

By far the largest Swedish settlement in the southeastern counties today exists along the west edge of LaMoure County between Kulm and Jud, embracing almost all of Swede Township and extending north and south into Norden and Raney townships. Their religious needs were served, for the most part, by the local Swedish Baptist Church.

As one would expect, the Lutheran religious tradition was embraced by most of the newly arriving Swedish groups; but, unlike their Norwegian counterparts, other religious bodies were present in surprisingly large numbers. Groups such as the Swedish Baptists and Swedish Evangelical Free Church could be found in almost every part of North Dakota.

In general, it can be said that Swedish families were often half-hearted in their attempt to stay on the farm; though they were among the first arrivals, the majority left the land and moved elsewhere. In many cases only a remnant is still present, and these individuals are frequently intermarried with their more-durable Norwegian neighbors.

SWISS

The influx of German immigrants to North Dakota brought with it a number of Swiss families who, like the Luxemburgers, tended to be submerged in the larger category of "German farmers." Often from Swiss rural communities in Minnesota and Wisconsin, they formed no real ethnic colony on the prairies. The only identifiable group in the state (and it involves only a few families) exists near Wimbledon in Barnes County, particularly in Pierce and Uxbridge townships. These came with the local German homesteaders, and they seem to have established no particular national organizations.

Ethnic Population Distribution
Northeast Section of North Dakota

1. Ukrainian
2. Belgian
3. Anglo-Ontarian (Many Scots) 60%: Anglo-American 15%: German, French, Norwegian, Pole
4. Anglo-Ontarian 35%: Icelander 25%: German 25%: Norwegian 15%
5. German 50%: Anglo-Ontarian 40%: Anglo-American 10%
6. Norwegian 50%: Anglo-American 50%
7. German and Norwegian
8. Anglo-Ontarian 80%: Anglo-American 20%
9. Anglo-Ontarian 50%: (few Anglo-American): German 30%: Norwegian and French 20%
10. Pole 50%: Anglo-Ontarian 50%
11. Anglo-Ontarian 35%: French 35%: Others 30%
12. German 50%: Anglo-Ontarian 30%: Others 20%
13. Anglo-Ontarian especially Scots
14. Anglo-Ontarian and Anglo-American 50%: Norwegian, German, Polish, Bohemian 50%
15. Norwegian and Anglo-Ontarian
16. Norwegian 30%: German 30%: Anglo-Ontarian 20%: Anglo-American 20%
17. Anglo-Ontarian and Irish, occasional other
18. Anglo-Ontarian 25%: Anglo-American 25%: Norwegian 25%: German 25%
19. Mixed: German, German-Russian, Anglo-American and occasional other
20. Mixed: Anglo-American, Anglo-Ontarian, Norwegian, Bohemian, occasional other
21. Mixed: Bohemian and several others
22. Finlander
23. Mixed: Anglo-Ontarian, Anglo-American, Norwegian, German, several Poles and Belgians
24. Anglo-Ontarian and Anglo-American 40%: German and German-Russian 30%: Norwegian 30%
25. Mixed: Anglo-American, Irish, occasionaly Anglo-Ontarian
26. Swede 40%: Anglo-American 30%: Norwegian 30%
27. Anglo-American 40%: German 40%: Anglo-Ontarian 10%, occasional other
28. Anglo-American 30%: Anglo-Ontarian 10%: Norwegian 30%: German 15%: Others 15%
29. Finlander 50%: Norwegian 50%
30. Mixed: Anglo-American, Bohemian and German
31. Mixed: Anglo-American, Anglo-Ontarian, Norwegian and German, occasional Pole
32. Anglo-Ontarian 50%: Anglo-American 30%: Irish 10%: Pole and German 10%
33. Mixed: Pole, German, Anglo-Ontarian, Norwegian
34. Irish 40%: Anglo-Ontarian 40%: Norwegian, German and others 20%
35. Mixed: Norwegian, Anglo-Ontarian, Anglo-American, French and others
36. Mixed: Anglo-Ontarian, German and Swede
37. Norwegian 40%: Dane 35%: Others 25%
38. Anglo-Ontarian 50%: Anglo-American and Irish 25%: Norwegian and German 25%
39. German 50%: Anglo-American 50%
40. Swede and Anglo-American
41. Mixed: Swede, also Norwegian, German
42. Forest River Hutterite
43. Mixed: Norwegian, German and Anglo-American
44. Anglo-American 25%: Anglo-Ontarian 25%: Norwegian 30%: German 20%
45. Norwegian 40%: Anglo-Ontarian 35%: Anglo-American 10%: German 15%
46. Mixed: Anglo-Ontarian and Anglo-American
47. Dane
48. Anglo-American 50%: Anglo-Ontarian 10%: German 20%: Norwegian 20%
49. Mixed: Anglo-Ontarian, Anglo-American and Norwegian
50. Mixed: Anglo-American, Anglo-Ontarian, Hollander, Norwegian, Bohemian and German
51. Hollander
52. Anglo-Ontarian 60%: German 25%: French 10%: occasional Icelander
53. Czech (Moravian)

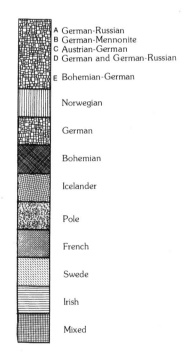

A German-Russian
B German-Mennonite
C Austrian-German
D German and German-Russian

E Bohemian-German

Norwegian

German

Bohemian

Icelander

Pole

French

Swede

Irish

Mixed

Shaded Areas
Are At Least
Ninety-Five
Percent Of The
Same National
Group Unless
Otherwise Indicated

Rural Residents As Of 1965

William C. Sherman   NDSU   Fargo, ND

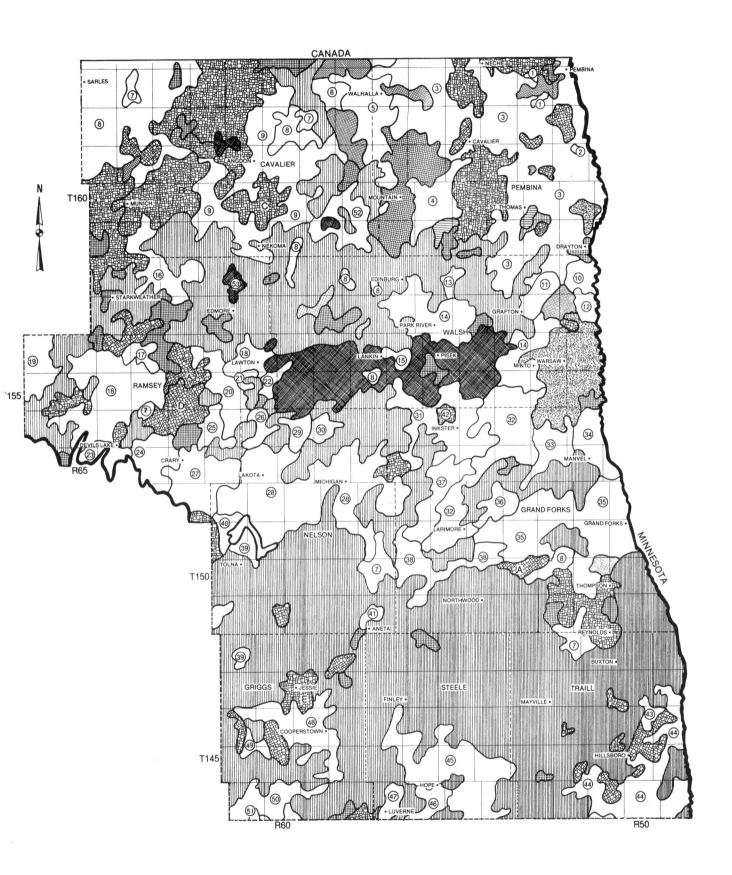

Township Names
Northeast Section of North Dakota

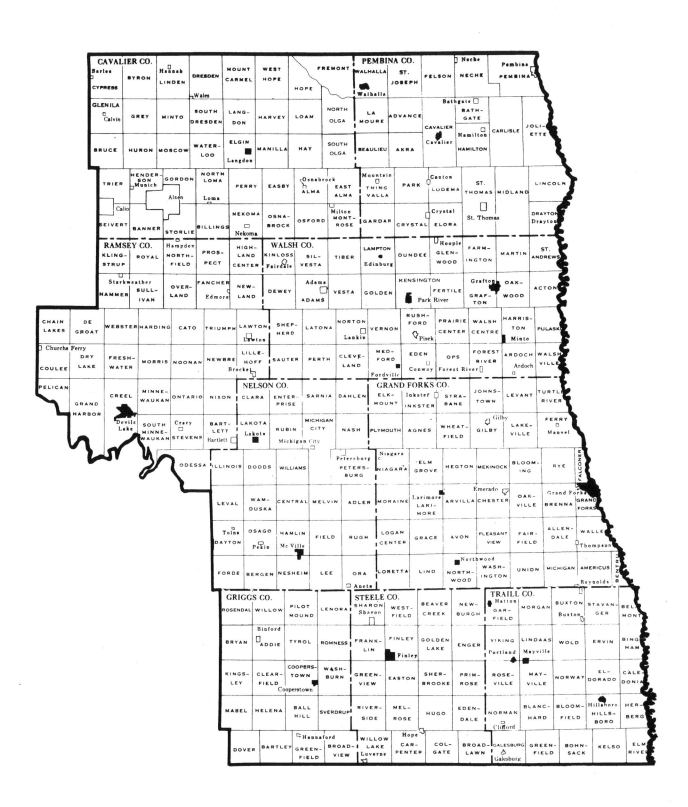

Commentary

ANGLO-AMERICAN

The northern portion of the Red River Valley in general, and Pembina County in particular, was first developed and populated by land seekers of Canadian origin. In fact, from the arrival of Alexander Henry in 1800 until the boundary clarification in 1823, the area around Pembina village was considered Canadian territory. After it was determined that the town and its immediate surroundings were part of the United States, Americans (or Yankees, as they were often called) began to show up in small and, later, in sizable numbers. A United States customs port of entry was built at Walhalla in 1851; and government officials, traders, and their families began more frequently to take up residence in the Pembina County region. Enterprising Americans became involved in the 1860's steamboat trade and in the Red River land commerce; they, with a number of Anglo-Ontarians, took part in the establishment of the first river towns. Americans were present in the early days of Frog Point, Acton, the Grand Forks Station, Quincy, and other such frontier posts. They were involved in handling the increasing amount of mail and commerce that moved up and down the valley.

As might be expected, many of these original entrepreneurs acquired parcels of land and became the first Anglo-Americans to settle in the region. For example, in Traill County, among the first four settlers to take land at Caledonia in early 1871, there was an American from Maine and another from Vermont. As settlement moved inland from that point, American squatters, with their Ontario friends, began to live along the Elm, the Forest, and the Goose rivers. The first settler in the present-day Portland area was an American who, with his family, arrived in 1871. Though most of the permanent settlers in the entire Red River region proved eventually to be people of immigrant background — Norwegians along the Goose and the Sheyenne rivers, Germans in Cavalier and Pembina counties, Bohemians in Walsh County, and Anglo-Ontarians in the Pembina region — many of the very first township residents were of Anglo-American background. They seemed comfortable in the American hinterland. Indeed, many were the descendants of people who had pushed westward over the Appalachians into the Ohio Valley and through Illinois and Wisconsin. Anglo-Americans proved to be ideal frontiersmen. They ventured forth as lone individuals or as families into what others saw as forbidding physical circumstances. They would build log cabins and cultivate small gardens; they survived by hunting game, selling hides, and collecting buffalo bones.

Some Americans, having eastern contacts and a degree of financial backing, looked at the Dakota frontier with profit-seeking eyes. Wamduska, Jerusalem, Odessa, and other townsites along Stump Lake and Devils Lake were examples of town speculation. The Great Northern and other railroads, everyone knew, would traverse the northern portion of North Dakota, and prosperous villages would arise along its course. Jumping ahead of the construction crews were Yankees who hoped to "cash in" on the railroad's arrival. In many cases the rail companies chose other routes, and the towns declined. Nevertheless, a few of these ambitious Americans remained on their plots of land as they awaited the arrival of land seekers from other nations.

Some Anglo-Americans came seeking not just 160 acres but sizable farm holdings. Early and successful Red River Valley bonanza farms were the model for many ambitious newcomers. For example, the first settler to stay in the Aneta region was a former Civil War colonel from New York who arrived in 1882 and acquired several thousand acres. The founder of Cavalier in Pembina County was a Missouri American of German extraction who, in 1875, moved along the Red River with Manitoba as his destination. Finding the Canadian land taken up by the Mennonite Reserves, he turned back and became the pioneer resident of the Cavalier area. The Mennonite Reserves, it is said, deflected many other American and Canadian settlers southward from the Manitoba line into the northeastern counties of Dakota.

American settlers also came in clusters, no doubt through the influence of aggressive land promoters. In 1909 an immigrant train arrived near Arvilla in Grand Forks County with seventy-two people from Rensselaer, Indiana. Niagara City, in Grand Forks County, was named after a group of settlers who came in the first part of the 1880's from Niagara County in New York. Such group-settlement experiences were frequent throughout the Dakotas.

The ethnic distribution in Griggs and Steele counties, even today, indicates clusters of non-Norwegians in the central parts of both of those regions. This dispersal pattern came about through the efforts of several large-scale land-development ventures. E. H. Steele purchased 50,000 acres from the Northern Pacific Railroad in 1880. His purchase gave him an abundance of odd-numbered sections in the central and eastern portion of what is now Steele County, and he thereupon established the village of Hope as headquarters for land-settlement activities. Steele's real estate firm advertised heavily in eastern periodicals; in response, great numbers of Anglo-Americans arrived within the next decade. Many left after a generation of farming, and their land is now owned by Norwegians. Nevertheless, a sizable amount of Anglo-Ontarians and Anglo-Americans still remain in southern Steele County.

Nearby, a similar activity took place. The Cooper brothers set up the Cooper Land Company in central Griggs County. They bought railroad land in 1882, platted the village of Cooperstown, and eventually owned or controlled something close to 20,000 acres. Under their direction a bonanza-type operation was established; but, after a few less than satisfactory years, land was sold to incoming settlers. The Cooperstown area today is surrounded by great numbers of the descendants of this Cooper venture. Part of the Cooper enterprise was the "St. Clair Settlement," which was home to sixty settlers, most of whom came in 1882 from the vicinity of St. Clair, Michigan.

Though they were often the first arrivals and were numerous in the first decades of settlement, Anglo-Americans departed from the region rapidly; and a more "foreign" type of settler took their places. Nevertheless, many of the eventual business and political leaders of North Dakota proved to be individuals whose roots went back to these first American land seekers.

The religious needs of the Anglo-Americans were, in most cases, taken care of by churches of American derivation. The Congregational church established many congregations. In newly founded Cooperstown, Congregationalists as early as 1884 gathered to plan a church organization. More aggressive and more practiced in the frontier religion of America were the Methodists. In Cavalier the first Methodist organization dates to 1880. Traveling missionaries gathered Methodists for worship in Grand Forks as early as 1871. They were active in Caledonia in 1874. Presbyterian church groups, too, were organizing wherever English-speaking people settled; dozens of congregations sprang up in the 1880's. Incoming Anglo-Americans often affiliated with the Episcopal Church. By 1884, churches of this denomination were already established in Forest River, Grafton, Larimore, and Mayville. St. Paul's Church in Grand Forks was by that time a thriving institution.

The English language denominations expanded with rapidity during the first years of homesteading. A surprising number — too many, in fact — of churches, parsonages, manses and rectories were built. Apparently, many local congregations received subsidies from "Mission Aid" organizations affiliated with their parent church headquarters. Because the English-speaking citizens tended to be the more affluent members of the community, a certain amount of initial local money was thereby, available. The English-language people were also the most prone to move away; in every local history a sad note marks the reference to many of their churches: "The members moved away." "The services were discontinued."

There were, however, other institutions of group interest. The Masonic Lodge, and, to a lesser extent, associations such as the Woodmen and the Odd Fellows sprang up in little villages, giving Anglo-American men outlets for their social needs and also "ethnic" identification centers. American women frequently established female counterparts such as the Order of the Eastern Star. In almost every settlement some women of American background affiliated with the Women's Christian Temperance Union. Less-formal types of literary and music clubs were an inevitable part of village life.

In retrospect, the early Anglo-American families seem to have been remarkably independent. Unlike their immigrant neighbors, they seldom lived in intensely ethnic clusters. For them, the world was full of opportunity. The "Yankees" realized that they were "true Americans." Their social institutions were not places of refuge but were often status organizations. Their clubs and even their religious groups separated the "Americans" from the "foreigners." In describing this class of people, the *Cooperstown Diamond Jubilee Book* said that their "eastern or English attitude has kept this group fairly distinct until the second Dakota generation."

ANGLO-ONTARIANS

Development of the Canadian West brought the Red River into prominence before settlers seriously thought of farming in Dakota. To move men and materials from Ontario to the Canadian frontiers in any quantity required the avoidance of the difficult lake and marsh terrain north of the Great Lakes and necessitated a trip through the United States via St. Paul. Initially, a wagon route carried assorted commerce from St. Paul to lower Red River ports such as Breckenridge and Abercrombie; from these villages stages and steamboats moved cargo northward to Ft. Garry. The first steamboat on the Red was launched in 1859. Later railroad construction allowed traffic to move directly from St. Paul to Moorhead and to Fisher's Landing, between Crookston and Grand Forks.

The Red River could, in some respects, have been called a Canadian waterway during the several decades preceding American homestead settlement. The North West and the Hudson's Bay companies had been operating along the river since the time of Alexander Henry, and for decades the Red River carts had traversed its length. Eventually, in the 1860's and 1870's, river outposts — clusters of primitive cabins a dozen miles apart — grew up between Georgetown and Pembina. These facilitated movement, supplied fuel, provided lodging, and assisted in the transportation of mail and freight. Caledonia, at the confluence of the Goose and the Red rivers in Traill County, came into being in 1871. Frog Point in northeastern Traill County and Quincy on the Elm River in southern Traill grew up at the same time. In Grand Forks County, the Grand Forks Station and the Turtle River Station were set up. In the Walsh County area, Rose Point (Acton) was established in 1871. Bowesmont in Pembina County was founded a few years later. Through these and other ports, river and stage traffic moved with regularity from Abercrombie, north to Winnipeg. The decade of the 1870's proved to be the boom period of river traffic. After railroad construction finally reached Winnipeg in 1879, boat traffic and river towns declined.

The Canadian public was, therefore, not unfamiliar with the Red River of the North. It had been in the "news" for several generations; "Pembina" and "Dakota" were terms in common usage. When in the 1870's Canadian citizens began moving westward to Manitoba's "homestead" lands, the settlers' journeys necessarily took them westward by way of the American railway system and ultimately through the Dakota-Minnesota portion of the Red River. It was not surprising, then, that some prospective Canadian prairie settlers should choose to take up American land rather than continue all the way north into the unknown hardships of the Canadian West. American railroad agents were active in Ontario at the time; they, too, often encouraged the choice of Dakota land. Yankee land agents were likewise present along the Red River route, trying to divert land seekers to American homesteads — to "kidnap" them, Canadian officials said. As a result, the northern Red River Valley, in both Minnesota and North Dakota, numbers among its present residents a great many citizens who have Canadian pasts.

Though some few Canadians came from English-speaking parts of Quebec and a small number were from the Maritimes, the great majority (ninety-five percent, if one were to guess) came from Ontario, which was the most "western" of all the older provinces. Among the Ontarians, people of British, Scotch, and Scotch-Irish background predominated, though often they were accompanied to Dakota by Catholic Irish. For simplicity's sake, since they intermingled freely, in this volume they will be classified (with apologies to the Irish) as Anglo-Ontarians.

It came about, therefore, that many of the very first English speaking settlers in the early Red River towns were of Canadian background. For example, around Caledonia, Walter Traill of the Hudson's Bay Company and George Weston of England took up the first land in present Traill County in 1870. So, also, in 1871 Antoine Girard from Acton, Ontario, was the first settler in Acton,

Walsh County. Every township along the Red and its tributaries in northeastern North Dakota numbered Ontario people among its original homesteaders. George Inkster settled the Inkster area in 1878, having come previously from Canada. In Walsh and Pembina counties, large-scale Ontario settlement took place. Drayton was founded by a group of settlers from Drayton, Ontario, in 1878. Levant Township in Grand Forks County was settled by people from Levant, Ontario. Perth, in Grand Forks County, was named after the Perth district of Canada. In Walsh County, Ardoch received its name from Ardoch, Ontario; Minto, from an Ontario town of the same name. Early Pembina County villages such as Carlisle, Hamilton, Joliette, McConnell, and St. Thomas were named after Canadian prototypes. Township names throughout the northeastern counties reflect much of the same origins.

Speaking English and being acquainted with Anglo-Saxon law and tradition, the Anglo-Ontarians had a special advantage. They mingled with ease among the

arriving Yankees, quickly moved into politics and business, and showed up almost immediately in leading territorial positions. The North Dakota Constitutional Convention saw almost a dozen delegates of Canadian background among its seventy-five specially elected members.

The spiritual needs of many of the Ontario people were taken care of by the Presbyterian Church. Scottish pioneers, in particular, were loyal to this religious tradition. Presbyterian groups organized along the Red River at Kelso, Quincy, and Grand Forks in the 1870's. At Pembina the first Presbyterian church building north of Bismarck and Fargo was erected in 1879. Early congregations were at the Forest River and the Turtle River in 1879. Presbyterian groups sprang up wherever the Anglo-Americans and Anglo-Ontarians settled: Minto, Bathgate, Neche, Arvilla, Grafton, Ardoch, Hillsboro. In 1885 the Pembina Presbytery, a Presbyterian jurisdictional division, numbered thirty-three congregations in the northern portion of Dakota.

The Methodist Church was affected also by this influx of Canadian settlers. Grand Forks saw its first Methodist Church in 1873. The Drayton Methodist Church was organized largely by Ontario people in 1879, and this church became central to Methodist affairs in the northeastern part of the state. Crystal, Thompson, Neche, and Devils Lake congregations were organized in the first part of the 1880's; these, too, served both American and Ontarian settlers.

Episcopal Church organizations also grew up, influenced somewhat by Canadian activities. Church authorities in Winnipeg urged the Episcopal clergymen of Emerson to conduct services over the line in Pembina in 1872. By 1875 occasional services were held in Grand Forks. The St. Paul's Parish in that city was organized in 1880. Within the next several years, Episcopal groups at Grafton, Larimore, Mayville, Forest River, Bathgate, and Devils Lake were organized into mission type congregations.

Robert and Wynona Wilkins in their Bicentennial History, *North Dakota,* say that by 1879 Canadians were so numerous in the region north of Grand Forks that more Canadian than American money was in use. The Grand Forks newspaper printed regular articles from London, Ottawa, and Toronto (Canadian) newspapers.

The Masonic Lodge was a social gathering place for American and, in particular, Canadian men of the times. A Pembina lodge was established under Canadian auspices in 1863. The Grand Forks lodge was organized in 1880, and at Hillsboro a lodge began in 1882. Lodges grew in dozens of towns throughout the region in the first two decades of settlement.

People of British Isles background, whether from Canada or the United States, were exceptional in that they felt fully at home in the Dakota territory. This was *their* land. They were not immigrants, but rather "old residents" moving into a new portion of America. Unlike the non-British settlers, they saw no desperate need for rallying points which would provide a protective institution in the new world. With them, church affiliation, most likely, sprang from the desire for religious meaning and less from ethnic identification needs. Lodge membership arose, likewise, from the desire to have a social outlet, rather than from a need for nationality reinforcement. Yet, an ethnic motive was probably present to a limited extent in that the church and the lodge gave the American and Ontarian settlers a sense of their "separateness." It allowed them to move among their own and to remind themselves and others that they were not "foreigners," but were of the old respected pioneer stock. Status, rather than ethnic protection, seemed to motivate their institutional arrangements.

Anglo-Ontarians in the northeastern part of North Dakota declined in numbers after the 1890's. Some left the area in search of better educational opportunities. Most went to some kind of urban life, and a few second-generation individuals went farther west to acquire new farmsteads. Their land, and that of their Anglo-American and Irish neighbors, was taken up eagerly by the local farmers of immigrant background whose limited options required that they remain on the prairies. Accordingly, the institutions of English-speaking people declined in rates far greater than those of their counterparts in other national groups.

Nevertheless, Anglo-Ontarians are still present in great numbers, particularly in certain regions of Pembina, Walsh, and Cavalier counties. In at least a half dozen townships the majority of the residents still trace their ancestry to Canada. In addition, Grand Forks, Traill, and Cass counties on the Red River, along with Towner, Rolette, and Bottineau counties on the Canadian border, contain hundreds of farm families of Canadian origin. The cluster of remaining Ontario farmers in Pembina, Walsh, and Cavalier counties is the largest settlement of its kind in North Dakota; indeed, this type of settlement is rare in central and western United States. Proportionately, forty percent of the rural residents in Pembina and Cavalier counties are of Anglo-Ontarian background.

In northeastern North Dakota a few signs of Scotland, England, and New England are still evident. Curling rinks, some organized as early as 1900, enliven small towns in the winter; and their teams compete internationally. Through much of the state, faded signs on buildings say "Opera House," and sometimes old newspapers mention a village racetrack or Chautauqua hall which once entertained and enlightened the local gentry. In Walsh County a British Isles Society meets regularly at Grafton. Its members hear the poetry and ballads of the past on two special occasions, Robert Burns' birthday and St. Patrick's Day.

BELGIANS

In 1880 some few Belgian settlers came to an area south of Joliette in Pembina County. Others joined them, and what could be called a Belgian settlement sprang up on the prairies. Their farms were scattered over a relatively wide area, and French and Anglo-Ontarian settlers were interspersed throughout the entire community. At least a dozen families were known to have been in the area. Less than half that number are present today.

BOHEMIANS

The largest Bohemian settlement in North Dakota is found in Walsh County, beginning near Minto and extending westward almost to Lawton in Ramsey County. A handful of first settlers came to what is now the Veseleyville area in 1880; they were joined soon afterwards by a large number of landseekers from the well-known Bohemian community at Spillville, Iowa. Other Iowa Bohemians (with an occasional Moravian and Slovak) came shortly afterwards, taking land in the Pisek area. In 1883 other newcomers founded the Bechyne settlement in Perth Township. Fellow countrymen arrived from New Prague, Montgomery, Heidelberg, Veseli and Owatonna in Minnesota, during early settlement days. A few years later, coming from some of the same southern Minnesota towns and also from the eastern seaboard, a number of Bohemian farmers took up land farther east in Shepherd Township.

With the arrival of the railroads, the towns of Pisek (1887) and Lankin (1905) became centers of Bohemian population, causing the original "inland" settlement clusters to lose their attractiveness. In each of the above towns, Catholic churches were founded which are active today. Veseleyville had St. Luke's Church, which was built in 1880. SS. Peter and Paul's Church in Bechyne was erected in 1886. St. John the Nepomucene Church of Pisek was built in 1886, and the St. Joseph's Church of Lankin was organized in 1906. A church in nearby Conway served Bohemians and Catholics of a variety of other national groups. Bohemians in the far western part of the county erected a rural church at Lomice in Section 24 of Shepherd Township in 1934.

There was a tension in Czech communities throughout most of the Dakotas between settlers of a "free thinker" background and those of a more active religious persuasion. Bohemian lodges, originally called the Czech Benevolent Society (CSPS) and later the ZCBJ (Západni Česka Bratrská Jednota), were founded at Conway in 1897, at Veseleyville in 1898, at Pisek in 1899, and at the rural Lawton community (Kosobud) in 1901. A few years later the same organizations were formed in Sauter and Shepherd townships. These lodges, each with its own social hall, were not only national centers, but also buried their dead, had educational and mutual support programs, and generally emphasized progress and freedom from religious restraint.

Local chapters of a rival religious organization, the Catholic Workmen's Lodge, were also set up. Pisek built its first Workmen's Hall in 1897; a second structure was erected in 1947. Veseleyville organized a Catholic Workmen's Society in 1896. Lomice organized one in 1902. Bechyne had a similar lodge in its early days. This division of ethnic focal points is characteristic of most Bohemian settlements in North Dakota and through much of the United States. The free-thinking tradition, going back to national and religious controversies which arose in the days of Huss, continued until recent times. Today, however, many religious-minded Czechs have memberships in an insurance oriented descendant of the ZCBJ organization, namely the Western Fraternal Life Association.

Likewise, the children of the many non-religious Czechs are practicing members of local Catholic or Protestant churches.

A much smaller group of Bohemians settled on farms a few miles south of the tiny village of Dresden in Cavalier County. These homesteaders — at least a dozen initial families — came from the Walsh County Bohemian community and from several midwestern states. No lodge seems to have been established; rather, the Dresden Catholic Church became the center of their social and religious life. They mixed with parishioners of other nationalities, and their traditional culture did not prevail. Bohemian families are still present in the Dresden area.

DANES

Present-day Willow Lake Township in southwestern Steele County is made up predominately of farmers of Danish extraction. These families are the great-grandchildren of a larger number of Danish settlers who came to the area of 1882. Apparently, they arrived in response to the advertising of the Red River Land Company, which had purchased railroad property and was offering it for sale at attractive rates. In 1902 a Danish Brotherhood Lodge was organized in the township. A Danish Lutheran Church was probably established at about the same time.

The Danes were not as aggressive as their Scandinavian neighbors, the Norwegians, who now own much of the land settled by the first Steele County Danish farmers. In addition, Norwegian farms surround the Danish pocket on every side.

A small Grand Forks County Danish community developed in 1903, when a group of settlers took up land in and around Moraine Township. This was a "second wave" kind of settlement, in which disillusioned first arrivals sold their land to incoming families. Contemporaries called the arrival of the new group the "Danish invasion." A pastor's house was built soon after their arrival, and the church congregation, which took the name Bethania, affiliated with the Danish Evangelical Lutheran Church of America. Sparsity of members and lack of internal loyalty caused the membership to remain small. After 1918 the congregation was served by non-resident ministers, but formal activities ended and members eventually joined local churches of Norwegian background. Danish descendants are still numerous in an area which starts in Moraine Township and extends into townships to the north and to the east.

DUNKERS (Brethren)

A surprisingly large migration of Dunkards, more properly called Brethren, came to North Dakota in the mid-1890's. Encouraged especially by Great Northern Railroad promotional activities, they established at least twenty colonies around the state. Frugal and industrious, these settlers were from midwestern states and were considered excellent candidates for prairie homestead life. Of German background, they were a highly visible people, the women having sun bonnets, the men having beards, and all having an exceptionally plain manner of dress.

At an earlier date, however, in 1885, what must have been North Dakota's first colony of Dunkards settled on farms south and southwest of Mayville in Norman Township, Traill County. Reports say they numbered about fifteen families and were brought to the area not by the railroad but through the efforts of the Grandin and Edwards real-estate firm. The colony built a church and survived for some twenty-five years; in 1900, forty-eight individuals were on its membership roll. In 1910 the church was no longer mentioned in Brethren official lists; most of its former members are said to have emigrated to Canada.

Cando, in Towner County, was the center of many later railroad Dunkard colonies which spread in every direction from that city. It was the hub of at least eight "daughter colonies," two of which were in Ramsey County. The Sweetwater Lake Congregation, north of Devils Lake, began in 1895 and had as high as eighty-five members in 1896. (Sixty were said to have come from Missouri.) By 1900 the community was in serious decline as members moved away and local disputes took their toll. Within a few years, activities ended completely.

A Salem Church was established in Klingstrup Township, Ramsey County, about eighteen miles east of Cando in 1899. A church was built in 1900, and membership in 1912 was recorded at 140; but here, too, numbers declined rapidly as members moved away. In 1930 the congregation was disbanded; only a cemetery remains. As elsewhere the Dunkard or Brethren settlers did not measure up to the full expectations of the railroad promoters. Perhaps their long acquaintance with American ways and the English language allowed them to move to "better places" when times became difficult. In contrast, the European immigrant homesteaders were forced to remain on their farm plots; their settlements proved to be more durable.

FINLANDERS

Pelto is a small community on the Soo Line located within Enterprise Township in northern Nelson County. This was the center of a small but very cohesive Finnish colony which was located primarily in Clara and Enterprise townships. The name "Pelto" is of Finnish origin; it is, in fact, a shortened version of the name of a farmer who lived nearby. The original settlers came in 1886 and centered their lives around the Prairie Blossom hall and the Finnish Evangelical Lutheran Church (established in 1899). The "Finn Hall," as it was called, featured a regular series of dances, plays, band concerts, and vaudeville performances. A kind of "free-thinking" and progressive atmosphere surrounded the place. The church, however, was the center of life for another portion of the community — those who rejected such entertainment and emphasized more religious-oriented activities. With the coming of the railroad, the hall was moved one-half mile southeast to the new Pelto townsite. Today, most of the original families have left. A cemetery still remains a mile and a half north of Pelto. Norwegian farmers now live interspersed with the descendants of the first Finnish settlers.

A few miles to the northwest of the Pelto community, a second collection of Finnish farmers live today on the edge of Ramsey County between Brocket and Lawton. This group is probably part of the original Pelto community.

FRENCH

A French gentleman, born on the Canadian frontier, may have been the first *bona fide* farmer in North Dakota. Charles Bottineau came in 1859 to the St. Joseph's (Walhalla) settlement in Pembina County to trade in furs. Seeing an opportunity for supplying food to the Canadian Red River settlers and the local employees of fur-trading posts, he hired Métis laborers and produced wheat, mutton, beef, and vegetables. Well before 1870, Bottineau had over one hundred acres of grain in production. His farm is said to have been several miles south of Leroy, not far from the Pembina River.

In the 1850's and the 1860's a few French-Canadians seem to have lived on the land near Pembina, Leroy (St. Joseph), Walhalla and modern-day Neche. (The area, of course, had many Metis people.) These French settlers were not agriculturalists in the strict sense. They were subsistence farmers; the Red River carts, the fur trade and the buffalo hunts continued to dominate their life expectations. Mobility was still central to their culture, and the permanence of full-time farming was alien to their thoughts. But even if they had desired such a thing, a stable farm life would have been difficult. Extensive agriculture was impossible since farm implements were in short supply. Also, French-Canadian women in the West were too scarce to lend a stabilizing family influence. Travel between Quebec and the Red River at that time was exceedingly difficult; only the hardiest of individuals would set out on the journey.

These earliest of French residents took land, as one might expect, adjacent to the Pembina River and occasionally to the Tongue and Red rivers. In sheltered areas, they with their Métis neighbors, cut wood and produced food for the trading posts and the Red River settlements. Father George Belcourt set up a flour mill in Walhalla at a remarkably early date (1856) to serve the needs of both the French and the Métis in the area.

The Assumption Catholic parish in Pembina, which dates back to 1818, served the needs of the Métis, the fur traders, and the later French-Canadian homesteaders. The Leroy Parish (1873), the earlier Walhalla church (1846), and the Neche church (1884), staffed by French-Canadian priests, were (and still are) centers of local French community life.

Sometime around 1870 a change took place. French-Canadian farmers (families and individuals) began arriving in the northern Red River Valley in considerable numbers. By this time a railroad route through the United States had made St. Paul, Minnesota, a terminal for western expansion. The Red River was well known to the Quebec populace, for the *voyageurs* had been returning from that region for several generations. French families in the 1870's began to consider seriously the idea of western settlement; and they were thinking not of small garden plots, but of permanent commercial-sized enterprises.

The French land seekers eventually set up colonies not only in the Pembina region, but also along the eastern edge of Walsh County, in northwestern Minnesota (Red Lake Falls), and in places farther north along the Red River (*e.g.*, Letellier and St. Jean Baptist). In fact, the Manitoba St. Boniface French community is made up primarily of the descendants of French agriculturalists who arrived during the 1870's and 1880's.

The Quebec-French settlers mingled rather easily with the earlier Métis families: both groups were Catholic and worshiped in the same church building; both could converse in the various French dialects. There were social barriers, however, and a class difference emerged, for, even though the two cultures had much in common, there were decided differences: the rough and tumble frontier life of native background versus the stable village life of the more sophisticated Quebec countryside.

The settlement patterns were often similar. Both groups avoided the more remote empty prairie, but rather chose to settle where a combination of water, woodland and prairie was available. In the very early settlements some parcels of land along the northern portion of the Red River were laid out in the typical "long lot" French design; starting at the water line, the land holdings stretched back in a narrow fashion through the trees to the open prairie.

Olga, near the South Pembina River, is a French settlement a dozen miles southwest of Walhalla. It was established by farmers who came to Dakota in 1882 after flood waters interrupted their earlier colony in Manitoba. A French priest led the movement to the United States and became Olga's first pastor. Olga can be considered an extension of the chain of Pembina River French villages; it claims to be the oldest town in Cavalier County. A log cabin church called *Notre Dame du Sacre Coeur*, built on the prairie above the rough terrain which marks the edge of the Red River Valley, was the initial community center. The little church, soon replaced by a larger frame structure, served the needs of the first French homesteaders, but it also became the religious center for the Metis who resided in the Pembina Hills to the east and north of the village. Within three years after its establishment, the parish is said to have numbered three hundred families. Nuns of French background taught in the local public school for several decades, beginning in 1914. In 1917 another frame church was built, which was destroyed by fire after five years. A more permanent ediface was later erected which exists today. Though greatly reduced in numbers, the descendants of the early French and Metis families still make up the Olga Catholic parish.

A small group of French families settled on farms south of Merrifield in Allendale and Walle townships in Grand Forks County. Another small cluster of families took land five miles west of Grand Forks in Blooming and Rye townships. These "French settlements" came about when a number of families of French (ultimately Quebec) origin came from the Hamel, Minnesota, area and from Massachusetts. Early arrivals homesteaded first in the mid-1870's. Their descendants are present today. No churches were erected in the settlements, but priests from Grand Forks often visited the two communities. Catholic services were held in Merrifield farm homes as early as 1877.

Oakwood Village, Walsh County, is the center of a French community which takes up the eastern half of Oakwood Township and the western portion of Acton Township. Its first French settler arrived in 1874, to be followed by others who came by wagon, oxcart and rail at the end of the decade. All the early arrivals were of Quebec French derivation, though some few had spent time in Minnesota prior to moving to Dakota. In 1881 a French priest from St. Boniface, Manitoba, assisted in building the Sacred Heart Church which formed the nucleus of the Oakwood community. In 1906, French nuns opened a day and boarding school which eventually included both grade and high school levels of education. The French language and tradition continued until the 1930's; French was part of the curriculum until the institution closed in 1967.

In perspective, North Dakota's French settlers, when compared to other national groups, seem to have been less aggressive in the acquisition of new land. They were frequently the very first to arrive and could have obtained large acreages; but they did not do so. The outlines of the earlier French settlements (Wild Rice, Oakwood) appear to be much the same as they were at the turn of the century; later settlements (Belfield, Little Fargo) have diminished considerably. French ambitions in agriculture were quite modest.

FRENCH-INDIANS (Métis)

The first agriculturally-oriented settlers in the northeastern part of the state, at least in recorded history, seem to have been the Métis — a people of mixed French and Indian background who settled around Pembina. Métis hunters planted gardens in the Pembina area as they sought to supplement the foods which were generally obtained from their buffalo hunts. Father Joseph Provencher, describing conditions around Pembina in a letter to Bishop Plessis in 1818, says: "The cultivated fields were not much larger than garden beds." Later in the century, turmoil in Canada, the scarcity of furs, and the decline of the buffalo hunts led growing numbers of Métis to squat on land in the vicinity of Pembina, along the Pembina River near Neche, around St. Joseph, and as far west as Walhalla. The Métis being a mobile people, their cabin sites were tiny plots scattered in irregular fashion where woods, water, and a bit of prairie could be found. In 1854, Father George Belcourt journeyed to Washington, D.C., to petition congress (unsuccessfully) to purchase land on "each side of the Red River" so that the "half-breeds might have a foedal [sic] right to each of the lots."

The 1850 Minnesota Territorial Census for Pembina County (which involved the northern half of present day North Dakota, but really meant the Pembina settlement area) classified only three individuals as farmers; great numbers of men were listed as "hunters." But even the hunters had families; and it seems that they, too, had their own special houses and garden plots. At least one Métis leader eventually went into farming in a relatively large way; Clement A. Lounsberry's *Early History of North Dakota* says Antoine Gingras had sixty acres in cultivation at Leroy in 1870.

Métis people lived in a semi-permanent manner elsewhere in the northern valley. They did, however, tend to gravitate to areas near the trading posts: the Kittson and Gingras posts at Pembina and Walhalla, but also at Georgetown and other river outposts.

Their religious needs were the concern of Canadian church authorities who had previously ministered to them for almost a century. The St. Boniface bishop sent priests from Manitoba as far south as Lake Traverse and west to the Turtle Mountains. Pembina already had a church for local Métis in 1818; a school was set up within the next decade. Father George Belcourt established the St. Joseph Mission at Walhalla in 1853 and soon afterward erected a school and church. An 1854 church directory says there were over 1500 people, mostly "half-breeds," attached to the Pembina parish.

In the 1850's and 1860's Métis individuals and families were to be found living along much of the Red River Valley. The Holy Cross Mission, near Ft. Abercrombie, was begun in the latter part of the 1860's in an attempt to take care of Catholic residents who were "primarily soldiers and half-breeds." By 1872 missionaries from Pembina (ultimately from St. Boniface) were conducting religious services for the French-Indian people who lived along the Red River at Grand Forks.

Land maps of 1893 indicate dozens of Métis families and individuals living on the land in Pembina County (interspersed with more recent arrivals, the Quebec French) in an area along both sides of the Pembina River from Pembina village to Neche, and from Leroy to Walhalla. In both areas, the Métis and French farm sites extended two to three miles outward from the river. In their midst, however, were the newly established farmsteads of people of British Isles (Ontario) backgrounds. In 1965 the identifiable Pembina County Métis farms were few in number, while the Quebec French had persisted. The portion of the Pembina River from Leroy to Walhalla is still French, so also the region immediately west of Pembina in Pembina Township. Few, if any, French are found along the river in present day Neche Township. Métis families are present in the area, but their land parcels are small and represent, in effect, village working families who live on rural house lots. Most of the Métis descendants now live in local towns such as Walhalla, Neche, and Leroy, and in larger cities like Grand Forks. The arrival of the non-French people with their survey procedures and homesteading requirements sounded the

death toll for most of the Métis settlers along the entire Red River. As a sort of epitaph, a Neche history book says the following: "Special mention should be made of the mixed-breed families who lived in the area long before the 1870's. Some of these people did take up title to land by exercising their pre-emption rights. . .It wasn't long, however, before they sold out to the settlers."

GERMAN (Reichsdeutsch)

Several very early Germans are said to have settled in Eldorado Township in Traill County on the Goose River in 1870. A scattered few arrived the next year. By 1875 a German-speaking Norwegian minister was visiting and preaching to some of these German families in their farm homes. In 1879 the initial members of what was to be a larger group of Germans took land in Bohnsack Township in southcentral Traill County. The St. John's German Lutheran Church was organized on the Elm River, and the Immanuel German congregation was founded on the Goose River northeast of Hillsboro. Both rural congregations built churches before the turn of the century and continued as active groups until 1947, when they merged and moved into the town of Hillsboro; both early congregations affiliated with the Missouri Synod. The German areas are intact today.

Farther north in Walsh County the river town of Acton saw a few German settlers arrive in 1879. A Lutheran congregation was organized in 1887, and this group worshipped in the Acton Public School building until a church was built in 1890. Missouri Synod German Lutherans still live in the Acton Township. In the mid-1930's, the church was moved to Grafton.

A large and cohesive group of Germans are present in the southcentral portion of Pembina County, especially in Lodema, Elora, St. Thomas, and to some extent in several adjacent townships. The earliest Germans among them are said to have come in 1880 from Iowa, Minnesota, Wisconsin, and Michigan; though some apparently came directly from Germany. Two rural German Lutheran congregations (Missouri Synod) grew up to serve them. The settlers in the eastern portion of the enclave formed the St. Paul's Church, four miles north and four miles west of St. Thomas, on Section 18 of St. Thomas Township; the Germans to the west set up St. John's Church, located three miles northeast of Crystal on Section 9 of Elora Township. These two country parishes began in 1882 when a pastor from Traill County gathered people together for periodic home worship. The St. Paul's congregation erected a small frame church in 1883 and a second larger church in 1889; the present modern structure dates to 1951. The St. John's community of rural Crystal erected its church in 1891. Both congregations are active today, and they share the services of one pastor. Both are located on their original church sites.

In 1947, the Our Savior's congregation in Cavalier was organized. This church is now the religious home of the farmers in the more northern part of the German area.

The two original congregations showed an intense concern for education. The St. Paul's families set up a parochial school in the mid-1890's, which continued for at least a generation. Enrollment reached as high as fifty students, and the classes stretched on for a full nine-month term. The rural Crystal Church also had a parochial school in the early years of this century.

Early Pembina County was a mosaic of national groups, many of which came from Canada. Great numbers of French, Scotch, Irish, and English were "coming down from the north." Actually, their route was a bit more indirect; most of them came from Canada by way of the American transportation system. Some Germans were part of this influx of land seekers. Northern Cavalier and Hamilton townships saw the arrival of what locals called the "Canada Dutch" in 1878 (perhaps in 1875). These German speaking farmers came particularly from the vicinity of Dashwood and Zurich, Ontario. They set up a little Zion Evangelical Church about one and one-half miles east of Cavalier; the congregation later affiliated with the Evangelical United Brethren tradition. By 1940 the church had closed its doors, when its membership merged with a sister church in Cavalier.

As early as 1881, a number of German Protestant land-seekers came to Union Township northwest of Reynolds in Grand Forks County. Their first church services were held in homes in 1882, and during that year the German Evangelical Congregation was organized. Most of the settlers who came throughout the decade were Germans from Wisconsin; some were Civil War veterans. The rural Holmes Church, as it was called, continues today, having once been affiliated with the Evangelical United Brethren and, more recently, with the United Methodist Tradition.

East of the Holmes German community a number of German Catholic farmers arrived in 1882 and took up land along with the earlier Irish and Anglo-American settlers. Some Germans and many non-Germans came from Michigan; the township still bears that name. The Catholic Germans joined the non-Germans in establishing Catholic parishes in nearby Reynolds (building a church about 1887) and in Thompson (St. Jude's Church, built in 1891). Many of these first German Catholics had lived in the United States for some years, and their two churches reflected little of the German culture. Instead, Irish priests attended their needs, and national traditions declined rapidly.

In 1884 a group of six German Catholic families and a few unmarried friends came to Cavalier County from Bruce County, Ontario. They founded the Mount Carmel community, which extends throughout Mount Carmel Township, westward through Dresden Township, and south almost to Langdon. Immigration continued, particularly from the Ontario towns of Formose and Mildmay. By 1887 some sixty-five German Catholics were present, and Catholic services were being conducted regularly in log houses on the banks of the South Pembina River. In 1889, the Mount Carmel Church was built; a resident priest served this congregation and the Holy Trinity Church at Dresden, which was erected in

1898. German Catholic settlers came not only from Canada but, through the encouragement of a German priest, from Stearns County, Minnesota, and other eastern states. An occasional German-Russian family joined the settlement. Their descendants live in the same area, and the German community still flourishes.

Also in Cavalier County, a decade later, a group of Catholic Germans took up a good part of the southwestern townships of Trier and Sievart. Their settlement extended southward into Ramsey County, and in an intermittent fashion towards Bisbee and Cando. German immigrants from Stearns County, Minnesota, were particularly in this later settlement activity; and they, like the Mount Carmel people, seemed to have come to the area through the advice of a German priest. Trier Township, where an original St. Boniface Church was erected in 1902, became a center for these German farm families. Priests with German Benedictine background served the local residents and also took care of Catholic congregations at Wales (church erected in 1900) and the later St. Boniface Church, which grew up in the new town of Calio in 1908.

East of Trier Township another group of Catholic Germans took up land after homesteading was complete. With the assistance of a local German banker, several dozen farmers came from St. Leo in Yellow Medicine County, Minnesota; they purchased land in the 1910's and centered their lives around St. Mary's Church (1916) in Munich.

The German Catholic areas persist today; the European origins of many of the first settlers are reflected in the names: Trier, Munich and Dresden.

Other Germans also came to Cavalier County. In the mid-1880's some German Lutheran families occupied land near the future town of Dresden. After several years in which traveling missionaries held religious services in various homes and even in a log granary, a formal congregation was begun in 1892; four years later the Immanuel Lutheran Church was erected a mile north of Dresden. This Missouri Synod congregation continued until 1956, when it merged with a Langdon Church. Other *Reichsdeutsch* homesteaders joined with the Volhynian Germans in South Dresden Township and established the St. John's Church a few miles northwest of Dresden; the first services took place in 1895, and the congregation is still active.

With the settlement of the Devils Lake vicinity, some Germans arrived from eastern states to take up land north and west of that city. A German Lutheran minister visited local farmers as early as 1887; organized services began in Grand Harbor in 1894, and a permanent Missouri Synod church began with the purchase of a Grand Harbor school building. A few miles to the northwest, another German Lutheran congregation started at Penn in the 1890's; a permanent pastor came in 1903. Both the Penn and Grand Harbor congregations continued at least until the 1960's.

A number of German families from midwestern states, particularly Iowa, moved into Griggs County from 1914 to 1917, especially in Kingsley and Clearfield townships. Early land company operations had brought Anglo-American land seekers to this Cooperstown region. The German "second wave" settlers represented a realignment as the American settlers moved away; Cooperstown still has concentrations of these pre-World War I Germans. This process of the replacement of early Anglo-Saxons by eastern-American-German farmers (occasionally Dutch, Norwegians, and others) took place throughout the first and second decades of the present century; almost every county in the eastern part of North Dakota saw some of this activity. Often individual farm families came, but sometimes whole groups made the transition to Dakota. By this late date, a need for ethnically centered religious or social institutions was at a minimum; the incoming farmers usually merged with the local citizenry.

More recently, in the 1930's, a government resettlement program brought German-Russians from central and eastern North Dakota into the land between Hillsboro and the Red River; these late-coming families stayed and many have become prosperous.

AUSTRIAN (GALICIAN) GERMANS

Between Langdon and Nekoma in Cavalier County there exists a collection of farmers whose origins are described variously as "Austria," "Galicia," and "Germany." The settlement extends over three townships; most are present in Perry, with some extending into Easby to the east and Loma to the west. The original families, some several dozen to begin with, were of German origin. Their ancestors moved to eastern Europe in the 18th century, into what was then the Austro-Hungarian Empire. They settled in that part of Galicia which is south of Lvov and north of the Carpathian Mountains, an area which centers around Kalusz, Dolina, and in particular, Stanislau. This part of the western Ukraine is now Soviet Russia, and earlier designations such as "Austria" are no longer meaningful.

Like so many other German groups in eastern Europe, their culture remained for the most part German; they were, in effect, an island of Germany in a Russian or Polish or Austrian world. In early North Dakota, however, their immediate past was at times evident, for some of their popular foods were clearly Ukrainian; *Borst, Holupsy,* and *Pedahayr.* They built, at first, not just sod houses or frame shanties, but very often adobe-type structures in the classic East European tradition.

The first settlers apparently came to Cavalier County from the Winnipeg area of Manitoba; they arrived during the mid-1890's. Later, other friends and family members came both from Canada and from eastern American states. No church or organization seems to have been founded which could serve the Galician farmers in an exclusive way; rather, being Catholic, they affiliated with the St. Alphonsus Church in Langdon. There, mingled with other nationalities, their religious and social needs were fulfilled. Perhaps the lack of an exclusive ethnic institution contributed to their rather rapid Americanization; their present-day descendants see themselves as

German in origin, but few are aware of the eastern European part of their heritage.

A second cluster of early Galician German families took up land in Pembina County. This group, Protestant in background, settled with other Germans in the northern portion of Joliette Township; they, too, mention Dolina in the western Ukraine as part of their past. A small German Evangelical Church (later Evangelical United Brethren) was a center of their life; this structure was at the railroad siding town of McArthur, six miles south of Pembina. Descendants of the German farmers remain, but the church is no longer present.

BOHEMIAN GERMANS

A number of Sudetenland Germans came to Griggs County and settled in Tyrol and Addie townships in the late 1880's. When the railroad was built from Cooperstown to McHenry in 1899, a greater number arrived. Mickelsdorf was the European home village for many of these families. Apparently, most of the first families had roots in the Bohemian-German settlement south of Casselton in Cass County. After working on farms in Cass County, they came north and purchased Griggs County railroad land. The town of Jessie became their social center. There they erected St. Laurenz Church in 1908. The church and the rural German community exist today.

GERMAN MENNONITES

Moscow, Henderson, and Gordon townships in Cavalier County are today inhabited predominately by farmers with a German-speaking Mennonite background. It appears that some of the original settlers, beginning in 1888, came from Russia by way of Manitoba; some came from the Freeman area of South Dakota, and some were from Minnesota and Nebraska. This collection of farm families make up the largest Mennonite settlement in North Dakota.

These were not colony people, but were families who lived separately on their individual farmsteads. The original farm homes were often of eastern European style; many were earthen structures with barn and house attached; some had thatched roofs and brick ovens.

The initial decades of settlement saw the erection of several open-country churches, including the Rosehill Church about six miles east and two miles north of Alsen, and the Bethel Church twelve miles west and south of Langdon. Alsen has the Swiss Mennonite Church; Munich, on the west edge of the Mennonite enclave, has the Salem Mennonite congregation; both date back to the first decade of this century. A slight division within the group is evident. The Rosehill Mennonites are affiliated with the Mennonite Brethren who have churches in German-Russian Mennonite areas such as Sawyer in Ward County, Harvey in Wells County, and McClusky in Sheridan County. The Salem, Swiss Mennonite, and Bethel churches are associated with the General Conference Mennonites, whose membership in North Dakota includes the Arena (Burleigh County) and Wolford (Pierce County) congregations. Though General Confer-

ence churches elsewhere in the state seem to have Mennonites of Pennsylvania origin among their memberships, the Cavalier County congregations are almost exclusively of German-Russian background. The cluster of settlements centers in Moscow Township, a name which reveals the home country of the first settlers.

The Rosehill Mennonite Brethren Congregation began in 1897 with a gathering of families who came by way of Minnesota and Nebraska. Its small church structure still serves the area as a place of worship. The Bethel congregation, which also began in 1897, built its frame church in 1899; services continued until the 1970's. The Salem Church at Munich counts among its members many people whose ancestors came from the German-Russian communities of Mountain Lake, Minnesota, and Henderson, Nebraska. The first arrivals came in 1898, and the Salem Church was built in 1906. The first members of the Swiss Mennonite congregation in Alsen came to the area in a less direct fashion. In 1898 an initial group of ten families left Freeman, South Dakota, and journeyed north by wagon to take up land near Starkweather in Ramsey County. There they formed the *Sweizer Mennonite Gemeinde* in 1904. In 1910-1911 they moved to the Alsen area and were finally able to build a church in 1919. This church is active today. Old-timers recall that the Swiss Church members spoke a dialect that differed substantially from the German which was in use in the other congregations. This may have been true initially, for a number of the earliest families traced their origins to Switzerland, hence the name Swiss Mennonite Church. All of the Swiss members have left the vicinity, and today's congregation is almost exclusively of Russian background.

A Mennonite Church of quite different orientation flourished for at least a generation on the east edge of the Mennonite enclave, ten miles west of Langdon. This small group of families, which was said to have come "mainly from Canada," wore beards and bonnets and had rather exclusive membership requirements. By the 1950's these Mennonites seem either to have moved elsewhere or to have been assimilated into the large mass of Mennonites. Today at least some descendants have affiliated with a recently established "strict" Mennonite church between Park River and Grafton.

GERMAN-RUSSIANS

A small group of German-Russians live south of Emerado in Grand Forks County in Chester, Pleasant View, and Fairfield townships. The original families came to the area from other North Dakota towns at the turn of the century, renting at first, but eventually buying their land. Their background was Protestant, and they were from the Black Sea region of the Ukraine. The Pleasant View German Evangelical congregation was organized in 1899. A church was built in 1913 and became a community focal point. Another group of Protestant German-Russians can be found in Cavalier County, southwest of Dresden in Minto and South Dresden townships. These people seem to be the descendants of a few families who came to the area after homestead days. No special ethnic center developed, for their numbers were small.

Some Catholic German-Russians came to the Ramsey County area north of Crary in the 1920's and the 1930's. In those decades German-Russian families were moving eastward from their Pierce County settlements, some working for the railroad in Devils Lake and others taking up land north and south of the railroad. A few of these late arrivals can be found scattered among non-Germans in an area ten and fifteen miles north of Lakota and Michigan. The group north of Crary, however, is the most numerous of the German settlers. These Ramsey County families looked to the Catholic Church in Crary as their religious center. There they joined with the remnants of the original Irish and Anglo-American settlers. Their ethnic heritage is minimal today.

VOLHYNIAN GERMANS

A group of Germans from eastern Europe occupies most of Felson Township in northcentral Pembina County. They seem to be, for the most part, descendants of Volhynian Germans who had settled in the border areas between Poland and the Ukraine. This frontier region, which switched back and forth between Russian and Polish jurisdictions, was the site of German colonists' settlements which began as early as 1801 and continued to increase in size throughout the nineteenth century. Apparently the first settlers in Pembina County had arrived in Winnipeg in 1895 and had obtained work on farms north of the border in the Gretna area. They later moved south to purchase American farms during the first decade of the present century.

The original Volhynian farmers were thus situated on both sides of the border. No rural church was erected; but, in keeping with their Lutheran background, these families organized a Christ Lutheran congregation in the town of Neche in 1908. This congregation sought to take care of the religious needs of the German settlers in both the Gretna and the Neche neighborhoods. In 1911 a church was built, and services in German continued through the first several generations. Pastors from the Manitoba Synod served the group until World War II, when allegiance switched to American religious affiliations. The congregation is active today. This is the larger of the two Volhynian German settlements in the state of North Dakota.

The other Volhynian group, some of whom came shortly before the turn of the century, settled a few miles north of Dresden in Cavalier County. These people, between fifteen and twenty families, also came from Canada; some were from the Gretna vicinity. A log structure served as the homesteaders' first place of worship. It was here in 1896 that a minister from Winnipeg began to hold services. In 1900 the St. John's Church was built four miles northwest of Dresden. It served both the Volhynians and other local Protestant Germans. The St. John's Church, like the Neche church, affiliated with the Manitoba Synod. The congregation is still active.

HOLLANDERS

Five Hollander families took up land in Dover Township, Griggs County, in the spring of 1914. They came from Fulton, Illinois, hoping to get a new start on farms vacated by earlier Anglo-American homesteaders. The original group was joined by other families, and a church building was begun in 1917. No regular minister lived in their midst; instead, elders of the community read the Sunday prayers in Dutch. A Reformed minister from Litchville would occasionally come to assist the congregation, but the church membership remained small. By 1963 the congregation no longer existed.

A small group of Hollanders, perhaps a dozen of Dutch Reformed background, moved from Iowa to Wheatfield Township in northcentral Grand Forks County in the 1910's. They erected a church on Section 26. The congregation was small, and it disbanded within a decade. The church building became a township school.

HUTTERITES

In 1949 a group of Hutterites came from Manitoba, Canada, to found the Forest River Colony in Inkster Township, Grand Forks County. An initial group of approximately one hundred adults and children began the settlement, and after a few years a second influx of members came especially from Paraguay. Within several years differences of lifestyles caused some departures, but those remaining continued the colony. The Hutterite families traced their origins to German-speaking parts of Europe. They, like so many other North Dakota Germans, came to North America after several generations of life in South Russia.

The Forest River community is organized along classic colony outlines. Their houses are clustered together; their property is held in common, and work assignments are clearly delineated. The colony's landholdings have increased in size to something over three thousand acres; and the community now flourishes, raising cattle, dairy herds, chickens, and geese. Eggs are produced which are distributed to stores throughout northeastern North Dakota. The colony now has its own school and conducts its own religious services.

ICELANDERS

The village of Mountain in Pembina County is the center of a sizable Icelandic community which includes almost all of Thingvalla, Gardar, and Akra townships and extends into Beaulieu Township. Some of the residents are found in South Olga and Montrose townships in Cavalier County. This collection of farms is probably the largest rural Icelandic community in the United States.

The history of this group begins in Canada in 1875, when settlers from Iceland took up homes along the west shore of Lake Winnipeg. They called their little colony "Gimli," the paradise in Icelandic mythology. Sickness, harsh physical conditions, and limited resources caused a number of the settlers to follow the advice of a young minister, Pall Thorlaksson, who suggested relocation in the United States. In June 1878, after a reconnaissance by local scouts, the first group of settlers came south to take up homesteads along the edge of the Red River Valley. Newcomers arrived from both Manitoba and Milwaukee, Wisconsin. Eventually three Icelandic towns grew up: Hallson, Gardar, and Mountain. In 1881, just three years after settlement, a local school district was established. Lutheran churches were organized in all three towns in the 1880's, and church buildings were erected within the next few years.

With the passage of time an American Icelandic Lutheran Synod developed, which drew together congregations throughout the upper Midwest. These small churches became social gathering places and helped perpetuate Icelandic traditions. Like some other Dakota immigrant groups, a "free thinking" movement was also present among the Pembina County residents; and this group set up a rival national center which was known as the Icelandic Unitarian Congregation. It was short lived, however, existing from 1895 to 1898; many of the adherents moved away.

A large room above a grocery store in Mountain was the setting during the 1880's and 1890's for frequent Icelandic lectures, dramatic events, and debates. In fact, Icelandic settlement life reflected a strong emphasis on the more "intellectual" sorts of national pursuits such as poetry and drama. A lending library and especially the school were of great importance. A debating society was organized in Mountain in 1886. A festival of regional interest is the Icelandic Independence Day on August 2nd, which has been celebrated at Mountain since settlement times. From the earliest days, Dakota men and women of Icelandic background attended universities in numbers far beyond their proportionate population size. Many became prominent state and national figures.

Today the Icelandic settlement contours match almost exactly the boundaries that can be seen on area maps of 1905 (see page 133).

IRISH

Land records throughout the entire northeastern section of the state almost invariably include Irish names among the very first homesteaders. The Irish came by two different routes. Some who were of American origin, journeyed from eastern states by way of Minnesota. Others, who were from Canada, traveled by way of the Great Lakes to Minnesota and thence by wagon, rail, or Red River steamboat to Dakota.

The Irish had an advantage in that they spoke English and were familiar with Anglo-Saxon ways before they arrived in America. Very often they were descendants of immigrants who had come to the United States in the 1840's during the Irish potato famine. Their familiarity with America allowed them to disperse acoss the plains in an easy manner, often with Anglo-American friends and neighbors. They found little reason to cluster into ethnic communities for mutual support. Their knowledge of America led them to view homesteading as a speculative venture; frequently, when their land titles were secure, they would sell their holdings and use the capital to set up small businesses such as hotels, saloons and dray services in local towns. Often they moved back to the larger American cities or continued farther west to more favorable climates and urban settings. For this reason it is almost impossible at present to find Irish settlements on the prairies.

Two exceptions, however, can be found in the northeastern portion of the state. Southeast of St. Thomas in

Pembina County a discernible cluster of Irish farmers remains. This small group, just a few miles outside of town, is the remnant of a great number of Irish who settled in that area in approximately 1880. The first arrivals erected the St. Thomas Catholic Church in 1886, having had religious services in farm homes for at least four years prior to that date.

Some few miles to the west, near the present village of Crystal in Crystal Township, another group of Irish farmers resides today. The St. Patrick's Congregation first met at Crystal in 1887. An Irish church had already been built at Stokesville, five miles west of Crystal, in 1888. Within a few years that church was closed and a permanent building, which is still an active religious center, was erected in the Crystal village.

One of the first non-French settlers in the northeastern part of the state was Michael Ferry, a man who in many ways typified the early Irish pioneers. Born in Ontario, Ferry came to the upper Red River Valley as a rodman with the St. Paul and Pacific railway engineering corps in 1868. After hunting and trapping for several months in Grand Forks County, he squatted on land along the Turtle River a year later. In 1874 near present-day Manvel he homesteaded in what is now known as Ferry Township. He was joined by a very large influx of Irish homesteaders who settled in nearby Turtle River and Levant townships. Though most of the original Irish settlers have departed, Turtle River Township to this day is almost half Irish; a large portion of Ferry Township is also of that national background.

Here and there in the state, old-time residents will point to parts of their country which once contained small, loosely-clustered groups of Irish farmers. One example is in Nelson County where a number of early Irish Catholic families settled a few miles northeast of Petersburg. Only a few of them remain today. Here, as elsewhere, the Irish found it easy to move to better surroundings.

JEWS

In Ramsey County, some twenty miles northeast of Devils Lake, a Jewish homestead colony was established in 1885. The location was east of Garske, centering in northern Cato and Harding townships, but also embracing the southern portions of Overland and Sullivan townships. Some Jews were also present in northeastern Webster Township. The term "Iola" (after a rural post office) has been used to describe this group; sometimes it is called "the Garske Colony." The settlement came about with the aid of Jewish agricultural agencies, which, at least during the initial years, assisted the farmers with low-cost loans. The colony was not an exclusive settlement, but rather a scattered series of farms interspersed among gentile farmers of various backgrounds. The major influx of Jewish homesteaders took place between the years 1887 and 1889; in all, over ninety adult Jewish men and women are known to have filed, in one way or another, on Burleigh County land. In one case, several cousins (or brothers) located their farmsteads on adjoining corners of their homestead acres; the resulting cross-

roads was known locally as "Little Palestine" or "Little Jerusalem."

The first Iola settlers were of eastern European background, speaking German or Russian. Some of them may have come from the Painted Woods settlement in Burleigh County, which had been established at an earlier date and which, by the late 1880's, was in a state of serious decline.

A rabbi traveled through the area to help with religious services. One may have been present on a full-time basis for a short time. A little cemetery was located on Section 27 of Sullivan Township. This cemetery was not in the middle but rather on the edge of the colony. Perhaps it was land available when the first colony deaths occurred and, thereafter, became the traditional burying place for people of Jewish faith. The cemetery remains as a weathered and lonely memorial to the struggles of dozens of pioneer families who once were in residence.

The Iola settlers were, in the main, ill-equipped to handle the harsh conditions of prairie frontier farming. This, coupled with bad weather and crop failure, caused many of them to leave the area as soon as their claims were "proved up" and they had learned English. After acquiring the cash sale price for their land, they moved to larger prairie towns (Devils Lake, Grand Forks, Fargo) or to more distant eastern or western American cities. Jewish farmers, at least a few, were active in Ramsey County until the mid-1920's. None remain today. Local opinion has it that they did very well after leaving the farms, and some became quite famous.

Other Jews were present in the northwest portion of the state, but never in such large numbers: instead, they were solitary business or farm families. Golden Lake in Steele County was named after a Mr. Golden who homesteaded nearby. Adler Township in Nelson County was named for an early Jewish pioneer who set up a hotel, blacksmith shop, and tavern on the trail between the Red River and Fort Totten in 1881. Soon, however, the arrival of a nearby railroad caused his businesses to decline. The settlement never flourished, but it was a post office for some time.

Jewish enterprisers were involved in the Wamduska speculative townsite on the edge of Stump Lake in the early 1880's. Hopes had arisen that the railroad would come through that region, and several business establishments were founded. The town was short lived and is now only a memory. Another speculative town, named Jerusalem, grew up nearby; a third was called Odessa. Neither seems to have had Jewish participation. All disappeared when possible railroad connections did not materialize.

MORAVIANS (Czech)

Though most North Dakota settlers of Czechoslovakian descent were Bohemian in background, an occasional Moravian or Slovakian farmer was found in the early Bohemian settlements. This was true of the Czech regions of Walsh and Richland counties. One cluster of early families, however, was almost completely Moravian in origin. A small group of Nebraska settlers of that background came to Prospect and Highland Center townships in Ramsey County in the 1910's. Their number was small, perhaps ten families; and no national church or lodge marked their presence. Rather, they affiliated with the Catholic parishes in Nekoma and Lawton. Edmore was their trade center. Their descendants still remain on the family farms.

NORWEGIANS

People of Norwegian background, without doubt, make up the largest number of rural residents in northeastern North Dakota. Traill County and Steele County, in the Red River Valley, share with Divide County, in the northwestern corner of the state, the honors of being the most Norwegian portions of North Dakota; the populations of all three counties are seventy percent or more of that nationality. Norwegians were not the earliest of settlers; the French-Indians, Anglo-Americans, Quebec-French, and perhaps even some Scots and Irish preceded them along the course of the northern Red River Valley. They were, however, the pioneer people in most of the Goose River regions and also along the Sheyenne. In fact, the Goose River can be called a Norwegian river, for the entire valley from Hillsboro through Mayville and beyond is populated almost exclusively by farmers with a Viking past. That term can also be applied to a large portion of the Sheyenne River, for the area from Luverne to Warwick is bounded by Norwegian farms on each side. In addition, the "lower" Sheyenne River is heavily Norwegian from Horace, in Cass County, through the northern parts of Richland County and from Fort Ransom north almost to Valley City. Over three-fourths of the Sheyenne Valley is peopled with the sons and daughters of Norway.

The junction of the Goose and the Red rivers was the location of Caledonia, an early Anglo-American trading village. Some Traill County farmland was taken up in that area in 1870. A year later, it seems, the first Norwegians arrived, setting up a colony along the river west of Hillsboro in Norway Township and farther west in Mayville Township. The Aal Lutheran congregation first met in local homes in 1872, and a church building was erected in the next decade. The Gran congregation, east of Mayville, was organized in 1873. Farther north the Red River town of Whynot in southeastern Grand Forks County had Norwegians in 1872. A Traill County Bruflat church came into existence at Portland in 1874.

Norwegian settlers moved quickly out along the Goose. In 1873 the first settlers were in Newburgh and Northwood townships near present-day Northwood in Grand Forks County. The Goose River Norwegian Evangelical Church (Hol Congregation) was organized on a local farmstead in 1874. Hol became a mother church for new congregations in Steele and Grand Forks counties. Within the next few years, as valley acreage was filled, Norwegians spilled out onto the flat land of the prairies. They were near Thompson in 1875. The Walle church group first met in that year. Fellow countrymen spread west along a Goose River tributary and settled in Beaver Creek Township, Steele County, in 1877. The

Little Forks congregation was organized eight miles southwest of Hatton in 1877. Norwegians were in the neighborhood of Lee on the Sheyenne River in Nelson County in 1880. Farther west on the same river, churches were founded in 1882 near McVille (New Luther Valley) and Pekin (Sheyenne Church). In the same year the Sigdal Congregation was organized in farm homes eight miles southeast of present-day Hamar.

As can be seen above, more than a dozen little country churches arose which served as focal points of Norwegian pioneer life. Local emphasis varied according to religious tradition — Haugean versus the more high-church orientation. Some churches reflected the region of origin in Norway — Hallingdal versus Telemark.

The newcomers might have been Norwegian in background, but they saw themselves as particular kinds of Norwegian. Their differing localities in Norway, separated by mountain ranges and water barriers, had given them special traditions which involved different dialects, clothes, and foods. Loyalty to these traditions led them, on occasion, to gather for special reunions. Thus, the Northwood area had a Selbu Lag convention in 1917, a Hadelands Lag convention in 1924, and at later dates a Halling Lag and a Nordhordlands Lag.

In the Northwood area, as in other Norwegian parts of eastern North Dakota, Norwegian parochial schools were set up in the summer time. During the school term, usually a month or six weeks, children were taught not only to read their catechisms, but also to spell and write in Norwegian. Many church congregations sponsored schools of this type until the late 1920's. Of more enduring influence was the Bruflat Academy, established at Portland in 1889. This parochial grade and high school became the alma mater of hundreds of second- and third-generation Norwegian-Americans.

A few Norwegian homesteaders settled south of Sheldon along the lower Sheyenne in Ransom County in 1873. Fellow countrymen moved into the Fort Ransom area soon afterwards, and some were up river in Barnes County in 1877. In 1878, Norwegians were at Romness along the Sheyenne in Griggs County, and in the Tolna area of Nelson County by 1881. The early Griggs settlers are said to have been from two groups: the first from Fillmore County, Minnesota, and from northern Iowa; the second from Stavanger, Norway, via rail to Granite Falls, Minnesota, and by wagon to the Sheyenne River and Sverdrup Township. By 1880 and 1881, Norwegians were near present-day Cooperstown (Haabet Congregation, 1880) and Hannaford (Wheatland Congregation, 1882). Everywhere little churches provided centers for local loyalties.

In addition to the Sheyenne and Goose River settlements, a small cluster of Norwegians settled in Walsh and Ramsey counties beginning in the vicinities of Grafton in 1878 (Landstad Norwegian Lutheran Church, 1881) and Hoople (South Trinity Church, 1879). Pleasant Valley Church southwest of the town of Park River began in 1880. A Norwegian Lutheran Church began farther up the Park River near Adams in 1884. Today a Norwegian belt extends from Grafton westward almost to Starkweather. But throughout this particular region competition for land was keen and Norwegian homestead areas were limited; the Bohemians, Poles, French, and Anglo-Ontarians had already been carving out pieces of territory for their own land claims.

Another group of Norwegian homesteaders took up land in western Grand Forks and northern Nelson counties. This series of farms began near Inkster and continued through Nelson County and extended a few miles into Ramsey County. The first Norwegian settlement there took place around 1881; and in subsequent years a series of Forest River churches sprang up which were called, appropriately, West, Middle and East Forest River congregations.

A cluster of Norwegians can be found today in the western townships of Ramsey County. These make up the eastern edge of a large settlement centered in and embracing much of Benson County. The earliest Norwegian settlers in Ramsey County came in 1882 and settled around what later became the towns of Devils Lake and Grand Harbor. A Big Coulee Lutheran Church started in 1883, and a Grand Harbor Church began in 1884. Churchs Ferry, on the boundary between Ramsey and Benson counties, received settlers in 1883. The Lake Ibsen Norwegian congregation near Leeds was organized in 1885. In every case, these first arrivals were jumping ahead of the railroad, which was completed to Devils Lake in 1883, after which construction was at a standstill for several years. As elsewhere, it seems that the first Norwegian "trail breakers" were those individuals and families who had already lived for a few years in Minnesota, Iowa, or Wisconsin. The "off the boat" immigrants came later.

A tightly knit group of Norwegian farmers occupy most of Hope and Loam townships in Cavalier County west of Walhalla. For several generations they have been surrounded by groups of French, Anglo-Ontarians, and Germans. Sometimes they are called the Vang community, for that tiny inland settlement has always been the center of their religious and social life. The Vang Norwegian homesteaders came in the 1880's from southern Minnesota, northern Iowa, and even from Canada. Both a Norwegian Lutheran and a Norwegian Baptist church served the early farmers' needs.

Perhaps the first Norwegians to arrive in Cavalier County were the members of an 1880's group from Jackson County, Wisconsin, who settled in the southeastern part of the county near what are now Milton and Osnabrock. St. Stephen's congregation, which was organized in 1882, built its church six miles south of Milton. Today, portions of Alma and East Alma townships are still decidedly Norwegian.

In Grand Forks County the land south and west of Manvel, extending through Mekinock (Ness Church, 1877), Honeyford, McCanna (Elk Valley Church, 1881), and farther southwest to Larimore, is occupied by Norwegians. Fellow countrymen from Blooming Prairie, Minnesota, settled in the Mekinock vicinity in 1877; and others were on the upper Turtle River in 1879. Here

several small churches arose to express the communities' religious and national bonds.

Settlement, at least in terms of homesteading activity, was complete in the northeastern North Dakota counties by the end of the first decade of this century. By that time the Norwegian land-ownership patterns were firmly established. There is evidence that the settlers from Norway did two things thereafter: they held on to their original land and, at times, expanded into neighboring agricultural areas predominantly occupied by other national groups.

The Gabrielson study of Norwegian land holdings in 1914 is described on page 135. A comparison of this early map and the 1965 map published in this atlas shows that the outlines of Norwegian-held land areas are surprisingly the same in the two time periods. In several regions, however, the Norwegian farm area had actually expanded. Comparing the two maps has certain limitations; one is a land-ownership survey and the other is a rural-resident analysis. Nevertheless, it would seem that in 1914 a considerable amount of land within the Norwegian communities was owned by non-Norwegians. The residents of many of these areas today are solidly of Norwegian background. One may suggest that the Norwegians "bought out" their non-Norwegian neighbors and that the areas are, in fact, today more intensely Norwegian than they were in 1914. Comparison of the two studies shows that the Norwegians' expansiveness was less successful in areas occupied by Polish, Bohemian, Icelandic and German farmers. They do seem to have moved extensively into land owned by the Irish (Manvel), Anglo-Ontarians (Grafton), and Anglo-Americans (southern Griggs, Steele, and Traill counties).

Despite the intense concentrations of Norwegians in so many townships, surprisingly few place names reflect the Norwegian presence. Only two of forty-one township names in Grand Forks County are Norwegian in origin. One of twenty-one township names in Steele County is Norwegian in background; three of twenty in Griggs County; and six of twenty-five in predominately Norwegian Traill County are of Norwegian background. Few, if any, village names show the presence of a Norwegian populace.

POLES

North Dakota's largest Polish settlement is in Walsh County. It began with the arrival of several men from Pine Creek, Wisconsin, in the mid-1870's (perhaps in 1876). These young men were the vanguard of dozens of families who followed in the ensuing decade. Almost all were born in Poland; some came directly from seaports, but the majority spent a few years, or at least months, in Wisconsin or Minnesota (Winona and Perham, Minnesota, are frequently mentioned). The Walsh County soil and terrain proved to be advantageous, and small farms became numerous and flourished in the area.

The trading post town of Acton on the Red River served as an initial business center for the Poles; but they soon established their own village of Warsaw, centering around a rural church which they called St. Stanislaus.

This Polish congregation first met in a farm house in 1879, and by 1884 a church building was erected (Harriston Township, Section 25). A second church — a magnificent brick edifice which seated 1,000 people — was built in 1900. It stands today as a "cathedral on the northern prairies" and is both a Warsaw parish church and an object of tourist fascination.

Warsaw was an "inland" settlement with no railroads; when the Soo Line crossed the southern extremity of the Polish settlement area, a siding received the name "Poland." The community center, however, remained at Warsaw. Poland had a post office and store for a few years, but these were discontinued in 1919.

In 1920, Catholic nuns from a Polish-speaking community started a grade school for day and boarding students in a large building which was erected near St. Stanislaus Church. The Polish language was taught in this school until the 1950's.

In Walsh County, Polish farmers eventually settled all of Pulaski Township, most of Walshville, Ardoch, and Harriston townships, and part of St. Andrews Township. The southern edge of the Warsaw settlement extends into Levant and Turtle River townships in Grand Forks County.

After the turn of the century, Polish families moved northward into Pembina County, where sizable holdings exist today in Lincoln Township, between Bowesmont and Drayton. The area immediately south of Drayton is half Polish. Later Poles moved onto adjoining farms in Walsh and Grand Forks counties, and their children reside there today in the midst of other national groups.

Minto, on the west edge of the Polish community, had an "Irish Church," St. Patrick's, established in 1880. In 1903 a second Catholic church — Sacred Heart — was erected in that town to serve the Polish-speaking people of the adjoining farm areas. The Irish church in Minto is now closed, and the traditionally Polish Sacred Heart Church alone serves the total Catholic population. Another "Irish" Church, St. John's at Ardoch, to the south, is predominantly Polish today.

In recent years, as individuals have acquired larger-sized farms, the total Polish population has diminished considerably. Through the decades, however, the outer boundaries of the community have changed very little. A refurbished St. Stanislaus Church stands in splendor at Warsaw, and elements of the Polish culture are very much alive. Polish hymns are sung regularly at services, and the old language is often heard at gatherings of middle- and older-aged residents.

SWEDES

An early townsite called Sweden was established in Glenwood Township in Walsh County, one mile west of the present village of Nash. It seems, however, that the founder (a homesick Swede who arrived in 1878) was one of what proved to be only a few Swedish settlers. The village has long since disappeared. A few Swedes are present in the nearby farming areas of Glenwood and Martin townships.

During Walsh County's homesteading days, a group of Swedes, many of whom came almost from dockside in seaport towns, settled as early as 1886 in Adams Township. A Swedish congregation called the Gustaf Adolph Church was organized in 1894. A church building was later erected, begun in 1902 and finished in 1906. Descendants of these Swedish pioneers, many with Norwegian spouses, still live in Adams, Dewey, and Silvesta townships. A new Gustavus Adolphus Church has been erected, and the congregation continues to flourish.

In 1887 a group of newly-arrived Swedish homesteaders, many from Renville County, Minnesota, held their first religious service in a farm home in Greenview Township, Steele County. Other families came to the area; and the Hofva Church was built around the turn of the century on Section 28, six miles south and four miles west of Finley. For several generations this congregation was affiliated with the Swedish Augustana Synod. It remains active today.

A Swedish Mission Church was built in 1914 on Section 30, Cooperstown Township, Griggs County, by a small community of Swedes who had previously held services in their homes. This congregation included a number of Swedish families, some having arrived as early as 1881, who lived on farms scattered throughout the central and southern part of the county. The Mission Church eventually closed after the main supporting families moved away. Today a few descendants of the original Swedish settlers remain, often inter-married with Norwegians.

An occasional handful of Swedish families are found elsewhere in the northeast, mixed with non-Scandinavian nationalities. In Nelson County a few families are present near Aneta; some Swedes remain on farms immediately west of Stump Lake, and others can be found in Clara Township farther to the northwest.

As a general rule, homestead areas in the northeastern portion of North Dakota, which were preponderantly of solid Norwegian background, had an occasional Swede. The proportion averaged about one Swede for every fifteen Norwegian settlers. Today the Swedish names often remain; but inter-marriage with Norwegians has taken place, and in most cases it is the Norwegian tradition which prevails.

SYRIANS (Lebanese)

A small group of Syrian families settled in Shepherd Township, Walsh County, during the homestead days of the 1890's. The census classified them as Syrian; but they were, in fact, Lebanese in origin. Perhaps twenty families were eventually present; some few lived across the line in Ramsey County. Edmore and Lawton became their trade center. Many started small shops in neighboring villages and later acquired large and substantial business interests in Grand Forks and elsewhere. These settlers were Arabic Catholics; their religious needs were served by itinerant Lebanese priests who made a circuit through Syrian communities from Crookston to Lawton, Rugby, and Williston. Eventually the Lebanese affiliated with local

Latin-rite Catholic parishes. The Shepherd Township settlers were often related to the Rugby Lebanese, and frequently marriages took place between the two groups. None remain today, except as wives of local non-Lebanese farmers.

UKRAINIANS

A small Ukrainian Orthodox Church congregation was organized in Pembina in 1927. This church was the religious center of a small number of families of Canadian origin who had taken land some six miles west and southwest of that town in the 1900's, well after early settlement times. A few farmers remain today, and their small Orthodox church still stands in the Pembina village.

Discussion and Bibliography

Reliability and Applicability

This volume presents a considerable amount of detailed information concerning every part of North Dakota. The matter of verification necessarily arises. The preparation of the atlas maps entailed the determination and proper placement of some 50,000 bits and pieces of data. Concern has been taken, in particular, with the distribution of North Dakota's rural households according to both location and national origin. The likelihood of a repetition of this study is, indeed, slight. Previous North Dakota historical investigations of this nature are rare; however, three smaller analyses do exist, and these can serve as a measure of reliability. The three studies are worthy of some comparative treatment.

The first is a land-ownership survey of Pembina County's Icelandic settlement published in the *Collections of the State Historical Society of North Dakota* (Vol. 1, pp. 110-111). This study portrays the extent of the settlement in 1888, 1896, and 1905. The maps, as reproduced on page 133 of this volume, show that the outline of the community remained rather stable through the years. The only change was one of consolidation; non-Icelandic farmers within the settlement boundaries were replaced by Icelandic agriculturalists. The Icelandic settlement, as seen in the northeast map in this atlas, is superimposed on the 1905 Pembina County map. The two are almost identical.

The second study is an analysis of ownership of land in a multi-county German-Russian portion of the state completed by William Sherman in 1965 ("Assimilation in a North Dakota German-Russian Community," Master's Thesis, University of North Dakota). Included in that investigation was the extent of German-held land in 1910 and also in 1960. The 1960 Pierce County portion of that study is printed on page 134, along with the same area as found in this atlas. The German settlement expanded considerably in the intervening fifty years: in 1910, nineteen percent of the land was in German-Russian hands; in 1960 the same group owned forty-five percent of the county farmland. As can be seen, the 1960 ownership map is almost exactly the same as the rural residency map as portrayed in this atlas. According to Sherman, the German expansion was at the expense of other groups. A 1910 Syrian community had disappeared, along with numerous Irish and Anglo-American individual farms. Yet the Germans did not move into the Norwegian areas east of Esmond, and the Silva Norwegian enclave remained intact.

As work on this atlas was being completed, a 1914 North Dakota Norwegian land ownership map was discovered in the archives of the University of North Dakota. This remarkable study by Alfred Gabrielson was first published as a two-page spread in the Norwegian language newspaper *Flam*. Although it seems to have been overlooked by scholars in recent decades, it proved to be the most valuable of all previous parallel works. The map, indicating *every* parcel of land owned by Norwegian farmers (even eighty-acre plots), was sponsored by a committee associated with the 1914 Norwegian centennial festivities. Gabrielson, a *Flam* report says, based his study on local tax lists and Register of Deeds books. Visiting *every* county, he apparently used the "sound of the name" approach and, in cases of doubtful national origin, received the assistance of county courthouse personnel. Gabrielson's data on northeastern North Dakota counties are reproduced on page 135 of this volume. The reader may compare them to the Norwegian settlements portrayed in this 1965 atlas study. The contours of the 1914 Norwegian settlements correspond closely with the results in this present study.

A comparison of the Gabrielson 1914 map and the 1965 atlas map gives rise to several observations. The Norwegians in the intervening years, like the Icelanders, "bought up" the land of the non-Norwegians in their midst. They intensified their hold on the areas which earlier Norwegian homesteaders had marked out for them. Areas which were partially Norwegian in 1914 seem almost completely Norwegian fifty years later. An analysis of local pre-World War I plat maps shows that farmers of British Isles background — American, Ontarian, and Irish — were most likely to be replaced. Furthermore, the Norwegian farmers broadened their areas of residence in central Nelson County and moved extensively into the Luverne Danish territory. They made no inroads, however, into the Bohemian or Polish areas of Walsh County, nor into the Icelandic and German portions of Pembina and Cavalier counties. The Germans of the Reynolds and Thompson vicinity, and the Germans of Jessie and of eastern Traill County also seem to have resisted Norwegian intrusion.

The above comparisons give a definite measure of credence to the present atlas. The contours of the Icelandic and the 1960 German-Russian settlements are almost exactly the same as the ones found in this 1965 study. The Norwegian settlements of 1914 are identical with those indicated in this atlas except where the Norwegians expanded into less-resilient ethnic groups along their borders.

HISTORICAL APPLICABILITY

In light of the above, a second set of observations can be made which may be of some value to the reader interested in history.

a. Some national groups were highly aggressive. Seeing agriculture on the Northern Plains as a favored enterprise, they consolidated their occupation of initial settlement areas and often expanded into the adjacent farmlands of less-enduring national groups. Examples are the Norwegians and German-Russians.

b. Some groups arrived, carved out a definite settlement area, and, after consolidating their hold on the region, underwent only slight expansion. Apparently their excess population moved to cities or more distant localities. Examples are the Icelanders, Bohemians, and Germans.

c. Some early national groups took up land, but seem to have been less than convinced of the desirability of Dakota agricultural life. They gave way to more aggressive groups and only a remnant remain: for example, the Swedes of the Hofva community in Griggs County and the Danes near Luverne.

d. Some groups came and left rather rapidly. Among them were immigrant settlers who, after acclimating to American ways, relinquished their holdings and moved to other parts of the country; the Jews in Ramsey County and the Syrians in Pierce County have all left the North Dakota prairies. Other groups were perhaps too familiar with America; knowing there were better opportunities elsewhere in the nation, the Irish and the Anglo-Americans sold their farms and moved away with little hesitation.

CONTEMPORARY RELIABILITY

This present atlas is a study of North Dakota's rural residents in the year 1965. As can be seen throughout the text, the author often writes in the present tense: "Norwegians still reside. . ."; "Bohemians live today in . . ." This manner of speaking arises from a basic presumption that the settlement outlines are, with rare exceptions, the same today (1982) as they were in 1965.

It is clear that a great amount of social change has taken place in the agricultural areas of the Northern Plains in the past two decades. Mechanization has been adopted to the extent that thousands of families have left the farms, and a large number of villages have virtually disappeared. Nevertheless, after carefully looking at townships in every part of the state and after consulting several dozen knowledgeable individuals, the author contends that, in spite of the readjustment in farmstyle and method, the ethnic boundaries in almost every case have remained the same. What has come about is this: local farmers have increased their holdings by buying out their neighbors. "Outsiders" are not moving in.

This conclusion is based on several observations:

1. The cost of land has increased to an extent that few outsiders have the capital needed to purchase viable farm enterprises. North Dakota's anti-corporation stance has made such acquisitions even more difficult.

2. The margin between success and failure in Great Plains farming ventures is often so narrow that a newcomer has to take almost impossible risks. Even if land is owned by outsiders, local farmers are needed to run the operations. Only a long-term resident can know the peculiarities of a piece of land — for example, the soil and moisture conditions which vary from field to field and from year to year.

3. Finally, all things being equal, local residents prefer to "sell out" to neighbors, not to strangers.

In short, the total number of farmers in a specific region may have declined, but the survivors tend to be people with roots in the local community.

The above statement needs to be qualified when applied to certain geographical areas: first, the "bedroom" rural community areas around the larger cities (in particular Fargo, Bismarck, Mandan, Minot, Dickinson, and to a lesser extent Grand Forks and Williston); second, the energy-producing areas, especially the regions adjacent to the Knife River, although this may be a temporary construction-phase situation.

Bibliographical Essay

Information concerning specific ethnic groups in North Dakota can be found in a number of journal articles, an occasional Master's thesis or small historical publication, portions of several volumes concerning nationwide groups, and in hundreds of random paragraphs in local histories. No single publication has as yet dealt systematically with the whole state and its multiplicity of groups. This atlas and the North Dakota Centennial Heritage volume on ethnic history (to be published in 1983) will be the first to attempt such a thing.

The materials for ethnic research are already at hand, however; and students of the subject will be using them extensively in future decades. Three basic sources are now available:

1. Microfilm copies of the *Federal Land Office Homestead Tract Books* have now been acquired by the Special Collections Department of the Chester Fritz Library at the University of North Dakota. This makes possible a complete and accurate portrayal of the first settlement patterns in every portion of the state.

2. A large collection of North Dakota's foreign-language newspapers has been accumulated at the State Historical Society in Bismarck and, to a lesser extent, at the Chester Fritz Library at the University of North Dakota. A summary of the newspaper holdings is presented in Carol Koehmstedt Kolar, *Union List of North Dakota Newspapers, 1864-1976* (Fargo: North Dakota Institute for Regional Studies, 1981). These newspapers hold the key to understanding the first-generation experiences of all the major North Dakota groups.

3. County, town, church, and school histories, occasioned often by jubilee observations, have been published in abundance in recent years. Perhaps a thousand items — small pamphlets and large volumes — have been printed. Unfortunately, no one single depository for them exists. The most complete collections are found in the archives of the State Historical Society at Bismarck, the North Dakota Institute for Regional Studies Archives at North Dakota State University at Fargo, and the Department of Special Collections of the Chester Fritz Library at the University of North Dakota in Grand Forks.

A carefully done, but popular treatment of all of North Dakota's major ethnic groups (and some minor ones) was recently published as a supplement to the *Bismarck Tribune* (February 16, 1982). The eighty-paged publication, entitled "We, the People," is a blend of personalities, historical data, and cultural features.

A series of occasional feature articles in the *Minot Daily News* has dealt with ethnic groups in the central and western part of North Dakota. Two authors are involved: Robert Cory, whose columns began in the 1950's, and Leonard Lund, who took up the subject in the late 1960's. The articles are accurate and well written. Both writers are still active. Unfortunately, no master list of the various columns has been compiled.

The general historical background and a certain amount of details concerning ethnic groups are included in Elwyn B. Robinson's indispensable *History of North Dakota* (Lincoln: University of Nebraska Press, 1966). Robert P. and Wynona H. Wilkins, *North Dakota: A Bicentennial History* (New York: W. W. Norton, 1977) complements the Robinson book and treats the subject in a lively and insightful way. Both of these works convey the political, social, and economic conditions which surrounded the immigrant groups as they set up their colonies throughout the Dakotas.

Since this atlas is concerned with ethnic settlement patterns in terms of location, times, and basic institutions, the author sought published materials which provided such information throughout the Midwest. Much of the information used in preparing the volume came from unpublished sources — interviews with hundreds of local informants — but some helpful publications are available. The major ones are listed below.

ANGLO-AMERICANS AND ANGLO-ONTARIANS

Stanley Norman Murray, *The Valley Comes of Age: A History of Agriculture in the Valley of the Red River of the North, 1812-1920* (Fargo: North Dakota Institute for Regional Studies, 1967), gives a good insight into the forces which brought Americans and Canadians into the early Red River Valley. The effect of the bonanza farms can be seen in Hiram Drache, *The Day of the Bonanza* (Fargo: North Dakota Institute for Regional Studies, 1964). Marcus Hansen, *Mingling of the Canadian and American Peoples* (New Haven: Yale University Press, 1940), discusses the "Manitoba Boom" which brought Anglo-Ontarians into North Dakota. The distribution of Anglo-Americans (and Anglo-Ontarians) is probably best seen in the history of their institutions. Of particular value are Robert P. and Wynona H. Wilkins, *God Giveth the Increase: The History of the Episcopal Church in North Dakota* (Fargo: North Dakota Institute for Regional Studies, 1959), and C. A. Armstrong, *History of the Methodist Church in North Dakota* (Fargo: The Author, 1960). Also of value is Harold Sackett Pond, *Masonry in North Dakota, 1804-1964* (Grafton: Record Printers, 1964). The Anglo-American influence in the early cattle industry has never been explicitly discussed, but the reader may get a sense of its importance in such books as D. Jerome Tweton, *The Marquis de Mores: Dakota Capitalist, French Nationalist* (Fargo: North Dakota Institute for Regional Studies, 1965).

GERMANS (REICHSDEUTSCH)

A helpful index to the presence of unhyphenated Germans is the chronicle of the Missouri Synod Lutheran Church in North Dakota. Two studies are available. The first is Benjamin M. Holt, *A History of the North Dakota District Lutheran Church — Missouri Synod, 1895-1900* (Fargo: The Author, 1966). The second is Lambert J. Mehl, "Missouri Grows to Maturity in North Dakota: A Regional History of the Lutheran Church — Missouri Synod" (Master's Thesis, University of North Dakota, 1953). Of some value for German and other ethnic groups in the western part of the state is Louis Pfaller, *The Catholic Church in Western North Dakota, 1738-1960* (Bismarck: Diocese of Bismarck, 1960). Information concerning some of the Catholic groups in the eastern part of North Dakota can be found in *Golden Jubilee Edition: Catholic Action News, 1889-1939* (Fargo: Diocese of Fargo, 1939).

EASTERN EUROPEAN GERMANS

Two volumes are indispensable for assessing the array of German-Russian settlements in North Dakota. The first is LeVern J. Rippley and Armand Bauer's translation of Richard Sallet, *Russian-German Settlements in the United States* (Fargo: North Dakota Institute for Regional Studies, 1974); the second is George Rath, *Black Sea Germans in the Dakotas* (Freeman, South Dakota: Pine Hill Press, 1977). Helpful for the Pierce, McHenry, and Benson county area is William C. Sherman, "Assimilation in a North Dakota German-Russian Community" (Master's Thesis, University of North Dakota, 1965). A discussion of some of the Catholic German-Russian settlements is found in George Aberle, *From the Steppes to the Prairies* (Dickinson, North Dakota: The Author, 1963). Two articles on the Dobrudja Germans in Wells and Sheridan counties were written by Lester C. Seibold, "Black Sea Germans from the Rumanian Dobrudja," *Heritage Review* (September 1978: 4-14; December 1978: 17-26). Cavalier County Mennonites from Russia are briefly discussed in Hazel J. Loynes, "Mennonite Settlements in North Dakota," *North Dakota Historical Society Collections*, III (1910), 324-336.

SCANDINAVIANS

The best source for the distribution of early Norwegians, and an invaluable aid in the preparation of this atlas, is Olaf M. Norlie (ed.), *Norsk Lutherske Menigheter i Amerika, 1843-1916*, II (Minneapolis: Augsburg Publishing House, 1918). Of special value for the eastern part of North Dakota is Carlton S. Qualey, *Norwegian Settlement in the United States* (Northfield, Minnesota: Norwegian-American Historical Association, 1938). Using much of Qualey's information with a few extra details is Walter J. Szczur, "Norwegian Settlement in North Dakota" (Master's Thesis, Montana State University, 1949). Early Red River Valley Norwegian settlements are discussed in Axle Tollefson, "Historical Notes on the Norwegians in the Red River Valley," *North Dakota Historical Society Collections*, VII (1925), 133-159. A valuable source is the North Dakota section of Martin Ulvestad, *Nordmaendene i Amerika, deres Historie og Rekord* (Minneapolis: History Book Co., 1907). The Swedish settlement experience is portrayed in a limited way in Myrtle Bemis, "History of the Settlement of Swedes in North Dakota," *North Dakota Historical Society Collections*, III (1910), 247-309. Much of this article was taken from Myrtle Bemis, "History of the Settlement of Swedes in North Dakota" (Master's Thesis, University of North Dakota, 1909). Danes in Cass County are discussed in Waldemar C. Westegaard,

"History of the Danish Settlement in Hill Township, Cass County, North Dakota," *North Dakota Historical Society Collections*, I (1905), 153-180. Icelandic life in Pembina County is chronicled in Thorstina Walters, *Modern Sagas: The Story of the Icelanders in North America* (Fargo: North Dakota Institute for Regional Studies, 1953). Of special value is Svienbjorn Johnson, "The Icelandic Settlement of Pembina County," *North Dakota Historical Society Collections*, I (1905), 89-131. One North Dakota Finnish community is studied in Waino Kontio, *History of the Rolla Finns* (Rolla, North Dakota: Rolla Historical Society, 1962).

SLAVIC SETTLEMENTS

Bohemians in early North Dakota are briefly discussed in Jan Habernicht, *Dejiny Cechuv Americkych* (St. Louis: Hlas Publishing Company, 1904). A survey of North Dakota's Bohemian lodges can be found in "A Brief History of Our Association," *Fraternal Herald, Magazine of the Western Fraternal Life Association*, Cedar Rapids, Iowa (July 1972): 3-12. Several Bohemian communities are described in William H. Elznic, "Bohemians in Richland County," *North Dakota Historical Society Collections*, IV (1913), 62-80. The Ukrainian experience in North Dakota is treated in Wasyl Halich, "Ukrainians in North Dakota, "*North Dakota History*, 18 (October 1951): 219-232. The story of the Crimean Bohemians can be found briefly in *Zlate Jubileum: Golden Jubilee of Saints Peter and Paul Catholic Church* (New Hradec, North Dakota: Jubilee Committee, 1948).

GERMAN-AMERICANS

The Dunkard (Brethren) settlement days are portrayed in Roy Thompson, "The First Dunker Settlement in North Dakota," *North Dakota Historical Society Collections*, IV (1913), 81-100. A more complete survey is found in Maryanna Hamer, *et al.*, *History of the Church of the Brethren on the Northern Plains* (Dallas Center, Iowa: Northern Plains District, 1976). Of special value is Ralph R. Petry, "A Study of the Trends and Forces in the History of the District of North Dakota and Eastern Montana" (Master's Thesis, Bethany Theological Seminary, 1940). The Old Order Amish difficulties on the Northern Plains are analyzed in John A. Hostetler, "The Old Order Amish on the Great Plains: A Study in Cultural Vulnerability," in *Ethnicity on the Great Plains*, ed. by Frederick C. Luebke (Lincoln: University of Nebraska Press, 1980), 92-108.

OTHER GROUPS

Several Jewish settlements are discussed in W. Gunther Plaut, "Jewish Colonies at Painted Woods and Devils Lake," *North Dakota History*, 32 (January 1965): 59-70. A little more information can be found in Lois Field Schwartz, "Early Jewish Agricultural Colonies in North Dakota," *North Dakota History*, 32 (October 1965): 217-232. Background information concerning North Dakota Jewish colonization is found in Robert J. Lazar, "From Ethnic Minority to Socio-economic Elite: A Study of the Jewish Community of Fargo, North

Dakota," (Ph.D. Dissertation, University of Minnesota, 1968). Hollanders in a small part of North Dakota are treated in Gerald Francis De Jong, "The Dutch in Emmons County," *North Dakota History*, 29 (January-April 1962): 253-265. The oldest French farming community in the state is described in Frank Richard, "St. Benedict of Wild Rice," *Red River Valley Historian* (Summer 1975): 2-8.

County Totals of North Dakota's Largest National Groups

North Dakota Rural Households – 1965	Adams	Barnes	Benson	Billings	Bottineau	Bowman	Burke	Burleigh	Cass	Cavalier	Dickey
Norwegian	215	371	555	12	647	105	227	90	449	304	96
Swede	7	58	87	5	37	10	89	102	88	16	33
Dane	—	28	17	—	15	6	63	11	41	3	14
Polish	—	5	2	2	4	10	—	6	15	5	1
Bohemian[1]	10	14	6	17	7	30	8	10	17	24	29
Ukrainian	—	5	1	121	1	—	—	17	2	1	1
German	24	355	55	17	188	69	56	98	412	323	101
German-Russian[2]	123	8	137	33	45	22	—	209	6	132	290
Anglo-Ontarian	2	55	7	—	110	—	19	44	142	221	15
Anglo-American	72	137	178	59	218	107	85	193	334	96	171
Irish	10	24	9	7	2	6	4	9	11	25	27
French	—	—	2	5	48	2	2	11	44	80	—
Hollander	1	43	—	—	—	—	7	—	9	—	2
Other	18	81	42	5	10	5	14	42	195	74	56
TOTAL	482	1184	1098	283	1332	372	574	842	1765	1304	836

North Dakota Rural Households – 1965	Divide	Dunn	Eddy	Emmons	Foster	Golden Valley	Grand Forks	Grant	Griggs	Hettinger	Kidder
Norwegian	449	150	192	28	104	38	712	47	386	81	86
Swede	14	16	38	26	15	3	48	3	18	4	10
Dane	14	2	3	2	8	1	30	3	1	3	8
Polish	—	1	1	2	6	4	50	6	—	5	4
Bohemian[1]	5	161	2	2	9	15	12	10	4	21	11
Ukrainian	—	48	—	1	—	2	—	—	—	—	4
German	34	58	60	28	87	60	187	44	43	74	61
German-Russian[2]	3	237	26	633	36	3	17	576	3	204	310
Anglo-Ontarian	7	6	6	1	18	2	183	—	12	—	1
Anglo-American	81	103	101	133	105	132	95	95	56	66	134
Irish	5	16	9	4	14	4	64	6	3	2	1
French	1	3	5	—	3	4	38	1	—	1	2
Hollander	—	1	—	123	2	—	4	3	5	—	17
Other	6	29	23	27	18	7	17	17	49	110	15
TOTAL	619	831	466	1010	425	275	1457	811	580	571	664

North Dakota Rural Households – 1965	LaMoure	Logan	McHenry	McIntosh	McKenzie	McLean	Mercer	Morton	Mountrail	Nelson	Oliver
Norwegian	220	33	309	2	393	222	11	84	575	550	28
Swede	68	5	12	—	16	98	12	10	23	27	11
Dane	16	1	7	1	2	7	—	5	14	3	4
Polish	12	—	—	—	1	5	5	3	1	—	1
Bohemian[1]	10	—	4	—	24	6	1	65	29	34	7
Ukrainian	—	—	18	—	34	112	4	1	1	—	—
German	288	5	205	13	74	130	51	292	107	90	131
German-Russian[2]	307	616	305	655	9	407	456	456	1	9	196
Anglo-Ontarian	4	—	11	—	8	11	—	10	2	10	1
Anglo-American	150	11	231	4	197	140	12	64	149	72	60
Irish	13	—	7	—	14	7	9	4	13	24	7
French	3	—	1	—	4	2	—	—	—	2	—
Hollander	7	—	6	—	6	—	—	2	5	—	3
Other	18	25	38	3	26	9	4	58	45	22	4
TOTAL	1116	696	1154	678	808	1156	565	1054	965	843	453

North Dakota Rural Households – 1965	Pembina	Pierce	Ramsey	Ransom	Renville	Richland	Rolette	Sargent	Sheridan	Sioux	Slope
Norwegian	150	225	363	342	176	610	223	227	33	37	74
Swede	13	30	22	50	36	56	19	83	8	—	11
Dane	1	1	12	18	46	24	5	11	7	—	4
Polish	18	—	10	—	2	11	4	46	—	—	6
Bohemian[1]	5	2	31	8	3	158	—	17	—	—	13
Ukrainian	17	—	—	1	1	2	1	—	18	1	—
German	276	40	157	212	117	803	76	205	16	19	60
German-Russian[2]	54	417	62	51	3	1	6	11	556	111	35
Anglo-Ontarian	348	15	56	35	17	31	11	19	—	—	3
Anglo-American	134	64	105	149	149	203	124	131	44	45	100
Irish	63	—	34	21	6	6	4	7	—	5	—
French	77	2	7	4	5	—	96	11	—	—	—
Hollander	5	—	5	2	2	4	—	5	5	—	2
Other	192	28	35	13	1	37	46	12	3	10	23
TOTAL	1353	824	899	906	564	1946	615	785	690	228	331

North Dakota Rural Households – 1965	Stark	Steele	Stutsman	Towner	Traill	Walsh	Ward	Wells	Williams	Total	Percent
Norwegian	50	518	156	173	715	675	529	242	590	13,879	29.9
Swede	3	13	18	38	16	79	40	12	42	1,598	3.4
Dane	4	20	9	5	2	5	69	2	10	588	1.3
Polish	5	—	38	—	—	285	2	2	2	588	1.3
Bohemian[1]	188	6	7	—	5	397	30	14	5	1,493	3.2
Ukrainian	29	—	2	—	—	—	78	—	8	532	1.1
German	49	34	395	209	146	91	285	176	111	7,297	15.7
German-Russian[2]	346	5	441	17	7	—	85	389	6	9,073	19.5
Anglo-Ontarian	5	20	32	24	25	108	14	8	12	1,691	3.6
Anglo-American	44	79	287	70	94	95	312	95	111	6,276	13.5
Irish	6	3	21	14	10	48	4	—	17	629	1.4
French	7	—	1	8	—	68	5	—	13	568	1.2
Hollander	3	—	20	1	—	—	1	—	6	307	.7
Other	180	3	62	91	5	15	34	26	39	1,967	4.2
TOTAL	919	701	1489	650	1025	1866	1488	966	972	46,486	

[1]Bohemian includes Crimean-Bohemian.
[2]German-Russian includes all kinds of Germans from Russia: Dobrudja, Black Sea, Volhynian, Mennonite, Marienburg, Volga.

County Totals of Every North Dakota National Group

Rural Households in North Dakota – 1965	Nor-wegian	Swede	Dane	Fin-lander	Ice-lander	Polish	Czech: Bohemian	Czech: Crimean Bohemian	Ukrainian
Adams	215	7	—	—	—	—	—	10	
Barnes	371	58	28	—	—	5	14	—	5
Benson	555	87	17	—	—	2	6	—	1
Billings	12	5	—	—	—	2	—	17	121
Bottineau	647	37	15	—	1	4	7	—	1
Bowman	105	10	6	—	—	10	30	—	—
Burke	227	89	63	—	—	—	8	—	—
Burleigh	90	102	11	21	—	6	10	—	17
Cass	449	88	41	1	—	15	17	—	2
Cavalier	304	16	3	—	16	5	24	—	1
Dickey	96	33	14	39	—	1	29	—	1
Divide	449	14	14	—	—	—	5	—	—
Dunn	150	16	2	—	—	1	—	161	48
Eddy	192	38	3	—	—	1	2	—	—
Emmons	28	26	2	21	—	2	2	—	1
Foster	104	15	8	—	—	6	9	—	—
Golden Valley	38	3	1	—	—	4	15	—	2
Grand Forks	712	48	30	—	1	50	12	—	—
Grant	47	3	3	9	—	6	10	—	—
Griggs	386	18	1	—	—	—	4	—	—
Hettinger	81	4	3	—	—	5	21	—	—
Kidder	86	10	8	—	—	4	11	—	4
LaMoure	220	68	16	—	—	12	10	—	—
Logan	33	5	1	23	—	—	—	—	—
McHenry	309	12	7	—	28	—	4	—	18
McIntosh	2	—	1	—	—	—	—	—	—
McKenzie	393	16	2	—	—	1	24	—	34
McLean	222	98	7	—	—	5	6	—	112
Mercer	11	12	—	—	—	5	1	—	4
Morton	84	10	5	—	—	3	65	—	1
Mountrail	575	23	14	28	—	1	29	—	1
Nelson	550	27	3	15	—	—	34	—	—
Oliver	28	11	4	—	—	1	7	—	—
Pembina	150	13	1	2	170	18	5	—	17
Pierce	225	30	1	—	—	—	2	—	—
Ramsey	363	22	12	10	—	10	31	—	—
Ransom	342	50	18	—	—	—	8	—	1
Renville	176	36	46	—	—	2	3	—	1
Richland	610	56	24	2	—	11	158	—	2
Rolette	223	19	5	4	—	4	—	—	1
Sargent	227	83	11	—	—	46	17	—	—
Sheridan	33	8	7	—	—	—	—	—	18
Sioux	37	—	—	—	—	—	—	—	1
Slope	74	11	4	—	—	6	13	—	—
Stark	50	3	4	—	—	5	—	188	29
Steele	518	13	20	—	—	—	6	—	—
Stutsman	156	18	9	3	—	38	7	—	2
Towner	173	38	5	75	—	—	—	—	—
Traill	715	16	2	—	—	—	5	—	—
Walsh	675	79	5	5	—	285	397	—	—
Ward	529	40	69	4	—	2	30	—	78
Wells	242	12	2	—	—	2	14	—	—
Williams	590	42	10	—	—	2	5	—	8
TOTAL	13,879	1598	588	262	216	588	1,117	376	532

Rural Households in North Dakota — 1965	Syrian (Lebanese)	Hollander	Luxem- burger	Belgian	Swiss	French	Anglo- Amer.[1]	Anglo- Ontar.[2]	Irish
Adams	—	1	—	—	—	—	72	2	10
Barnes	—	43	2	—	16	—	137	55	24
Benson	—	—	—	—	3	2	178	7	9
Billings	—	—	—	—	1	5	59	—	7
Bottineau	—	—	—	—	3	48	218	110	2
Bowman	—	—	3	—	—	2	107	—	6
Burke	—	7	6	—	—	2	85	19	4
Burleigh	—	—	—	1	—	11	193	44	9
Cass	—	9	17	1	1	44	334	142	11
Cavalier	—	—	3	4	—	80	96	221	25
Dickey	—	2	2	—	2	—	171	15	27
Divide	—	—	—	5	—	1	81	7	5
Dunn	—	1	—	—	—	3	103	6	16
Eddy	—	—	10	—	1	5	101	6	9
Emmons	—	123	1	—	4	—	133	1	4
Foster	8	2	3	—	3	3	105	18	14
Golden Valley	3	—	—	—	—	4	132	2	4
Grand Forks	—	4	—	—	—	38	95	183	64
Grant	—	3	—	—	2	1	95	—	6
Griggs	—	5	—	—	—	—	56	12	3
Hettinger	2	—	—	—	—	1	66	—	2
Kidder	1	17	—	—	—	2	134	1	1
LaMoure	—	7	7	2	1	3	150	4	13
Logan	—	—	—	—	—	—	11	—	—
McHenry	—	6	—	—	6	1	231	11	7
McIntosh	—	—	—	—	—	—	4	—	—
McKenzie	3	6	—	1	—	4	197	8	14
McLean	—	—	—	—	—	2	140	11	7
Mercer	—	—	—	—	—	—	12	—	9
Morton	.	2	—	—	—	—	64	10	4
Mountrail	12	5	—	—	—	—	149	2	13
Nelson	1	—	2	—	—	2	72	10	24
Oliver	—	3	—	—	—	—	60	1	7
Pembina	1	5	—	6	—	77	134	348	63
Pierce	1	—	—	—	—	2	64	15	—
Ramsey	1	5	—	6	2	7	105	56	34
Ransom	—	2	—	—	—	4	149	35	21
Renville	—	2	—	—	—	5	149	17	6
Richland	—	4	13	1	3	—	203	31	6
Rolette	1	—	—	—	—	96	124	11	4
Sargent	—	5	—	2	—	11	131	19	7
Sheridan	—	5	—	—	—	—	44	—	—
Sioux	—	—	—	—	—	—	45	—	5
Slope	—	2	1	1	—	—	100	3	—
Stark	—	3	—	—	1	7	44	5	6
Steele	—	—	—	—	1	—	79	20	3
Stutsman	—	20	8	2	6	1	287	32	21
Towner	2	1	—	1	—	8	70	24	14
Traill	—	—	1	—	—	—	94	25	10
Walsh	1	—	—	—	—	68	95	108	48
Ward	—	1	—	2	2	5	312	14	4
Wells	—	—	5	1	—	—	95	8	—
Williams	13	6	10	—	—	13	111	12	17
TOTAL	50	307	94	36	58	568	6,276	1,691	629

[1]Contains some 1st generation English, Scotch; and also some Protestant-Irish.
[2]Contains some Quebec Anglo-Saxons.

Rural Households in North Dakota – 1965	American-Indian[3]	German (Reichs-deutsch)	German-American Mennonite	German-American Dunker	German-American Moravian	Hungarian German Burgen-land	Hungarian German (Banat)	Austrian (Galician) German	Bohemian (Sudeten) German
Adams	—	24	—	—	—	—	13	—	—
Barnes	—	355	1	—	—	44	—	—	8
Benson	7	55	—	24	—	—	1	—	—
Billings	—	17	—	—	—	—	—	—	—
Bottineau	—	188	—	—	—	—	—	—	—
Bowman	—	69	—	—	—	—	—	—	—
Burke	—	56	—	5	—	—	—	—	—
Burleigh	—	98	—	—	—	—	3	—	—
Cass	—	412	2	—	121	1	—	—	33
Cavalier	—	323	—	—	—	—	—	44	—
Dickey	—	107	—	—	—	—	—	—	—
Divide	—	34	—	—	—	—	—	—	—
Dunn	—	58	—	—	—	—	25	—	—
Eddy	—	60	—	—	—	7	—	—	—
Emmons	—	28	—	—	—	—	—	—	—
Foster	—	87	—	1	—	—	—	—	—
Golden Valley	—	60	—	—	—	—	—	—	—
Grand Forks	—	187	—	—	—	—	—	—	—
Grant	—	44	—	—	—	—	2	—	—
Griggs	—	43	—	—	—	—	—	—	44
Hettinger	—	74	—	—	—	—	102	—	—
Kidder	—	61	—	—	—	—	—	—	—
LaMoure	—	288	—	—	—	—	—	—	—
Logan	—	5	—	—	—	—	—	—	—
McHenry	—	205	—	—	—	—	—	—	—
McIntosh	—	13	—	—	—	—	—	—	—
McKenzie	—	74	—	—	—	—	—	6	—
McLean	1	130	—	—	—	—	—	—	—
Mercer	—	51	—	—	—	—	—	—	—
Morton	1	292	—	—	—	—	50	—	—
Mountrail	—	107	—	—	—	—	—	—	—
Nelson	—	90	—	—	—	—	—	—	—
Oliver	—	131	—	—	—	—	—	—	—
Pembina	—	276	—	—	—	—	—	8	—
Pierce	—	40	22	1	—	—	—	—	—
Ramsey	—	157	—	—	—	—	—	—	—
Ransom	—	212	—	—	—	2	—	—	—
Renville	—	117	—	—	—	—	—	—	—
Richland	—	803	—	—	—	—	—	—	—
Rolette	3	76	20	—	—	—	—	—	—
Sargent	1	205	—	—	—	—	—	—	—
Sheridan	—	16	—	—	—	—	—	—	—
Sioux	5	19	—	—	—	—	1	—	—
Slope	—	60	—	—	—	—	12	—	—
Stark	—	49	—	—	—	—	163	—	—
Steele	—	34	—	—	—	—	—	—	—
Stutsman	—	395	—	—	—	1	—	—	—
Towner	—	209	—	—	—	—	1	—	—
Traill	—	146	—	—	—	—	—	—	—
Walsh	—	91	—	—	—	—	—	—	—
Ward	—	285	14	2	—	—	1	—	—
Wells	—	176	—	—	—	13	—	—	3
Williams	—	111	—	12	—	—	—	—	—
TOTAL	18	7303	59	45	121	68	374	58	88

[3]In reservation counties, many rural non-farm families are not included.

Rural Households in North Dakota — 1965	German-Russian-Black Sea	German-Russian (Dobrudja)	German-Russian-Mennonite	Minor Groups[6]	Unknown[5]	Total
Adams	123	—	—	—	5	482
Barnes	7	—	—	1	10	1,184
Benson	137	—	—	2	5	1,098
Billings	33	—	—	2	2	283
Bottineau	45	—	—	1	5	1,332
Bowman	22	—	—	—	2	372
Burke	—	—	—	—	3	574
Burleigh	197	—	12	8	9	842
Cass	6	—	—	—	18	1,765
Cavalier	27	—	105	—	7	1,304
Dickey	282	—	—	8	7	836
Divide	3	—	—	—	1	619
Dunn	237	—	—	—	4	831
Eddy	22	4	—	1	4	466
Emmons	633	—	—	—	1	1,010
Foster	36	—	—	—	3	425
Golden Valley	3	—	—	1	3	275
Grand Forks	17	—	—	—	16	1,457
Grant	576	—	—	—	4	811
Griggs	3	—	—	—	5	580
Hettinger	204	—	—	—	6	571
Kidder	309	—	—	11	4	664
LaMoure	307	—	—	1	7	1,116
Logan	616	—	—	—	2	696
McHenry	292	13	—	1	3	1,154
McIntosh	655	—	—	—	3	678
McKenzie	9	—	—	1	15	808
McLean	407	—	—	1	7	1,156
Mercer	452	4	—	—	4	565
Morton	456	—	—	—	7	1,054
Mountrail	1	—	—	1	4	965
Nelson	9	—	—	—	4	843
Oliver	196	—	—	—	4	453
Pembina	21	—	—	28	10	1,353
Pierce	417	—	—	—	4	824
Ramsey	62	—	—	9	7	899
Ransom	40	—	—	13	9	906
Renville	3	—	—	—	1	564
Richland	1	—	—	—	18	1,946
Rolette	6	—	—	13	5	615
Sargent	11	—	—	1	8	785
Sheridan	472	52	32	—	3	690
Sioux	111	—	—	—	4	228
Slope	35	—	—	6	3	331
Stark	346	—	—	6	10	919
Steele	5	—	—	—	2	701
Stutsman	412	—	—	54	17	1,489
Towner	8	9	—	7	5	650
Traill	7	—	—	—	4	1,025
Walsh	—	—	—	—	9	1,866
Ward	49	—	36	—	9	1,488
Wells	329	30	30	1	3	966
Williams	6	—	—	—	4	972
Total	8,663	112	215	178	319	46,486

[5]This figure probably contains members of less known groups (e.g., Balkans)
[6]See list of Minor Groups on next page.

Minor Groups

Armenian, Kidder 2, State Total 2; *Austrian,* Burleigh 4, Eddy 1, McKenzie 1, Slope 1, Towner 2, State Total 9; *Black,* McHenry 1, Pembina 1, State Total 2; *Bulgarian,* Burleigh 1, Kidder 8, State Total 9; *Croatian,* LaMoure 1, Slope 3, Stark 2, State Total 6; *Czech (Moravian),* Ramsey 9, Slope 2, State Total 11; *Estonian,* Stark 3, State Total 3; *French-Indian (Métis),* Benson 2, Rolette 13, State Total 15; *German-Russian (Marienburg),* Barnes 1, Kidder 1, Stutsman 29, State Total 31; *German-Russian (Volga),* Dickey 8, Ransom 11, State Total 19; *German-Russian (Volhynian),* Cavalier 6, Pembina 25, State Total 31; *Greek,* Mountrail 1, Ransom 1, State Total 2; *Jew,* Burleigh 2, Pembina 2, State Total 4; *Hungarian,* Bottineau 1, Sargent 1, State Total 2; *Italian,* Burleigh 1, Stark 1, State Total 2; *Latvian,* Towner 2, State Total 2; *Lithuanian,* Stutsman 1, Towner 2, Wells 1, State Total 4; *Rumanian,* Foster 1, McLean 1, Towner 1, State Total 3; *Serbian,* Billings 2, State Total 2; *Silesian Pole,* Stutsman 24, State Total 24; *Slovenian,* Ransom 1, State Total 1.

Rural Farm and Rural Nonfarm Including Places of Less than 1000.

**Persons Per Square Mile
(from U.S. Census, 1970)**

COUNTY	1970	COUNTY	1970
Adams	2.2	Mountrail	2.3
Barnes	4.6	Nelson	5.8
Benson	5.9	Oliver	3.2
Billings	1.1	Pembina	6.0
Bottineau	4.0	Pierce	3.3
Bowman	1.8	Ramsey	4.7
Burke	4.2	Ransom	4.3
Burleigh	3.7	Renville	4.3
Cass	7.8	Richland	6.1
Cavalier	4.0	Rolette	11.1
Dickey	3.3	Sargent	7.0
Divide	2.3	Sheridan	3.3
Dunn	2.5	Sioux	2.3
Eddy	3.4	Slope	1.2
Emmons	3.7	Stark	4.6
Foster	3.6	Steele	5.3
Golden Valley	1.2	Stutsman	3.6
Grand Forks	6.2	Towner	3.0
Grant	3.0	Traill	6.6
Griggs	3.8	Walsh	6.7
Hettinger	3.3	Ward	6.2
Kidder	3.2	Wells	4.2
LaMoure	6.3	Williams	3.1
Logan	3.2		
McHenry	4.1		
McIntosh	3.1	NORTH DAKOTA	4.0
McKenzie	1.6		
McLean	4.7		
Mercer	3.5		
Morton	3.7		

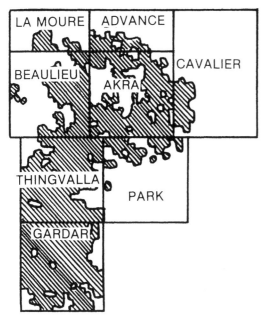

**Land Held By Icelanders
Pembina County—1905**

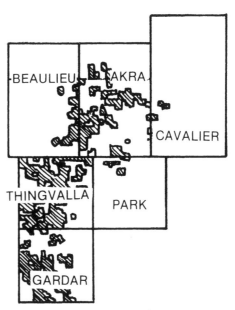

**Land Held By Icelanders
Pembina County—1888**

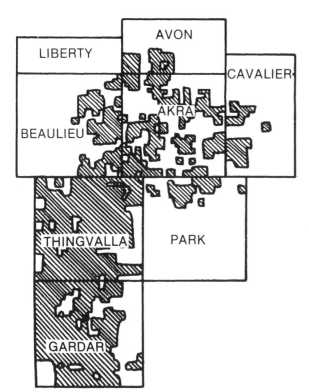

**Land Held By Icelanders
Pembina County—1896**

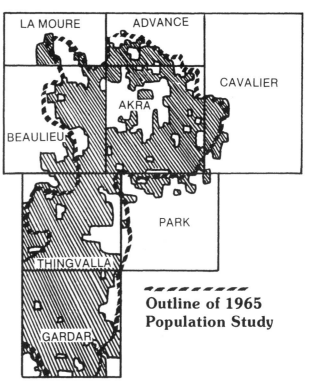

**Outline of 1965
Population Study**

**Land Held By Icelanders
Pembina County—1905
1965 Ethnic Atlas Area Superimposed**

1888, 1896, 1905 Data from Sveinbjorn Johnson, "The Icelandic Settlement of Pembina County," North Dakota Historical Society *Collections*, I (1908), 110-111.

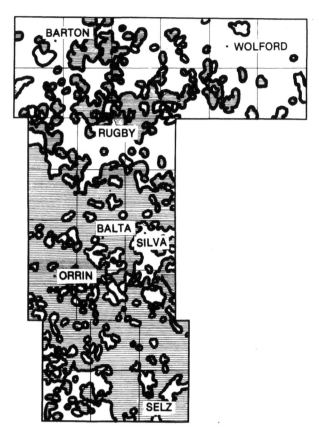

**In 1960, Pierce County
Land Owned by German-Russians**

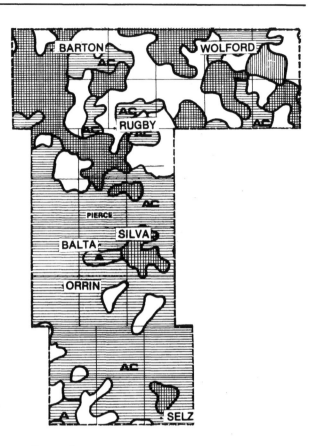

**Population Distribution
Pierce County, 1965 Ethnic Atlas**

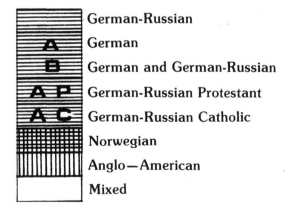

German-Russian

German

German and German-Russian

German-Russian Protestant

German-Russian Catholic

Norwegian

Anglo—American

Mixed

1960 Data from William Sherman, "Assimilation in a North Dakota German-Russian Community" (Unpublished M.A. thesis, University of North Dakota, 1965) Appendix.

Land Owned by People of Norwegian Birth or Descent in Northeastern North Dakota, 1913-1914

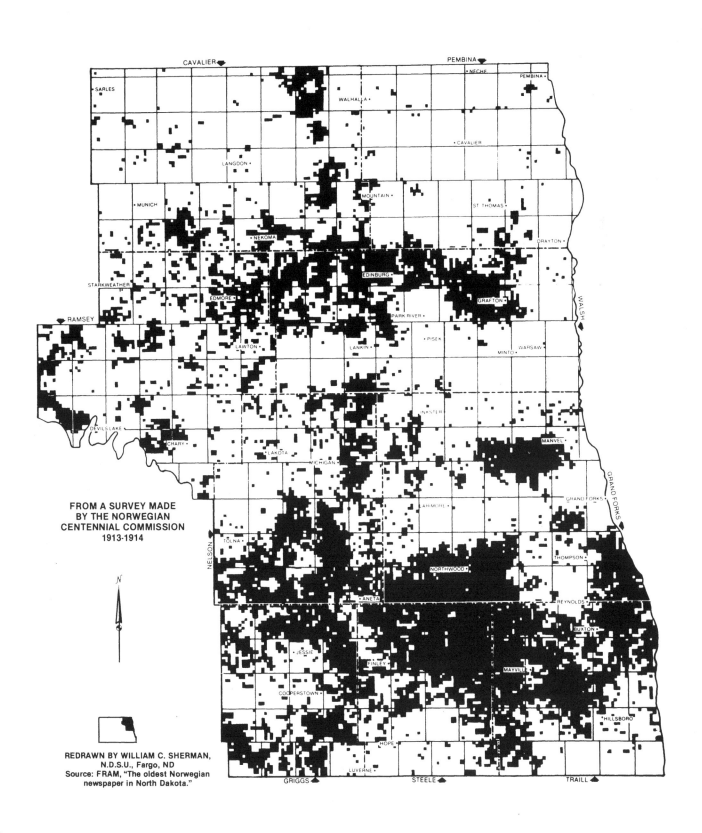

FROM A SURVEY MADE
BY THE NORWEGIAN
CENTENNIAL COMMISSION
1913-1914

N

REDRAWN BY WILLIAM C. SHERMAN,
N.D.S.U., Fargo, ND
Source: FRAM, "The oldest Norwegian
newspaper in North Dakota."

Identifiable Ethnic Settlement Areas in North Dakota as of 1965

Major settlements are italicized. Settlements which extend into several counties are hyphenated.

AMERICAN-INDIAN	*Benson, Dunn, McKenzie, McLean, Pembina, Sioux,* Rolette, Williams
ANGLO-AMERICAN	*Barnes-Cass, Bottineau, Burleigh, McHenry, McKenzie-Billings-Golden Valley-Slope-Bowman, Ransom,* Benson, Burke, Cavalier, Dickey, Divide, Eddy, Emmons, Foster, Grand Forks, Grant, Griggs, LaMoure, McKenzie, McLean, Mercer, Morton, Mountrail, Nelson, Oliver, Pembina, Pierce, Ramsey, Renville, Richland, Rolette, Sargent, Steele, Stutsman, Towner, Traill, Walsh, Ward, Wells, Williams
ANGLO-ONTARIAN	*Cavalier, Pembina,* Barnes, Bottineau, Burke, Burleigh, Cass, Grand Forks, Griggs, McHenry, Nelson, Ramsey, Renville, Rolette, Steele, Stutsman, Towner, Traill
BELGIAN	Divide, Pembina
CZECH: BOHEMIAN	*Mountrail, Richland, Walsh-Ramsey,* Bowman, Burke, Cavalier, Dickey, Foster, Morton, Ward
CZECH: CRIMEAN BOHEMIAN	*Dunn-Stark*
CZECH: MORAVIAN	*Ramsey*
DANE	*Burke, Ward-Renville,* Cass, Divide, Grand Forks, Richland, Steele
FINN	*Burleigh, Mountrail, Rolette,* Dickey, Emmons, Logan, Nelson, Ramsey, Towner
FRENCH	*Bottineau, Cass, Cavalier, Rolette, Walsh,* Billings, Grand Forks, Pembina, Stark, Towner
FRENCH-INDIAN (Métis)	*Pembina, Rolette,* Williams
GERMAN (REICHSDEUTSCH)	*Cavalier, Morton, Oliver, Pembina, Richland,* Barnes, Benson, Bottineau, Bowman, Burke, Burleigh, Cass, Dickey, Eddy, Emmons, Foster, Golden Valley, Grand Forks, Griggs, LaMoure, McHenry, McLean, Mercer, Mountrail, Pierce, Ramsey, Ransom, Renville, Sargent, Slope, Stutsman, Towner, Traill, Ward, Wells, Williams
GERMAN-AMERICAN BRETHREN (DUNKER)	Benson, Towner
GERMAN-AMERICAN MENNONITE	*Rolette-Pierce,* Cass, Ward
GERMAN-AMERICAN MORAVIAN	*Cass*
GERMAN, AUSTRIAN (GALICIAN)	Cavalier, Pembina
GERMAN, BOHEMIAN (SUDETEN)	*Cass,* Griggs
GERMAN, HUNGARIAN (BANAT)	*Stark-Hettinger,* Morton
GERMAN, HUNGARIAN (BURGENLAND)	*Barnes,* Wells

GERMAN (STEARNS COUNTY)	*Ward-Renville*, Golden Valley, Towner, Williams
GERMAN-RUSSIAN (BLACK SEA)	*McIntosh-Emmons-Logan-Stutsman-Kidder-LaMoure-Dickey, Mercer-Oliver-Stark-Morton-Grant-Hettinger, Sheridan-Pierce-McHenry-Benson-Wells-McLean*, Adams, Benson, Bottineau, Burleigh, Dunn, Grand Forks, Ramsey, Ransom, Sioux, Slope, Ward
GERMAN-RUSSIAN (DOBRUDJA)	*Wells*, Sheridan
GERMAN-RUSSIAN (MARIENBURG AREA)	Stutsman
GERMAN-RUSSIAN (MENNONITE)	*Cavalier*, Burleigh, Sheridan, Ward, Wells
GERMAN-RUSSIAN (VOLGA)	Dickey, Ransom
GERMAN-RUSSIAN (VOLHYNIA)	Cavalier, Pembina
HUTTERITE	Grand Forks
HOLLANDER	*Emmons*, Barnes, Burke, Grant, Griggs, Kidder, Stutsman
ICELANDER	*Pembina-Cavalier*, McHenry
IRISH	*Pembina*, Foster, Grand Forks, Ramsey
LEBANESE (SYRIAN)	*Mountrail, Williams*, Foster
LUXEMBURGER	Cass, Eddy, LaMoure, Sargent, Williams
NORWEGIAN	*Barnes-LaMoure-Ransom, Divide-Williams-Burke-Mountrail-Ward-Renville, Traill-Steele-Grand Forks-Griggs-Nelson-Eddy-Foster, Walsh-Ramsey-Cavalier, Wells-Benson*, Bottineau, *McKenzie, Richland-Ransom, Adams-Hettinger*, Bowman, Burleigh, Dunn, Kidder, Logan, McHenry, McLean, Morton, Pierce, Rolette, Sargent, Sioux, Slope, Stutsman, Towner
POLE	*Sargent-Richland, Walsh-Grand Forks*, Bowman, Foster, LaMoure, Golden Valley, Stutsman
SCOT	Pembina, Walsh
SWEDE	*Burke, LaMoure, McLean, Renville*, Benson, Bottineau, Burleigh, Cass, Dickey, Divide, Eddy, Emmons, Mercer, Ransom, Richland, Rolette, Sargent, Stutsman, Towner, Walsh, Williams
SWISS	Barnes
UKRAINIAN	*Billings-Stark, Burleigh-McLean, Dunn-McKenzie, McLean-Ward-Sheridan-McHenry*, Pembina, Williams

National Settlements Once Present But No Longer Clearly Identifiable as of 1965

NOTE: The British Isles (American, Ontarian, Irish, Scot) community lists are deceiving in that dozens of small settlements once existed. No serious chronicle of their names and locations has ever been made. A few are mentioned below.

AMISH (OLD ORDER)

Rolette and Pierce (Island Lake Township)

ANGLO-AMERICAN

Burke (North Star Township)
Dickey (Kentner Township)
Dickey (Yorktown)
Emmons (Williamsport)
Kidder (Buckeye and Union Township)
Logan (Napoleon)
McIntosh (Ashley)
Pierce (Juanita Township)
Ransom (Owego)
Richland (Fairmount)
Sargent (Hamlin)
Stutsman (Gray Township)

ANGLO-ONTARIAN

Barnes (Hemen Township)

BLACK

Grand Forks (Larimore)
McKenzie (Alexander)

BOHEMIAN

Burleigh (Summit Township)

BULGARIAN

Kidder (Steele)

DANE

Richland (Fairmount Township)

DUNKARD (BRETHREN)

Burke (Bowbells)
Eddy (Brantford)
Foster (Carrington)
Ramsey (Sweet Water Lake)
Ramsey (Klingstrup Township)
Ransom (Englevale)
Rolette (Ellsworth Township)
Traill (Norman Township)
Wells (Bowden)
Williams (Spring Brook)

ESTONIAN (CRIMEAN)

Stark (Daglum)

FINN

Grant (Delabarre Township)

FRENCH

Stark (Gaylord)
Wells (Dover)

GYPSY

Stutsman (Homer Township)

HOLLANDER

Barnes (Pierce Township)
Grand Forks (Wheatfield Township)
Griggs (Dover Township)
Stark (Zenith)

ICELANDER

Renville (Eden Valley Township)

IRISH	Eddy (Tiffany)
	Mercer (Knife River)
	Nelson (Pittsburgh)
	Wells (Carrington)
JAPANESE	Mountrail (Manitou Township)
JEW	Burleigh (Andrews-Richmond Township)
	Bowman (Rhame)
	Bottineau (Starbuck Township)
	Morton (Devaul Township)
	McIntosh (Ashley)
	McLean (Painted Woods)
	Ramsey (Garske)
LEBANESE (SYRIAN)	Pierce (Meyer-Reno Township)
	Rolette (Dunseith-Belcourt)
	Sheridan (Lincoln Valley)
	Walsh (Shepherd Township)
MENNONITE	Barnes (Rogers)
	Burke (Portal)
	Mountrail (Lostwood Township)
	Stutsman (Lowery Township)
	Ward (Baden Township)
MORAVIAN (GERMAN AMERICAN)	Mountrail (Tagus)
	Ward (Aurelia)
GERMAN-HUNGARIAN (BURGENLAND)	Morton (St. Anthony)
NORWEGIAN	Emmons (Pursian Lake)
	Emmons (Larvik)
	McIntosh (Norwegian)
SCOT	Richland (Antelope Township)
	Walsh (Edinburg)
SWEDE	Bottineau (Antler)
	Mercer (Fort Clark)

Index

List of Photographs

Photograph Credits

Photographs on pages 15, 40, and 106 are used through the
courtesy of Haynes Foundation Collection, Montana Historical
Society, Helena, Montana

Photographs on title page and on pages 13, 23, 32, 52, 75, 84,
117, and 123 are from the Farm Security Administration
Collection, copies from the Department of Special Collections,
Chester Fritz Library, University of North Dakota, Grand Forks,
North Dakota

Photographs on pages 57, 71, 87, 95, 101, and 111 are from the
Hulstrand "History in Pictures" Collection, Institute for Regional
Studies, North Dakota State University, Fargo, North Dakota

Photographs on pages 21, 28, 30, 37, and 65 are from the Archives
of the Department of Special Collections, Chester Fritz Library,
University of North Dakota, Grand Forks, North Dakota

The photograph on page 90 is from the Fjeld Collection at the
Institute for Regional Studies, North Dakota State University,
Fargo, North Dakota.

Photographs found elsewhere in the book are from the private
collection of William C. Sherman.